THE BREAKDOWN OF CARTESIAN METAPHYSICS

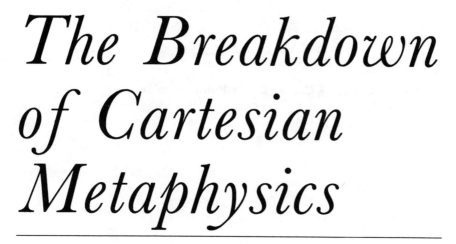

The Breakdown of Cartesian Metaphysics

by

Richard A. Watson

HUMANITIES PRESS INTERNATIONAL, INC.
Atlantic Highlands, NJ

First published in 1987 in the United States of America by Humanities
Press International, Inc., Atlantic Highlands, NJ 07716

© 1987 by Humanities Press International, Inc.
Reprinted 1988
Library of Congress Cataloging-in-Publication Data

Watson, Richard A., 1931–
    The breakdown of Cartesian metaphysics.

    Bibliography: p.
    Includes index.
    1. Descartes, René, 1596–1650.   2. Metaphysics—
History—17th century.   3. Philosophy, Modern—17th
century.   I. Title.
B1875.W35   1987   194   86–7382
ISBN 0–391–03370–0

PRINTED IN THE UNITED STATES OF AMERICA

Contents

Preface

The Breakdown of Cartesian Metaphysics combines the methods of historical research with analytic techniques to cast light on why and how Cartesianism failed as a complete metaphysical system. Western philosophy is, of course, ineradicably Cartesian at its core, but in the end Cartesian ontology is empty and Cartesian epistemology is a deception.

In Part One, I discuss methods and goals of the history of philosophy. I intend the present book to be more than just a work on Descartes and Cartesianism. It is also a work in historiography in that I describe and illustrate the combined use of methods of both conventional and of analytic history of philosophy. That is, I come to conclusions about the development and actual historical fortunes of Cartesianism, and I also examine·Cartesian arguments and positions by means of logical analyses that go beneath the surface of the texts. I believe that the best history of philosophy is and must be both analytical and conventionally historical. Thus this book is meant to be an illustration of work in the genre of analytic history of philosophy set in solid historical context.

The main body of this study is Part Two, which consists of analyses of the late 17th century Cartesian system and of criticisms of it. The primary conflict within the system is between two principles: that mind and matter differ in essence, and that sensations and ideas are modifications of the mind. Basing themselves on the generally accepted principles that essential likeness between entities is required for them to interact causally, and that likeness is required between an idea and its object for the one to represent the other, critics argued to the conclusions that on Cartesian grounds bodies cannot cause us to have sensations and ideas, we cannot cause our bodies to move by thought, and mental ideas cannot *resemble* and therefore cannot *represent* material objects. Because Cartesians wished to maintain the dualism, they either professed occasionalism as did Malebranche, or they were driven to assert that mind and body can interact because God makes it so, and that ideas inexplicably represent their objects without resembling them. This inability to explain how mind and body can interact causally, and how representative ideas make their objects known, contributed to the historical downfall of Cartesianism.

The primary critic of Cartesianism was Simon Foucher, a sceptic who published the first criticisms of Malebranche's occasionalism and of Leibniz's monadism. I examine Foucher's interactions with Malebranche and Leibniz in detail. I also follow the arguments and fortunes of several representative and important orthodox Cartesians: Robert Desgabets, Louis de La Forge, Jacque Rohault, Pierre-Sylvain Régis, Antoine Le Grand, and Antoine Arnauld. None of them could solve the problems facing Cartesianism.

Then I examine briefly some post-Cartesian developments. Bayle, Berkeley, and Hume each used Foucher's arguments with devastating results; the strictures of Berkeley and Hume against Locke on ideas derive largely from their basic agreement with Foucher that representation can be explained only by resemblance between idea and object. This notion also lies behind Norman Kemp Smith's critique of rationalism, and has played a vital role in the development of logical empiricism.

In Part Three, I examine Cartesian theology. Descartes himself got into difficulty with his several attempts to explain transubstantiation according to the principles of Cartesian physics. Then Louis de La Forge carried Cartesian theology to its logical conclusion: the soul that survives after death remembers nothing of this mundane personal life, but spends eternity contemplating only the general ideas of God, the soul, and intelligible extension. This position was as hard for the general public to accept as was the Cartesian contention that animals are machines.

Finally, in Part Four, I use logical analyses to conclude that the breakdown of Cartesian metaphysics stems from the logical incoherence of the Cartesian system. I argue, first, that Cartesian ontology is vacuous, that analysis of Descartes's ideas shows that the substances of Descartes's ontology—God, mind, and matter—are empty of content. This is a new result in Cartesian scholarship. Second, I argue that Cartesian epistemology is a sham, because on the basis of Descartes's grounds for doubt that he establishes in the First Meditation, he can literally know nothing, neither existence nor essence, not even of himself. This conclusion has been reached by Huet and Santayana, but no one has taken it as far as I do here.

I mean for this work to be provocative of discussion, as earlier presentations of some of these ideas have certainly proved to be. While most contemporary philosophers will approve of my method, my conclusion that Cartesian metaphysics reduces to nescience goes against the standard views of many contemporary scholars. I am thinking, for example, of recent books by Hiram Caton, E. M. Curley, Harry G. Frankfurt, Lüder Gäbe, Brian E. O'Neil, Jonathan Rée, Geneviève Rodis-Lewis, Bernard Williams, and Margaret Dauler Wilson. All of these commentators ultimately try to save Descartes by defending his claim to reason and certainty. In my estimation, they do so by failing to take his scepticism seriously; they try to save Descartes from himself. On the contrary, I show Descartes without crutches.

I conclude that Cartesian metaphysics as a complete system breaks down because of Descartes's inability to establish epistemological certainty; because of the logical incoherences of his ontological dualism; and finally, because just as his physics failed to fit the facts of experience and experiment, so also did his theology fail to conform with Christian hopes and dogma. In the end, reason fails Descartes. It is important to show how and why, because while nobody today is a Cartesian, Western philosophers continue to be centrally concerned with problems of epistemology and ontology set by that cautious Frenchman René Descartes, the indisputable father of modern philosophy.

Acknowledgments

My work on Cartesianism began under the direction of Richard H. Popkin, whose *The History of Scepticism from Erasmus to Descartes* is a seminal background study behind the present book. I thank him, and also Robert G. Turnbull and Gustav Bergmann who taught me the importance of analysing historical arguments. Various parts of this text have been commented on by Harry M. Bracken, Edwin B. Allaire, Phillip D. Cummins, Gregor Sebba, Craig Walton, David Fate Norton, James R. Groves, Jerome P. Schiller, Henry G. van Leeuwen, Margaret D. Wilson, and Patty Jo Watson. I very much appreciate their help. The text was not merely typed several times, but also commented on by Dorothy Fleck, Shaaron Benjamin, and Deanna Dejan; such secretaries are integral to the scholarly enterprise and cannot be thanked to much.

Work like this could not be done without the generous help of many librarians, and I thank those at the following libraries: University of Iowa Library, Niedersächsischen Landesbibliothek, Bibliothèque Nationale, Honnold Library of the Associated Colleges of Claremont, Hoose Library of Philosophy at the University of Southern California, University of Michigan Library, Washington University Library, Stanford University Library, University of California Library at Berkeley, Princeton University Library, and the Center for Advanced Study in the Behavioral Sciences Library.

I should like to thank the editors of *Journal of the History of Philosophy*, *Revue internationale de philosophie*, *Archives internationales d'histoire des sciences*, *Encyclopedia of Philosophy*, *Encyclopaedia Britannica*, *Southwestern Journal of Philosophy*, *Studia Cartesiana*, *American Philosophical Quarterly*, *History of Philosophy Quarterly*, Martinus Nijhoff, Johnson Reprint Corporation, and McGill-Queen's University Press for use of material that has appeared in different form in their publications.

During the twenty-five years I have been working on Cartesianism, I have received grants and fellowships from the University of Michigan, Washington University, the American Council of Learned Societies, the National Endowment for the Humanities, the National Science Foundation, the Princeton Center of International Studies, and twice from the Center for Advanced Study in the Behavioral Sciences. I thank them all very much.

In particular, I thank the successive directors of the Center for Advanced

Study in the Behavioral Sciences—Ralph W. Tyler, O. Meredith Wilson, and Gardner Lindzey—who have supported my Cartesian studies for many years. Their personal interest in the work of Center Fellows and their influence on institutional design have shaped the Center in the Stanford Hills into a scholar's Shangri-La.

Part One

Method

chapter 1

Method in the History of Philosophy

Il y a plus à faire à interpréter les interprétations qu'à interpréter les choses, et plus de livres sur les livres que sur tout autre object: nous ne faisons que nous entregloser.

—Montaigne

1 INTERPRETATION OF TEXTS

The history of philosophy consists of interpretations of texts presented in the historical context of their origin and development. The historical context may be relatively static as when a philosophical system or problem is presented as it was understood at a certain time, or dynamic as when the development or influence of a philosophical idea is pursued through time. Comprehensive systems usually make the most sense and are seen to be most consistent when examined as belonging to a given milieu. Isolated themes, such as the mind/body problem or representational ideas, can often be pursued fruitfully by following their development through time and, so to speak, cross-systemically.

The value of these studies is at least twofold. First, one's depth and breadth of comprehension is always increased by viewing ideas as they were understood and developed in historical context. This is because no set of ideas, not even those of pure mathematics, can be understood outside all historical contexts. Second, advancement in philosophy is always a matter of understanding. Philosophical systems and problems have origins in, and their elaboration and solutions unfold in, historical contexts. One can pick up along the line and do philosophical work without knowing much history of philosophy—as one can solve problems in mathematics without under-standing its foundations—but if one is to understand the basis of a problem or system, and its interrelations with other problems and systems, then one must look at historical origin and development. The interrelations of the branches, and the significance of the blossoms of the tree of philosophy cannot be comprehended without knowledge of its trunk and roots. Using another common metaphor, philosophy in its broadest sense—knowledge of the principles and relations of things—has an architectonic, the foundations of which must be comprehended if one is to stand securely in the higher parts of the structure, whether merely to understand, or to contribute to the construction that is still going on.

One should not carry these metaphors too far. The architectonic of philosophy may be discontinuous and unbalanced. Some work can proceed if one claims knowledge of little more than a foundational principle such as the law of non-contradiction, or that A = A. My point is that neither consistency of system nor elegance of solution is sufficient to the understanding of philosophy. This is because philosophical ideas and problems arise in contemplation of, and are about, the world as experienced by human beings. Human experience is temporally and historically extended, so that philosophy is necessarily tied to historical context.

The primary opposition to this view is the claim that philosophical understanding is best gained by examining the logical form of ideas, problems, and systems, apart from their historical context. One can certainly extract and understand syntactical structures, and examination of these abstract forms does help one understand philosophy. But the structures in themselves are not philosophy as it engages human beings in their attempts to understand the world in which they live. That is, either philosophy is understood in an historical context, or it is pure mathematics. Some philosophers consciously choose the latter view. I think they contribute an enormous amount by isolating the formal structures of philosophical systems and arguments, but even formal results develop in, and can be understood only in, historical contexts.

2   PRESUPPOSITIONS OF INTERPRETATION

Historians of philosophy interpret texts that are taken to have been written with the intent of presenting a philosophical system, position, problem, or argument. These interpretations are in part based on, but differ from, examinations of philosophers' lives and bibliographies, descriptions of philosophical milieus, attributions and verifications of texts, and historical semantics. If an historian pursues biography and bibliography, general history, or lexicography, he must know various archival, library, bibliographic, historiographic, lexicographical, and other research methods. But he can also take the results of such pursuits by others on trust. That is, the interpreter must discover, accept, or assume a large body of background knowledge which includes—besides placement of the text in a given philosophical environment—knowledge of the language as the philosopher knew it, and knowledge of the general historical situation in which the text was written. This includes at a minimum familiarity with the anthropology, art, biology, economics, literature, mathematics, physics, politics, religion, social organization, and whatever else is assumed necessary to situate the text in its times. An historian of philosophy also must have in mind a general view of where the texts fit in the overall history of philosophy.

Other special knowledge in philosophy includes basic familiarity with logic, epistemology, ontology, ethics, esthetics, etc., and with the general outlines of rationalism, idealism, empiricism, and so on. Further, an historian must have skills in various methods of analysis, such as dialectical, Ideal Language, Ordinary Language, and so on, to be able to follow explicit arguments and construct arguments implicit in the texts, analyze them, and derive their implications.

It is tedious to spell all this out, but it is important to do so for several reasons. The primary reason is to make explicit the large body of presuppositions or accepted background knowledge on which any interpretation is based. And by showing that the task of gaining this background by original research or even by studying original sources is overwhelming, I make evident that through sheer mortality an historian is required to accept a considerable amount on trust. Perhaps it is true, for example, that to undertake wide-ranging thematic studies in the history of Modern Philosophy one should know thoroughly Latin, French, English, German, Italian, and Spanish, and also perhaps Hebrew and Arabic, with Greek, of course, assumed. I should suppose that any scholar's heaven would consist in having the abilities and the time, unflagging enthusiasm, and the incredible memory required to become proficient in all the fields and languages pertinent to the subject of investigation. All historical interpretations, however, are based necessarily on a large amount of secondary knowledge. The history of philosophy, then, consists of interpretations that are in some part constructed, tested, and confirmed with respect to background that is not itself challenged or proved in the study in hand, but is accepted on authority and trust. Some of it, moreover, is inevitably made up.

3 GOALS OF INTERPRETATION: THE AUTHOR'S INTENT

Given a background that consists of general historical and philosophical facts and methods, an historian can proceed. The traditional first task is to attempt to present an interpretation of the text as the writer himself understood it. Thus some historians strive to present "what the philosopher really meant" or "the author's true intent." Sometimes this is thought to be reached by providing some sort of "literal" reading of the text, and sometimes it is produced by use of a special key of interpretation. In either case, one must assume that the writer intended to say something and knew what he was saying, and that he presented it clearly and consistently. One might think that if a philosopher did in fact do this, then there would be no need for interpretation. However, the writer's intent and knowledge of what he had to say may not have been secure, and he may have written inconsistently and unclearly. Even a philosopher's immediate contemporaries often have trouble understanding his writings, so interpretation is necessary. And for those of us who are not contemporaries of the writer, the text is historically removed, which makes interpretation necessary using historiographic methods.

What all this means is that although it is possible that there is one clear and intended meaning of a given text, and probable that the author intended for there to be one of *the* correct interpretation, it is not usual that a philosopher manages to present his intended meaning in an unambiguous text. It is even more unlikely that an interpreter—contemporary or historian—can confidently and justifiably claim to have discerned *this* meaning. This is because the interpreter is faced with texts, all of which are at least partially ambiguous and removed in time. A wide variety of plausible interpretations also results from the fact that historians have a wide choice of assumed backgrounds in which to situate and against which to test their interpretations. *The* intended, unambiguous meaning of the author is a will-o'-the-wisp. Even if an interpretation exactly presented it, the fact that interpretation must be based on selected assumptions would make it impossible ever to know that one had exposed *the* intended meaning of the philosopher. Nevertheless, the primary goal must be an attempt to present the author's original meaning, otherwise the history of philosophy would not have even a theoretical anchor. Given this general goal, there are three major specific goals of interpretation.

4   GOALS OF INTERPRETATION: COMPREHENSION OF SYSTEM

The first specific goal deriving from the general attempt to present what philosophers mean is to give comprehensive expositions of philosophical systems. That is, one way to make sense of texts is to show how they fit together in a philosophical system. The basic assumption here—beyond the presupposition that the texts do comprise a system—is that the system is consistent. In fact, it may not be. Inevitably, there will be some things the author says that are not consistent with the system as presented, and the interpretation may be warped from the author's actual intent in order to keep it consistent. There is also the assumption that the system is in some sense complete. The interpreter may fill in lacunae, inferring what the philosopher would have said on certain neglected topics. Thus systemic interpretation always requires argument to establish the precedence of the proffered exposition over other possible interpretations, and to claim consistency and completeness.

There is always a variety of plausible interpretations based on different background assumptions because no system ever shows itself uniquely and neutrally in any text. The system must be picked out. But although some systemic notions may be suggested by the text itself, historians of philosophy always implicitly or explicitly bring to the text several possible systemic frameworks of interpretation. The texts, or various possible meanings of the texts, are then fitted to these frameworks, and their exposition is ultimately justified by showing how well the texts fit the chosen framework.

There is a certain element of circularity in this process, the choice of framework being determined by the meaning of the text, and the meaning of the text being conditioned by choice of framework. One might start with the assumption, for example, that Descartes is a rationalist. The Cartesian system is presented then as a variety of rationalism, and this interpretation is challenged or abandoned only if, say, a major empiricist element appears in the texts that both cannot be explained in rationalist terms and which seriously contradicts the rationalistic interpretation. This circularity is not vicious, however, if one first poses a variety of possible textual meanings against a variety of systemic frameworks. The ideal is to propose various hypothetical frameworks, and then to test and confirm or disconfirm them by checking to see which provides the best background for making the most complete and consistent sense of the texts. Such balancing of textual meanings against interpretive frameworks is done at least implicitly by anyone who reads and makes sense of a text.

Of course the assumed framework—the foundational or skeletal structure of the interpretational architectonic—is, like the general historical background, itself an interpretation. It may require examination in turn. For example, it might be suggested that the general frameworks of rationalism and empiricism are not adequate or appropriate structures for making sense, say, of the texts of Descartes and Locke. A radically new categorial scheme might then be offered to replace the old rationalist/empiricist dichotomy, so that Locke and Descartes might be classed together as, say, hypothetico-deductive scientists. But then the new framework itself is an interpretation that can be challenged. In one sense there is no end to modification and substitution, but in another sense there is an end. For no interpretation—no exposition, no explanation, no explication—is presuppositionless. Once an old framework is abandoned, one must start with other assumed interpretive or methodological principles whose justification rests, as always, in the fruitfulness, completeness, and consistency of their application, and not on their being based on more fundamental principles, ad infinitum.

5 GOALS OF INTERPRETATION: UNDERSTANDING OF DEVELOPMENT

The second specific goal is based on conclusions about philosophers' meanings and systems. Historians of philosophy are concerned to understand the development of philosophical themes, ideas, problems, and arguments, as these appear in the various systems of various philosophers. The basic assumption here is that a given theme does appear in the texts of different philosophers and in different systems of philosophy. This assumption permits comparative studies, but most often interpreters presume that philosophical themes, ideas, problems, and arguments develop or evolve through the course of history. The background framework for the presentation of development, then, includes a grand schema encompassing various philosophical systems, and a criterion of development according to which one can evaluate change as either progressive or retrogressive.

Some of the grandest works in the history of philosophy are thematic studies. There is a majesty and sweep of coverage when, for example, Norman Kemp Smith follows the idea that logical necessity is the model of empirical causality from Descartes to its debacle in Kant,[1] and when Richard H. Popkin bases the development of Cartesianism on the revival of Pyrrhonism.[2] These interpretations are often overwhelming in their impact. This is because the comprehensiveness of their coverage is the primary criterion for confirming their application. Again, there is a sense in which this approach is circular. However, it is easy to see the defects in grandschemata interpretations that do not comprehend development adequately, as is the case in some Marxist and Thomist works. Thus a test by comparison with alternative interpretive frameworks is possible.

Nevertheless, it is sometimes difficult to get critical purchase on an interpretation, whether it be of system or of development. It is always possible to find isolated passages that seem to contradict an overall interpretation, but in the context of the framework, it is also almost always possible to explain these passages away or to give them meanings consistent with the interpretation. The only effective way to challenge an interpretation is to provide an alternative interpretation that comprehends the material more completely and more fruitfully than does the interpretation under attack. In the end, each interpretation may be plausible, and several may complement one another rather than stand in opposition. There is a limit, after all, to how much can be embodied in and covered by a clear interpretation. Density of understanding may depend not on the densest of interpretations, but on a variety of clear interpretations that illuminate different aspects from different points of view.

Sometimes criticism internal to a system can be destructive; for example, when Pyrrhonian sceptics derive absurdities from given principles. But only constructive substitution of a positive interpretation holds up. If there is no alternative, then even a defective interpretation is usually accepted rather than none.

I have spoken of fruitfulness as a criterion several times. By this I mean that an interpretation suggests further extensions of meaning, system, and development not evident in the original interpretive context. In detail, an interpretation is fruitful when it makes possible explanations of what happened before and after the texts were written and why, when it helps to make sense of other ideas and movements contemporary to the writing of the texts, and when it can be used to explicate further philosophical problems and solutions. These suggestions can then be checked by extending the scope of the interpretation, and if it is found that the expected meanings or systemic intricacies or developments do show up in further examination of the texts or in further texts, to that extent the interpretation is fruitful, and to that extent it is confirmed.

Obviously, this is to view the history of philosophy in much the same way as one views the natural sciences. Interpretive principles and hypotheses are proposed and tested and, on the basis of the evidence, are so far confirmed or disconfirmed. Methods are usually accepted or not on the basis of their fruitfulness. Interpretations are usually accepted or not on the basis of their explanatory comprehensiveness. And as there is no empirical way of reaching certain truth in physics, neither is there any empirical way of attaining certainty about the interpretation of a text. Interpretations are always open to correction, modification, and replacement. If this were recognized and accepted by historians of philosophy, there might be less rancor involved in the comparative criticism and interpretation of texts. This is not at all to argue that one interpretation is just as good as another. Some interpretations are better than others in proportion to the extent to which in given contexts they fruitfully help us understand the texts.

6   GOALS OF INTERPRETATION: FORMAL STRUCTURE

The position that philosophy is analysis, and that philosophical understanding is reached through analytical interpretations has never been successfully challenged. All understanding consists in selection, organization, and categorization of material with relation to some criteria. Thus all understanding is in the form of an argument for the inclusion of some elements and the exclusion of others in an idea, a theme, or a system. One way of explicating a system, for example, is to analyze it into its basic elements and principles of selection. Such analyses can result in metaphorical models—for example, the comparison of a system to a tree or to a building—and they can also be represented mathematically. When such a structure is exhibited in mathematical terms and is examined with respect only to its syntactical features, operations, and relations, a great deal can be learned about how arguments and systems do or do not work. Points of inconsistency stand out, and both solutions of problems and extrapolations of systems are suggested. These are beautiful results, and certainly one goal of historians of philosophy is to present detailed interpretations of original intent, established system, and confirmed development so that formal structures can be derived and exhibited by analysis.

Moreover, on the assumption that all philosophical ideas, problems, arguments, systems, and developments do have formal structures, syntactical models can be used by historians as part of their interpretive frameworks. Here again the structures are posed hypothetically, and they both are tested by, and direct the interpretation of, the formal elements of the texts under interpretation.

Can one go too far with formal analysis? I do not think so, but some would say that philosophers such as Wilfrid Sellers,[3] Jaakko Hintikka,[4] and Gustav Bergmann[5] proceed according to principles of structural history that lead them to draw and quarter the historical texts. Bergmann, for example, proposes what he argues is the Ideal Language that underlies Malebranche's system, and then on this basis exposes deficiencies in Malebranche's thought that derive from Malebranche not understanding his own Ideal Language.[6] Bertrand Russell's *A Critical Exposition of the Philosophy of Leibniz*[7] is a classic interpretation in this genre. I cannot see that anyone who keeps an eye for history will be harmed by such exercises. Why not even construct imaginary philosophers named Maleniz or Leibranche as Robert G. Turnbull has been known to do?[8] Surely the more possibilities one is aware of, the better one is prepared to figure out what this or that text means. And such models do provide possible means of understanding and solving philosophic problems. Of course, that any formal model is a good historical interpretation must be demonstrated. And such demonstration depends on the interpretation's making comprehensive sense both logically or analytically and in assumed historical contexts.

Those philosophers who believe that comprehension of formal models is the sole kind of understanding that should be called philosophical do go too far. There is some justification for their claim, because given the assumptions of consistency and completeness of system, crucial relations are most elegantly shown syntactically. There are an infinite number of such structures, and indeed their comprehension is a form of philosophical understanding. However, among them are some formal structures—sets of elements, operations, and relations—that are of special interest because they are the structures of those few systems that have been of crucial importance to human beings in their attempts to understand and control the world. Those particular structures that in fact have been used by human beings to categorize their experience and interactions with the world in which they live are—by that use—roughly, but justifiably, designated as philosophical structures to distinguish them from an infinite number of other structures, none of which enjoys a syntactically preferred place over the others, all of which provide *philosophical* understanding of themselves by exhibiting their own structures, but of which only those few that have played a role in human history have philosophical significance for humankind. Obviously, in this sense, the whole syntactical set *is* of philosophical importance because it has recently played a role in the development of philosophy. But it has gained this importance only by playing that historical role, and neither thereby nor in itself can it be set above or apart from members of the subject of structures that also play roles in history.

7 PROBLEM-ORIENTED HISTORY OF PHILOSOPHY

In other words, to produce an illuminating interpretation, an historian of philosophy must pick a text from which an interpretation of an explicit system, theme, problem, or line of development can be composed, tested, and confirmed. I might have said "from which an interpretation can be inferred," but I think most interpretations are constructions based only in part on texts, rather than being pure inductions or abstractions from texts. However derived, the interpretive model—to be plausible—must be a skeleton on which the flesh of the text can be reasonably shaped. One cannot make sense of any text without such an interpretive framework. This is problem-oriented history of philosophy.[9]

For example, in *The Downfall of Cartesianism, 1673–1712*,[10] I take critical problems in Cartesian epistemology that arise out of Cartesian ontology, and by providing a structural interpretation, I make sense both of their impact and of various failures to solve them. Thus I construct a model Late Seventeenth Century Cartesianism that no Cartesian explicitly acknowledged, but on which I show that all Cartesians depended. This model contains contradictory principles, which explains both how some of the problems of Cartesianism arose, and also why Cartesians could not solve them. Thus the Cartesian notion of representative ideas is contradictory because Cartesians are committed to both the principle that representation depends on resemblance, and the principle that ideas cannot resemble material objects. And the skeleton that supports the Cartesian corpus is the ontology of substance and modification, which explains why Cartesians (and

Berkeley) are not worried about how the mind (a substance) can have direct acquaintance with its own ideas (modifications of mind), and why Malebranche feels little need to explain how we are acquainted with ideas in the mind of God.

This interpretation requires acceptance of the view that a given philosopher does not always mean what he or she appears to say, does not always know completely what he or she is saying, or say completely what he or she knows, and does not always write consistently. One begins with the hypothesis that a philosopher's works, or some associated selection of them, form a unity, but one need not assume that every sentence in those texts will support this assumption of consistency. If, for example, a passage in a Cartesian text resembles a Scholastic formula, this resemblance could be intentional or accidental, and crucial or insignificant. One must ask whether or not the penumbra from other systems has any influence on the system being examined. I find that the Cartesians reject many Scholastic categories for the good reason that they cannot make sense of them in a Cartesian context. If they then resort to some of these rejected categories in later attempts to explicate something that they find difficult to explain with Cartesian categories (for example, how Cartesian matter and Cartesian mind can interact), then one can defensibly argue that they are just using empty words in a desperate attempt to bridge gaps in their explanatory apparatus. One may conclude, as I do about Cartesianism, that the system under examination is in fact inconsistent.

In this approach I have been influenced, as have been many others, by two seminal historians of philosophy: Norman Kemp Smith and Richard H. Popkin. Each exhibits great respect for his own grasp of philosophical systems, problems, and movements, and each marshals comprehensive support for plausible interpretations. They do attempt to discover the intentions of the philosophers, but they do not fuss excessively about literal or original meanings, and they do not look only at what the philosophers say. They look also at the philosophers' underlying positions and purposes, at what the philosophers do, at how they associate ideas, and at how their overall systems integrate in the wider historical and philosophical contexts. Such work often requires one to decide what a philosopher must mean or depend on when he says, or means to say, this or that.

This was impressed on me about twenty-five years ago when I was casting about for a dissertation topic. Popkin charmed me into working on Simon Foucher with a disquisition that went something like the following: Only when you have worked through the texts of a tenth-rate philosopher will you begin to learn what is required to be an historian of philosophy. You must work on some thinker who possibly does not even know himself what he is getting at, and who does not express himself clearly, or consistently, or completely. When you can begin to make sense of what that kind of thinker is all about, then you begin to be an historian of philosophy.

8 HISTORY OF PHILOSOPHY AND ANALYSIS

Gregor Sebba in *What Is 'History of Philosophy'?*[11] distinguishes "doctrinal analysis . . . the study of philosophical concepts, propositions, doctrines, and systems, to determine their precise meaning, structure, and internal verity" from "historical analysis proper." Doctrinal analysis "stands *between* philosophizing and writing history of philosophy."

Doctrinal analysis takes its material as a mathematician takes theorems and calculi; it treats them as timeless, *i.e.*, non-historical statements; inasmuch as validity is concerned, doctrinal analysis seeks to determine whether the propositions it examines hold or do not hold as they are given.[12]

This is similar to the distinction philosophers and historians of science make between the logic of justification and the logic of discovery, and to the distinction philosophers of language make between the questions of validity and meaning that arise in syntactics and semantics, and the questions of action and influence that arise in pragmatics. Sebba asserts that with doctrinal analysis, one can examine texts as non-historical entities to determine the meanings expressed therein, the logical relations among the included propositions, and the validity of the arguments contained. This raises two questions. Can a text be posited as a non-historical entity? And, how are texts given? I argue that texts can be subjected to doctrinal analysis essentially as Sebba defines it, but not ahistorically and thus not as non-historical entities. The results of any such analyses are necessarily determined in crucial ways by the fact that a text is always given (even if anachronistically) as an historical entity in historical context.

What is a text? It is neither merely a physical book nor a set of marks on paper. We say that texts are *given*, but in fact all texts are *taken*. A text is taken to mean something in an assumed historical context according to an assumed framework of interpretation. The text itself is neither timeless nor non-historical, it is not neutral, it is itself an interpretation. The same book of marks on paper may very well provide a text for a Whig that is different from the text it provides for a Tory.

But *given* a text, can it not then be examined as a timeless, non-historical entity? Perhaps. But if it is analyzed the results are in turn compromised by an historical context. This is because methods of analysis are themselves neither non-historical nor neutral. The doctrinal analyst who uses Idealist logic reaches conclusions about the validity of arguments different from those reached by one who bases his analysis on the logic of *Principia Mathematica*.

The meaning and validity even of a *given* text, then, depends on the injection of an historically determined method of analysis.

But *given* a text, and *given* a method of analysis, cannot one then isolate timeless meanings, structures, and relations? Probably I am handicapped by not being a Platonist. But I think that many philosophers are prone to forget that the present itself is an historical context. If one is given a text and assumes a given method of analysis, his application of that method to that text itself depends on his ability to apply the method to the text, and this in turn depends on and is conditioned by the present historical context in which he understands that he has before him on the one hand a text, and on the other, a method.

How does one know that the marks are symbols, and that they have order and place that are meaningful? We bring to the text the methodological principle that similar marks have similar meanings, but we also have to bring to the method the principle that it itself is consistent, and this is not shown in the method itself, but is an interpretation of it. This interpretation, this understanding of the method and of how it is to be applied to the text, is conditioned by the historical context of the present. Our understanding of purportedly *non-historical* texts and methods is possible only in the context of categories of meaning and convention in the present historical context. Moreover, this historical present is itself various, as is dramatically illustrated when one contrasts the interpretations of texts by, say, a Carnapian born and trained in the United States, and a Heideggerian born and trained in France.

Platonists, Idealists, Rationalists, Empiricists, Positivists, Thomists, Marxists, Ideal Language Philosophers, Ordinary Language Philosophers, all *take* texts in different ways. And even if all agreed to utilize the *same* method of analysis, each, from his own historical context, would interpret that method and apply it differently from the others. But is agreement not possible? Surely these are all intelligent people, and all could agree to apply the same method to the same text in the same way, as one works out linear equations in the domain of real numbers. Apparently agreement works for mathematics. It does not work for philosophy, and the reason is that philosophy is not about non-historical abstract structures. Philosophy exists only in historical contexts.

(And as far as that goes, what the set of international mathematicians agree is that for a special purpose in a limited domain they will apply the meanings and conventions of the same, limited, historical context. All philosophers usually agree also in very general or limited domains. For example, most would agree that Descartes is a philosopher and that his writings are texts. But full agreement on specific philosophical issues is unlikely because of the variety of meanings derived from the variety of human historical contexts. When agreement is imposed in philosophy, it is called totalitarian.)

Thus I would say of doctrinal analysis exactly what Sebba says of historical analysis, that its object must be treated as "historical fact, as an object in time to which its precise position in the flux of change is essential and constitutive."[13] Whether the text is rarefied and extenuated as in mathematics, or whether it is taken "literally" to have just plain, ordinary meanings of the sort everybody uses in everyday speech, at least the present historical context, itself informed by the sedimented remains of the past, provides the framework for the interpretation of the text. A non-historical text outside any historical context of interpretation or understanding or intent is meaningless, and a method that does not rest on principles accepted and understood in an historical context is—as a guide to analysis—empty.

9 HISTORY AND SCEPTICISM

The primary assumption of the history of philosophy is that there was a past. It is worthwhile for historians to consider the implications of the fact that this assumption can be challenged. In *Scepticism and Historical Knowledge*,[14] Jack W. Meiland argues that historical interpretations are constructed in the present out of materials that in themselves give no indication that there was a past. On the assumption that there was no past he shows how historiographic methods can still be used to evaluate these constructions, so that some can be seen as better *historical* interpretations than others. This thesis deserves to be taken seriously in its own right, but Meiland's book can also be seen as containing a cautionary tale for historians who do believe that there was a past. Historical interpretations *are* constructions, and they do derive from material that must be examined now, in the present. I said previously that historians make up part of their interpretations. I mean that they make inferences to fill in gaps consistently for completeness. Scrupulously or unscrupulously, with the best of intentions or through lack of care, historians perpetrate fictions. All historians stand with their toes across the line separating scholarly interpretations from historical novels. There are criteria for discernment, but it is nevertheless still possible to construct arbitrary interpretations out of historical data and to assign arbitrary meanings to texts. Outright hoaxes are rare,[15] but the imposition of meaning on a text from a dogmatic interpretive framework is common.

What if one should try to make up an interpretation—to impose a non-historical interpretation on a text? I argue that even if one attempts ahistorically to assign a non-historical meaning to a text, this still puts the text in the historical context of its assignment, a context that makes the assigned meanings understandable. But granted that not-quite-pure doc-trinal analysis can be undertaken and is important to the understanding of texts, what historian of philosophy would want to assign meanings, anyway? Historians of philosophy are primarily interested in what authors mean, in systems and developments, and in formal structures of actual arguments. It is presumed that interpretations are to present meanings as they were understood in the historical context of the composition of the text. And it would not be to do history at all if one allowed assignments—as contrasted to historical interpretations—of meanings to texts.

We do, however, assign meanings, although seldom arbitrarily or capri-ciously, and never non-historically. Throughout this chapter I allude to the common cautionary maxim of historians, which is to be aware of one's own historical context and to beware of importing contemporary meanings into interpretations of historical texts. One must also beware of quaint errors, such as treating Aristotle anachronistically as a nineteenth-century British don. Nevertheless, even the best historical interpretations are assignments. Historians interpret the texts; they attempt to present them as they were understood in the historical contexts of their origins, and they try to avoid presenting them as though they were written in the historical present. But no matter how carefully made, all interpretations are matters of choice and assignment from a variety of plausible possibilities.

I have already expressed my scepticism about the possibility of ever knowing just what an author originally meant. (If you need convincing, try to figure out whether or not Pierre Bayle, or Descartes, for that matter, was a sincere believer in Christianity.) I think it impossible, also, knowingly to fasten onto *the* uniquely relevant aspects of any historical context. However, my doubts do not lead me to the conclusion that attempts to discern authors' meanings and justified historical interpretations ought to be abandoned. On the contrary, that various plausible interpretations of any text are possible makes the history of philosophy all the more interesting. Whether incompati-ble or complementary, these different interpretations are the history of philosophy.

I believe also that it is impossible not to import meanings and viewpoints from the historical present into one's historical interpretations. But we are aware that they are there and can make whatever allowances are possible. Furthermore, these conditioned interpretations themselves become a part of the history of philosophy, as indicated by the epigraph for this chapter. Plato's Socrates, Descartes's Aristotle, Kant's Hume, Husserl's Descartes, and Sartre's Heidegger are as important and as influential as the originals.

Finally, everyone's reading of any text, or of an interpretation of a text, is itself a new interpretation, engendered out of the background and historical context of the reader. Some of us get to the same place, but none of us takes exactly the same route as anyone else.

The goal of discovering *the* meaning of a text in the historical context of its origin is a necessary ideal and anchor for the history of philosophy. The only danger in positing it is that someone might take it seriously as an attainable end, using it as a standard against which all interpretations are to be measured, and thus denigrate all mortal interpretations. In practice, however, historical interpretations are measured as to their plausibility and comprehensibility in providing understanding of texts in historical contexts of which we are a part. This does not preclude (as some austere historians would) presentation as the history of philosophy of connections, structures, influences, implications, and ideas that the philosophers who wrote the texts never had explicitly in mind. One builds such interpretations in assumed historical contexts with the data at hand. I believe that such context-controlled constructions are appropriately presented as the history of philosophy.[16]

Part II

The Downfall of Cartesianism

chapter 2

The Epistemological Background of Seventeenth-Century Cartesianism

1 INTRODUCTION

Phenomenalism, idealism, spiritualism, and other contemporary philosophical movements originating in the reflective experience of the *cogito* bear witness to the immense influence of Descartes. However, Cartesianism as a complete metaphysical system in the image of that of the master collapsed early in the eighteenth century. A small school of brilliant Cartesians, almost all expert in the new mechanistic science, flashed like meteors upon the intellectual world of late seventeenth-century Europe to win well-deserved recognition for Cartesianism. They were accompanied by a scintillating comet, Malebranche, the deviant Cartesian, now remembered as the orthodox Cartesians are not. However, all these bright stars faded upon the philosophical horizon, almost as soon as they appeared. The metaphysical dualism of Descartes was to be neither preserved nor reconstructed.

There are many reasons why the Cartesian system did not survive the victory over Scholasticism that Descartes, Malebranche, and the others had won. Newtonian physics very soon replaced Cartesian physics. The practical interest and success of the new science, which the Cartesians themselves had nurtured, drew men down from the lofty realms of metaphysics. On the popular front, Cartesianism was attacked and ridiculed for the view that animals are unthinking machines. In the schools of Paris and elsewhere, there was the general but severe opposition of pedants, deriving from political as much as from philosophical concerns. The Church put Descartes's *Meditations* on the Index, and the Cartesian explanation of transubstantiation was taken as a meddling with Church tradition, if not as an attack upon Church doctrine.

The most important reason for the rapid decline of the Cartesian metaphysical system is that it is epistemologically and ontologically incoherent in several ways. Criticism of these incoherencies came from varied sources during the second half of the seventeenth century and are so thorough that the close of the century is also the end of the Cartesian era.

Problems within the Cartesian system derive primarily from conflicts among metaphysical principles. The major difficulties stem from the dualistic system of mind and matter in which the ontological categories of substance and modification are exhaustive, and which includes epistemological and causal likeness principles. If every representation must be in some way like the object it represents, and if every cause must be in some way like its effect, then the Cartesian metaphysical system incorporates an unbridgeable gap between mind and matter. The Cartesians, orthodox and deviant alike, could explain neither how two substances unlike in essence could causally interact nor how one could know the other.

The main attack came from a source the Cartesians at first refused to take seriously. L'Abbé Simon Foucher, Chanoine de la Sainte Chapelle de Dijon, was an eccentric and obscure sceptic; he said he was an Academic in the tradition of Socrates and Philo. He wrote several critical works, making in each more or less the same points against Cartesian metaphysics. Foucher's sceptical technique is to admit the Cartesian ontological principles and then to show that contradictions arise when they are combined with Cartesian epistemological and causal principles. According to these principles, Foucher argues, it should be impossible for mind and matter to interact, and for mind to know matter. In fact, however, we experience the interaction and have the knowledge. Thus, Foucher concludes, the Cartesian metaphysical system is based on incompatible principles, one or some of which must be false. Its major systematic breakdown derives from the inability of Cartesians to perfect an epistemology commensurable with their ontology.

How can two unlike substances causally interact? How can mind know matter? The two major answers offered by the Cartesians are developed from either the denial of the likeness principles or the alteration of the ontological framework. Neither of these answers is intelligible within the Cartesian context. Ultimately, the Cartesians appeal to God to support the Cartesian machine. Certainly God is far from being extraneous in the Cartesian system. Many opponents, however, thought it unphilosophical to rely on His inexplicable ways to explain events that are evidently impossible according to Cartesian principles.

The Downfall of Cartesianism is thus a study of failure. Its binding thread is the development of the Cartesian way of ideas in the face of these problems. I follow the fortunes of Cartesianism through the critical years from 1673, when Simon Foucher published his first critique, to 1712, when Malebranche published the last additions to his system. The body of this study is historical; its heart is a logical analysis of how and why the Cartesians failed to solve their problems. The analysis deals primarily with Foucher's criticisms of Cartesian metaphysics. My purpose is to show that Cartesian failures to answer Foucher's sceptical objections led to the downfall of the Cartesian metaphysical system. The arguments Foucher originated became thereafter very important in the history of modern philosophy. Bayle included them in his *Dictionnaire*, and those against the distinction between primary and secondary qualities were taken from Bayle for explosive use by Berkeley and Hume. Thus, I follow the further development of the way of ideas through

Locke, Berkeley, and Hume to show what the post-Cartesians believed was necessary to replace Cartesian metaphysics as a whole.

There is one other major study that shows reasons for the downfall of Cartesianism. Norman Kemp Smith argues that Cartesianism as a complete metaphysical system failed because causal relations cannot be rationalized.[17] He carries his study through Hume and Kant to show that the Cartesian dream is impossible of realization. The Cartesian metaphysical ideal is a logic that exactly represents the world, that is, an axiomatic system of ideas from which absolutely certain conclusions can be deduced about the world.[18] Not only must the ideas truly represent the essences of things in the world, but also the relations of logical necessity in the deductive system must truly represent necessary causal relations in the world. Kemp Smith's argument is that the downfall of Cartesianism is due to the fact that necessary logical relations in deductive systems are eternal, whereas causal relations in the world are temporal. Cartesian rationalism must inevitably fail because eternal relations in logic cannot be representations of temporal relations in the world.

I have little argument with Kemp Smith's conclusions. He illuminates one major defect, sufficient for the failure of Cartesianism. I illuminate another major defect, and show not only that it is a sufficient reason, but also that in the context of late seventeenth-century philosophical controversy it is the actual cause of the downfall of Cartesian metaphysics. This defect is that the Cartesians could give no intelligible explanation of how ideas represent their objects. Their inability is traced to two connected doctrines of traditional substance philosophy.

First, the Cartesians are bound to the principle that representation depends upon or is the same as resemblance or likeness between an idea (whatever it is) and the object it represents. Part of my argument for this rests on evidence that they are bound also to the principle that causal interaction depends upon likeness between cause and effect. When the later Cartesians abandon the principles that there must be likeness between an idea and its object, and between a cause and its effect, they can no longer explain how mental ideas can represent material objects, nor how a mind can causally interact with a body.

Second, the Cartesians have a notion of a mind's being directly acquainted with ideas that makes direct acquaintance dependent upon or identical with the relation of a substance to its modifications. Because it seems to the Cartesians obvious that a mind is directly acquainted with its own modifications, they never doubt that a mind has knowledge of its own ideas, which are *in* the mind as modifications *of* it. When they abandon the notion that ideas are mental modifications, the Cartesians can no longer explain how a mind can be directly acquainted with and thus know ideas.

The downfall of Cartesianism, then, comes because criticism of the

Cartesian metaphysical system leads to demands for an explanation of representation not based on resemblance of idea to object, an explanation of causal interaction not dependent on likeness between mind and body, and an explanation of direct acquaintance that does not make it identical with the relation of a substance to its modifications. Cartesians can provide no such explanations.

Having said this, I can now point out that Kemp Smith comes to the conclusions he does because he, also, accepts the principle that resemblance is necessary for representation. He insists that eternal, that is, timeless, logical relations cannot represent temporal causal relations because of the lack of resemblance between them. It is enough here to say on this subject that a deep-seated philosophical concern underlying the present study is embodied in the question, "*Is* resemblance necessary for representation?" I suspect so, for despite myriad recent criticisms of so-called picture theories of representation, I know of no representation system that does not depend on some sort of likeness, for example isomorphic relations between elements, commensurability, coordination, and so on.

In broad terms, I move in this study from a consideration of problems arising from an ontology of two substances different in essence to a consideration of problems arising from an ontology of two categories, substance and modification. The Cartesians are concerned about relationships between two substances, but they see no problems arising from the relationship between a substance and its properties or modifications. Berkeley's treatment (deriving from Malebranche) of the relationships between mind and idea, and between mind and notion, is illuminated by a consideration of the extent to which he takes these relationships for granted in the Cartesian way (as substance to modification), and of the extent to which he sees difficulties in the relationship between substance and modification. Berkeley's solution to Cartesian problems by the introduction of an entity external to substance and modification is, like that of Malebranche before him, not successful; Malebranche belittles, and Berkeley denies, the dualism of substances, but neither philosopher can break entirely with the ontological pattern of substance and modification. The final breakdown of Cartesian metaphysics comes with Hume, who, in completely abandoning the ontology of substance and modification, parts company with substance philosophy to become the father of contemporary philosophy.

The Downfall of Cartesianism may thus seem to be a title both too broad and too narrow for what is covered in Part Two. Nevertheless, after the publication of the last of Malebranche's *Eclaircissements* in 1712, the ascendancy of the complete dualistic Cartesian metaphysical system is over and done. That is, by then the sceptical critics had exposed problems the Cartesians could not solve. However, I make no claim that all aspects of Cartesianism disappeared or stopped developing, for it is evident that much of Western philosophy today is in a very broad sense Cartesian. And of course other factors mentioned above contributed to the downfall of the metaphysical system. Nevertheless, I do claim that the more strictly epistemological difficulties analyzed herein are crucial philosophically and historically.

The title might be thought to be too narrow also from another viewpoint. The downfall of Cartesianism is intimately linked to the inadequacies of substance philosophy. Malebranche recognizes at least vaguely the ontological paucity of a system in which the categories of substance and modification are all-inclusive. I trace the major failures of the Cartesians to their inability to break out of this ontological pattern. Philosophers later in the Cartesian tradition do break with this pattern, and in carrying this study through Hume, I show that the downfall of Cartesianism is a major movement toward the collapse of a strain of substance philosophy that Descartes inherited from his Scholastic predecessors.

2 CHARACTERIZATION OF A SCHOLASTIC EXPLANATION OF PERCEPTION AND KNOWING

Although Descartes's substance philosophy derives from Scholastic patterns, the Cartesian system is in many respects developed in opposition to Scholastic explanations in physics and particularly to those of perception. Therefore it is useful to give here a short characterization of a Scholastic theory of perception. The Aristotelian account presented is essentially that of St. Thomas Aquinas,[19] although the Cartesian attacks show clearly that the Peripatetics were variously interpreted. Some of the arguments for and against the Cartesian theory of perception even take as a foil a theory more Epicurean than Aristotelian.

All material substances, goes the Thomistic account, are composed of a union of form, which is a principle of organization, and of matter, which has a capacity to be organized. Each particular material thing or substance necessarily has only one essential form, which gives the thing the being it has. Substantial change can occur when one essential form replaces another, the matter remaining the same. Besides its essential form, a material thing can have an unspecified number of accidental forms, or qualities. Traditionally, these are reducible to four sets of opposites: heat and cold, wetness and dryness, denseness and rarity, heaviness and lightness. The first of each pair is an active quality that can act on its passive opposite; the quantitative proportions of these qualities in a thing determine its nature. By Descartes's time, the ranks of accidental forms were swollen with any number of occult powers, real accidents, sensible qualities, thisnesses, and so on. Each of these qualities, when actually qualifying a thing, excludes all other qualities of its same general kind; that is, whiteness in a material thing causes it to be white, and greenness cannot be in the thing (nor any other color) in the same way at the same time as whiteness, and so on. It should be noted that the thing remains substantially the same whatever accidental forms qualify it, so long as the essential form that gives it being as a substance remains the same. Of the essential forms that give being to material substances, only one can exist separately from union with matter. This unique substantial form is the human soul. Matter itself is featureless, without quantity, extension, or dimension, until united with form; however, because its priority is only logical, matter cannot exist outside the union.

The central point in the Thomistic account of perception is that the sense organs and the intellect can in some way receive the essential form of a material thing or substance without its matter. In the process of knowing, the impossibility of a substance having more than one form is in some way transcended as the knower takes on besides his own essential form the form of the known, and the known shares its form with the knower. The mechanics of this process are complicated. In a knowing situation, there must be a knower, a material thing known, and a medium. The material thing expresses itself through the medium to cause a material impression upon one of the sense organs of the knower. This impression causes the knower's Imagination to form sense imagery consisting of a material image, or phantasm. The knower's Active Intellect illumines the sense imagery, abstracting from it to form in the knower's Possible Intellect the intelligible species, which is the essential form of the thing known; this essential form exists in the Possible Intellect with intentional being, while at the same time it exists in and gives natural being to the thing known. Thus, the thing itself is known through the intelligible species; this amounts to the knower's having direct knowledge of the thing's essential form. If, in reflection, the intelligible species itself is made an object of thought, then it is referred to by a mental word, that is, by a concept.

Three aspects of this explanation should be noted. First, the first intention in knowing is the essential form of the thing known; the intelligible species is not a representative being, but is itself the known essence. Intelligible species themselves can be objects of second intention, in which case they are referred to by concepts, which are representative beings.

Second, the Scholastic contention that the action of the material thing causes a material image to be conducted through the medium to the sense organs is to that extent like the Cartesian mechanical account of perception. In each case, it is clear that no Epicurean material species travels from the thing known to the knower. The Scholastics then require that the phantasm formed by Imagination contain as abstractable the essential form, or intelligible species, of the thing to be known. For the Scholastics, knowing is not the way of a representation that inheres merely in the knower; the intelligible species *is* the known thing's essential form shared by the knower. That is, the known thing's form has intelligible, or intentional, being in the knower. In the Cartesian account, however, the representative idea that arises is only a modification of the mind, which is not the same as, nor even essentially like, the known thing's form as the Cartesians understand it (that is, for the Cartesians, the idea of a material thing is unextended; the form of a material thing is its extended shape).

Third, the Scholastic account of perception is consistent with the maxim "Nihil est in intellectu quod non prius fuerit in sensu." If material things did not act through a medium on the sense organs, nothing would be known. However, the maxim does not mean that anything sensible or material like the thing known is found in the Intellect; what is known are immaterial natures.

For the Scholastics, sensible qualities modify material things. These properties may be only nonessential accidents, but they do exist in material things *as* they are sensed. The Cartesians object strenuously to this attribution. They argue—primarily by reference to the variability of sensible qualities—that it leads to inconsistencies. To avoid the absurdity of a material thing having contrary sensible qualities at the same time, they make a distinction that is later popularized by Locke as the distinction between primary and secondary qualities. The Cartesian distinction between modifications of the body and modifications of the mind and the subsidiary distinction between sensations and ideas are the major tools for dislodging Scholastic physics. They are also used in an attempt to provide an infallible way of knowing material things. Foucher analyzes these Cartesian distinctions to make major criticisms of the Cartesian way of knowing by ideas. And because the distinctions are an essential part of the foundations of Cartesian metaphysics, the contradictions exposed by Foucher reflect the basic contradictions of Cartesianism. Because the distinction between primary and secondary qualities plays a central role in the following chapters, I examine briefly its development before Descartes.

3 THE DISTINCTION BETWEEN PRIMARY AND SECONDARY QUALITIES BEFORE DESCARTES

The distinction between primary and secondary qualities is generally taken to be a differentiation of sensible qualities from mathematical qualities. The sensible, or secondary, qualities are colors, odors, tastes, sounds, and tactual feelings including pleasure, wetness, heat, roughness, and pressure, that is, all the objects of our senses. Some—if not all—of the secondary qualities obviously do not belong to material things. Mathematical qualities include size, shape, and motion or rest, that is, all properties of material things that are amenable to quantitative or mathematical representation. All these primary qualities do belong to material things. The distinction is made even by the Scholastics, who claim that material things have as their properties both primary and secondary qualities, and further, that the mathematical qualities are also sensible.

In the Cartesian tradition the distinction is much more exclusive than it is in Scholastic terms. Descartes finds the secondary quality and the perception of it to be one; the sensible quality and the sensing of it are the same; the direct object of a sensation is the sensation itself. And because sensations are modifications of the immaterial mind, material things have none of the secondary qualities as such. They do have, however, the primary qualities of which we have representative ideas, but not sensations. To speak of secondary qualities in material things for Descartes, as for Locke, is either to speak falsely or to refer to those collections of primary qualities that give rise to sensations in our minds when material things interact causally with our sense organs.

One of the first modern expressions of the distinction is found in Galileo's *Il Saggiatore*. He reasons as follows:

> I want to propose some examination of that which we call heat, whose generally accepted notion comes very far from the truth if my serious doubts be correct, inasmuch as it is supposed to be a true accident, affection, and quality really residing in the thing which we perceive to be heated. Nevertheless I say, that indeed I feel myself impelled by the necessity, as soon as I conceive a piece of matter or corporeal substance, of conceiving that in its own nature it is bounded and figured in such and such a figure, that in relation to others it is large or small, that it is in this or that place, in this or that time, that it is in motion or remains at rest, that it touches or does not touch another body, that it is single, few, or many; in short by no imagination can a body be separated from such conditions: but that it must be white or red, bitter or sweet, sounding or mute, or a pleasant or unpleasant odour, I do not perceive my mind forced to acknowledge it necessarily accompanied by such conditions; so if the senses were not the escorts, perhaps the reason or the imagination by itself would never have arrived at them. Hence I think that these tastes, odours, colours, etc., on the side of the object in which they seem to exist, are nothing else than mere names, but hold their residence solely in the sensitive body; so that if the animal were removed, every such quality would be abolished and annihilated.[20]

Galileo goes on to say that all that is needed "to excite in us these tastes, these odours, and these sounds" is "size, figure, number, and slow or rapid motion."[21] Heat in the material thing is nothing more than the rapid motion of minute bodies. Without a living animal having sense organs in active contact with material things, there would be no sensations or secondary qualities. Galileo's distinction is far from clear. It is plainly evident that he believes the material world would be adequately composed of the primary qualities alone, but it is not evident what status the secondary qualities have. Galileo does not deny that we sense primary qualities, and he does not deny that some bodies—those that are living animals with sense organs—have or at least receive secondary qualities. He simply states that material bodies cannot be conceived of without primary qualities, although they can be conceived of without secondary qualities. This conceptual necessity implies that material bodies necessarily must actually have primary qualities, whereas their possession of secondary qualities is unnecessary and superfluous. This conceptual necessity implies that material bodies cannot be conceived of except as having primary qualities, although they can be conceived of as not having secondary qualities whose possession is thus unnecessary and superfluous. Finally, the variability of the secondary qualities makes them suspect, whereas the constancy of the primary qualities speaks for their abiding material reality.

Although Galileo writes primarily as a physicist, he is usually believed to have been the great physicist he is because of his metaphysical convictions.[22] His study of Archimedes, Plato, and the Pythagoreans, and above all his own success in solving physical problems with mathematics, evidently convince him that the underlying reality of the material world is mathematical. If geometrical atoms are the basic units from which material things are made, then the real primary qualities of these material things are those that can be represented mathematically. Even if we say cautiously that Galileo has a mathematical method, rather than a mathematical metaphysics, it is still not unfair to suggest that he finds those qualities that we call primary to be persistent in his conception of material things because of his mathematical way of viewing the material world.

Gassendi, also, distinguishes between primary and secondary qualities. For Gassendi, all material things are made of conglomerations of atoms in the void. The primary qualities of atoms are size, figure, weight, and a certain swiftness of motion; order and position are primary relations among the atoms. The primary qualities of material things are merely the summations of the primary qualities of the atoms that make up the material things.[23] Although all these qualities are quantitative, Gassendi does not seem to have chosen them because they are amenable to mathematical representation, in this differing from Galileo. Gassendi places his stress upon the constancy of the primary qualities. He reasons that if atoms had colors and tastes and other sensible qualities, then there would not be such a variation of these qualities in material things during generation and corruption, which are merely changes in the internal arrangements of the atoms making up things.[24] The sensible, or secondary, qualities, then, do not belong to material things; they result from the primary qualities of, and the structural relations among, the atoms of which perceptible material things are made.

In its mechanical aspects, Gassendi's theory of perception is similar in many ways to Descartes's, but Gassendi's void is a striking contrast to the Cartesian *plenum*. Gassendi believes that action can take place in the material world only through the motion and contact of material things; he denies both the efficacy of Scholastic internal occult qualities and action over a distance. Because in his system there is no all-pervading medium through which motions might be conveyed—upon which the Cartesians insist—it is obvious, he says, that for a thing to be perceived, something material must travel from the thing to act upon, and thus make it known to, the knower. He thus develops an Epicurean doctrine of emission. Each material thing continually emits atoms arranged in patterns similar to the structure of the thing. These groups of atoms travel in straight lines with a uniform speed. If they strike a sense organ of a human being before they are deflected or scattered, then distinctive motions are transferred from the sense organ along the nerves to the brain where they cause a material image—a plication, *image impresse*—to be formed. This in turn causes the soul to have a sensation and an *image expresse* that conforms to the thing known and represents it as it is objectively in the soul.[25]

The sense organs do not respond merely to the arrangements of the emitted atoms, but each organ also responds to atoms of special types. The sensation of heat arises from the impression upon the touch organs of atoms distinguished by their primary qualities as heat atoms; there are similarly special atoms that give rise to sensations of cold.[26] It must be stressed, however, that secondary qualities can be said to belong to material things only in the sense that certain arrangements of primary qualities of atoms or groups of atoms uniformly give rise to certain sensations if proper contact is made with sense organs. After such contact is made, the mechanical aspects of perception proceed in the body much as they do upon the Cartesian account. In no sense do the atoms travel to the brain; their journey is done when they strike the sense organs. Outside the body, the major difference is that on the Cartesian account there is always a medium through which motions can be transferred to sense organs without the necessity of flying material atoms or species.

Gassendi believes that the human soul has two parts: a sensitive corporeal part and a reasoning incorporeal part. The sensitive part is spread throughout the body, and although the sensorium is centered in the brain, in some way the organs as well as the brain experience sensations. This means that secondary or sensible qualities are properties of a material thing to the extent that the sensitive part of the soul is material, although these secondary qualities do not picture or represent the primary qualities that cause them. The spiritual images, or ideas, that do represent the material things, and thus make them known, arise in the incorporeal part of the soul. These images, Gassendi says, are always mixed with "quelque image de corporéité" because of the two-part nature of the soul in its union with the body.[27] While such an account may give rise to grave theological and metaphysical problems, it does not leave Gassendi with the problem—which the Cartesians face—of how there can be an immaterial image of a material thing.

A final remark should be made about what might be called a Scholastic version of the Epicurean theory. In such a theory, the flying atoms or species would be said to have sensible secondary as well as mathematical primary qualities. Some of the Cartesians—perhaps mistakenly—believe that they have to combat such a theory. In any event, Gassendi, like the Cartesians, believes that the attribution of sensible qualities to material things by the Scholastics is one of their greatest mistakes. And as do the Cartesians, he offers his system with its careful distinction between primary and secondary qualities, and its notion of mechanical causality in the material world, as a reasonable alternative to the contradictory Scholastic account.

In the following chapters, I speak more often of sensations and ideas than of secondary and primary qualities. In most cases it is clear that sensations either are secondary qualities or represent secondary qualities, and that ideas represent primary qualities. This usage suffices for the Cartesians. When groups of primary qualities are referred to as secondary qualities because they cause sensations, these passages are well marked. Deviations are also apparent when I discuss non-Cartesians who believe that there can be sensations of primary qualities and ideas of secondary qualities. The distinction also often carries the implication that primary qualities are real properties of material things, whereas secondary qualities are not. Such categorization is implicit in much of the discussion that follows, although one should remember that for the Cartesians, secondary qualities are real properties of spiritual things. And, as I show above, some of the Scholastics believe that secondary qualities are real properties of material things, while, as I show in the next chapter, Foucher doubts that even primary qualities are real properties of material things.

chapter 3
Simon Foucher (1644–1696)

1 LIFE AND WORKS

Simon Foucher is important in the history of modern philosophy as a sceptic who originated epistemological criticisms that are fatal to the Cartesian way of ideas. His method is that of the traditional sceptic: He assumes the principles of the system under analysis and then reasons to contradictory conclusions. His arguments against the distinction between ideas and sensations are utilized by Bayle, Berkeley, and Hume. Any history of the Cartesian way of ideas, and any analysis of the causal, representative theory of perception, must take into consideration the significant contribution of Simon Foucher.

Simon Foucher was baptized in the parish of Notre-Dame of Dijon on 1 March 1644, the son of Nicolas Foucher, a merchant, and Anne Richot.[28] He took orders at an early age, at which time he was made honorary canon of the Sainte Chapelle of Dijon. His interest in classical letters and philosophy soon led him to Paris, where he took a bachelor's degree at the Sorbonne in the faculty of theology. He spent the remainder of his life in Paris, dying, it is said of overwork, on 27 April 1696. He was buried in Saint-Nicholas-des-Champs.

Foucher spent his adult life in commerce with some of the main philosophers and philosophical problems of his time. Baillet says that in 1667, upon the return of Descartes's remains to Paris, Foucher was asked by Rohault to deliver a funeral oration.[29] If true, this suggests that the young Foucher, not long arrived from the provinces, must have very soon come into contact with the important Cartesians. Rabbe believes that Foucher was at this time a Cartesian whose great promise was awarded with the honor of giving the funeral oration.[30] Gouhier, on the other hand, believes that Foucher must already have been an Academic sceptic.[31] Gouhier believes that Foucher was chosen because he was a non-Cartesian who disliked Scholasticism and was favorable to Descartes's method of doubt. Foucher could thus be counted on to give a relatively nonpartisan account of Descartes as a great and pious man. Gouhier bases his speculations upon Foucher's statement that he had begun arguments with Rohault in 1667 concerning knowledge of the world of extension, which suggests that he was not a Cartesian then. It is also improbable that he left the Jesuit college in Dijon as a Cartesian. There is no record of Foucher's giving the oration, and one can wonder whether he were

33

ever asked, and if so, whether he ever prepared it. Foucher was somewhat vain about his writing, and although we have no copies of his first *Disserta- tions sur la recherche de la verité, ou sur la logique des academiciens* of 1673, he refers to this book several times in other writings. He published two long poems and left a drama in manuscript.[32] Because he did believe that Descartes was a great man, it seems likely that if he had been asked to give the oration or had prepared it he would have left a reference to it. Neither Clerselier nor Rohault mentions it. All of this is negative evidence however; there is no positive ground for doubting Baillet's simple statement that Foucher was asked, and the reasons given above are adequate to explain why he was. It is at least very probable that Foucher attended Rohault's weekly lectures on Cartesianism in 1667 and 1668, and he could have been an intimate of Rohault at that time.

In Paris, Foucher was the chaplain of some religious men who lived on rue Saint-Denis. Huet knew Foucher and although he had respect for him, he did not believe that he was a very good historian, claiming that Foucher hardly knew the names of Carneades and Arcesilaus, and that he knew even less of Pyrrhonism. Huet once tried to get Foucher a position with Charles de Sainte-Maure, Duke of Montausier and tutor to the Dauphine, but after a long visit and dinner during which, Huet says, Foucher fought with everyone and tried continually to talk of things unsuitable to the place and to the people present, the Duke did not even wish to hear Foucher's name spoken again.[33] Menage thought Foucher was a good historian, but Huet's opinion is more accurate.[34]

Leibniz was in Paris on a diplomatic mission during the years 1672–1676.[35] There he met Lantin and La Mare, Conseillers to Parlement from Dijon. Foucher was Lantin's friend, and it was probably through Lantin that he met Leibniz. In the later correspondence between Foucher and Leibniz, Lantin is often mentioned. Leibniz corresponded with Foucher for two reasons. First, he valued his criticisms and was stimulated by his ingenious arguments. Second, Foucher was active in trying to get Leibniz admitted to the Académie des Sciences. Foucher was in contact with Theve- not, was a friend of Jean-Baptiste Du Hamel, who was working on a history of the Academie, and knew Gallois, who was responsible for the appearance of Leibniz's contributions in the *Mémoires de l'Académie*. The exchange of letters between Foucher and Leibniz lasted from 1676 to 1695, and culmi- nated in the publication of extracts from them in the *Journal des Sçavans* from 1692 to 1696, including the first public exposition and criticism of Leibniz's theory of monads and pre-established harmony.[36]

Foucher's first published work is a long poem upon the death of Anne of Austria, published in Paris in 1666.[37] Nearly every verse is inspired by a

Latin quotation, which is given in the margin. *Cupio dissolvi & esse cum Christo* accompanies the earnest lines:

> Son corps la captivoit, une divine flame
>   En sçait rompre les noeuds,
> Ces indignes climates étoient pour sa grande Ame
>   Un sejour ennuyeaux.[38]

One might speculate about the young canon's literary ambitions. Perhaps he heard of Anne's death while still in Dijon and wrote the poem. Receiving praise in Dijon, he may have set off for Paris, manuscript in hand, with high hopes for the future. It is an intriguing picture, although highly speculative.

In 1672 Foucher published an eighteen-page letter entitled *Nouvelle façon d'hygrometres*, in which he describes several instruments for measuring the humidity of the air. This work was reprinted in 1686 along with five further letters on the same subject.[39] Foucher's interest in experimental physics was probably fostered by Rohault's lectures.

In 1673 Foucher had a small number of copies of his *Dissertations sur la recherche de la verité, ou sur la logique des academiciens* printed in Dijon. He distributed it personally; it was not put up for sale. He remarked to Leibniz (probably in 1685) that he no longer had even one copy.[40] There is none available today, but the substance of this work is incorporated in Foucher's other *Dissertations*.[41] Foucher no doubt distributed his *Logique* of 1673 among the philosophers in Paris; in it he speaks of the need for workers in "la recherche de la verité." Considering the similarity of the titles (although it is not an uncommon title), Foucher perhaps had some grounds for thinking that Malebranche's *Recherche de la vérité* of 1674 was in response to the call in the *Logique* of 1673. He seems to believe in his *Critique de la recherche de la verité* of 1675 that the *Logique* could not have been unknown to Malebranche. However, if Foucher truly believed that Malebranche had written at least partially from the inspiration of the *Logique*, then one wonders just how close Foucher's contact with the philosophic world of Paris was. Malebranche spent several years writing the *Recherche*. The first volume was finished in 1673, and the manuscript was in circulation; there must have been some gossip about the work Malebranche was doing. It seems likely that many knew that the author of the *Recherche* was Malebranche and that a second volume was nearly ready for the press. Malebranche, at least, did not feel that it was necessary to put a volume number on the work he published in 1674. In any event, it is clear that for lack of intelligence of one kind or another, Foucher took the 1674 volume of the *Recherche* as a complete work and criticized it as such. In Chapter 5, I give a more substantial excuse for his doing this than the speculation that he frequented the wrong cafés. If he did not know beforehand about the first volume of the *Recherche*, however, Foucher certainly had prior warning of the second of 1675. Ouvrard reports that Foucher could hardly wait for it to appear and that he was unapproachable for some time after it did.[42] Foucher's *Réponse pour la critique à la preface du second volume de la recherche de la verité* appeared in 1676. Malebranche removed the offensive preface in the fourth edition of the *Recherche* in 1678, so Foucher removed his preface in the second edition of the *Réponse* of 1679; he still believed, however, that the *Réponse* deserved a second printing.

In 1675 there also appeared Desgabet's *Critique de la critique de la recherche de la vérité*. Foucher replied to Desgabets in 1676 in his *Nouvelle dissertation*, and again in his *Dissertation . . . contenant l'apologie des academiciens* of 1687. Finally, in 1693 appeared Foucher's last work, *Dissertation . . . contenant l'histoire des academiciens* in four parts incorporating the substance of all the *Dissertations* that had gone before plus some new material. There is a great deal of repetition in Foucher's critiques, responses, and dissertations.

Foucher also wrote two works on moral philosophy, one in verse, to show that the pagan philosophers have principles similar to Christian ones.[43]

2   FOUCHER'S ACADEMIC SCEPTICISM AND HIS POSITIVE POSITION

Having examined Foucher's life and works, I now consider his Academic scepticism and his positive position. Foucher is known as the restorer of the Academic philosophy.[44] He says that he is an Academic in the manner of Plato, not that he is a Platonist, but that he follows the Platonic method of philosophizing.[45] By this he seems to mean primarily that he, and the other Academics, reject the senses as a source of knowledge, depending only on reason. He also asserts that all Academic philosophy is founded in Socratic ignorance; the Academic philosopher knows little more or less than anyone else, except that he knows his own ignorance.

Foucher's major *Dissertations* were written to give expositions of the Academic philosophy. They are, in turn, *La Logique des academiciens* (1673), *L'Apologie des academiciens* (1687), and *L'Histoire des academiciens* (1693). His sources for these works are Cicero, Plutarch, Sextus Empiricus, Diogenes Laertius, and Augustine.[46] The following is a short exposition of Foucher's positive views as he adapts them from the Academic philosophers. I make little attempt here to question his interpretations, beyond remarking that they are somewhat free, perhaps because one of his intents is to show that Academic principles are most fitted to lead one to Christianity.

A very short outline can be given of the principal Academics. Foucher paraphrases their views as follows:

Socrates:	*Je sçais que je ne sçais pas.*
Arcesilaus:	Je ne sçais pas même que je sçais que je ne sçais pas.
Carneades:	Je doute si je sçais que je ne sçais rien.
Philo:	Je sçais peu de chose & j'en ignore beaucoup.
Antiochus:	Je sçais plusieurs choses & j'en ignore plusieurs.[47]

After Socrates on principle, Foucher agrees most with Antiochus and Philo.[48] He admits that Arcesilaus ended as a Pyrrhonist, but like Carneades, Arcesilaus began in Socratic ignorance. However, even the Pyrrhonians cannot actually be said to be opposed to the Academic dictum to search for the truth, for they make no dogmatic assertions at all.[49] Among the church fathers, Augustine can be counted as "Chef d'Academie."[50] He was really for, not against them, and he worked to show that Academic principles can be accommodated to those of Christendom.[51] Lactantius did the same, and further stressed that knowledge cannot be based on probabilities. With this, Foucher is in full agreement. Descartes is an Academic in that he correctly commences in metaphysics by rejecting all propositions that can be doubted, but unfortunately he does not abide by this rule and so falls into dogmatism.[52]

Foucher is a sceptic, but in a limited sense. He distinguishes Academic beliefs from two extremes of dogmatism: that everything can be known and that nothing can be known. The Academics are not extreme:

> C'est ainsi que les Academiciens combatoient les prejugez des Dogmatists, & tachoient de les reduire dans un doute raisonnable: non pas pour les y arrêter entierement; mais au contraire pour les obliger d'en sortir de maniere à n'y rentre jamais. Il est vray que les Academiciens doivent douter d'une tres grande quantité des choses, mais c'est parce que ces choses sont douteuses, & il se trouve neamoins que les principales veritez leur son connuës, de sorte que leurs doutes regardent seulement les matieres de sciences, & les propostions dogmatiques que l'on pourroit faire sur les sujets de pure speculation humain.[53]

Foucher believes that we do have some certain knowledge but doubts that we have or can have knowledge of the essences of external things. Let us begin, then, with what the Academic knows for certain.

Philosophy should begin with an examination of first principles.[54] The first principle, "la grande maxime," of the Academics is: "[Academiciens] ne reconnoissent que la verité évidente pour regel, & à son défaut la foi, *in fide & veritate*."[55] It is most reasonable to follow evident truths in matters of knowledge, the laws of one's country in matters of life, and faith in matters of religion. Among first principles that are certainly known are five that Foucher gives as the laws of the Academic philosophers:

1. *Ne se conduire que par demonstration en matiere de Philosophie.*

2. *Ne point agiter les questions que nous voions bien ne pouvoir decider.*

3. *Avoüer que l'on ne sçait pas, ce que l'on ignore effectivement.*

4. *Distinguer les choses que l'on sçait de celles que l'on ne sçait pas.*

5. *Chercher toûjours des connoissances nouvelles.*[56]

Foucher also stresses three important axioms:

1. *Judicium veritatis non est in sensibus.*

2. *Non opinaturum esse sapientem.*

3. *Verba non dant conceptus, sed supponent.*[57]

Socratic ignorance and reasonable doubt, then, are far from leading the Academic philosopher to deny that we have knowledge. These five laws and three axioms are offered, like the first "grande maxime," as self-evident truths. The fifth law expressly states that the business of a philosopher is to search after truth: "chercher la verité n'est autre chose que philosopher."[58] Thus, "les Academiciens sont plus éloignez des prejugez que les autres Philosophes, puis qu'ils dêcident moins & qu'ils ne se hazardent pas à suive de simples vray-semblances."[59]

The three axioms, like the truths of mathematics, Foucher calls dogmas of the Academics. The first means that knowledge of the essences of things cannot be gained from sense experience. The second does not deny that in the actions of life we must often act by opinion, but this can go easily with suspense of judgment concerning the truth.[60] The third means simply that words are the arbitrary signs of the ideas they excite, and that we must have these ideas before words can be applied to them. Simple ideas come only through experience, but complex ideas can be constructed by putting together simple ideas or the words that are signs of them. Foucher says that this means that two kinds of logic are required:

> L'une que doit servir à nous acquerir les idées que nous n'avons pas, ou à éclaircir celles que nouns avons confuses. L'autre à exposer & décrire les idées que nous avons afin de découvir aux autres les veritez que nous connoissons dés-jà. L'une est proprement la recherche de la verité, & l'autre retient plus proprement le nom de Logique, concernant le discour & l'arrangement des propositions.[61]

The first (which we might call the logic of discovery) is the more important; this search for or clarification of new knowledge is best pursued with Academic principles. The second (which we might call the logic of justification) is harmful without the first; such analyzing and demonstrating of logical relations among ideas is most highly developed by the Peripatetics.

In metaphysics, the Academics recognize such truths as the existence of a good and just God, and of two sorts of being, one created, the other uncreated. In morals, they recognize such truths as that the goods of fortune are not capable of rendering us happy, that one should not contradict oneself, nor suppose what is in question, nor conduct oneself by prejudices in matters of knowledge, and that we are obliged to make good use of our reason. The major dogma, again, is that evident reason is necessary in matters of knowledge, with the concomitant reasonable conclusions that probabilities are sufficient for the particular actions of life and for the establishment of historical facts, and that reason should be silenced in matters of religion.[62] One must restrict reasonable doubt in order to live, but it is better to doubt too much than to doubt too little in the search for knowledge.[63]

We have seen the first principles; Foucher says that we must now inquire into the search for truth. What we are looking for when we search for truth is a way to determine whether or not our judgments are true; that is, the goal of philosophy is to learn how to avoid error in judgments.[64] This means that we must find a criterion of truth. After the criterion is found, we are to use it to discover knowledge of the essences of external things, and then to discover a necessary order in that knowledge.[65] Let us proceed in order.

There are good signs, Foucher says, that we will be able to find the criterion. We do know some truths—for example, mathematical truths—so we know what truth is in general. Foucher says that this saves us from having to seek a criterion for our criterion, and so on. No one has ever doubted that 2 + 2 = 4 is necessarily true, or that 2 + 2 = 5 is necessarily false; mathematical truths are true, even if they exist only in our minds.[66] The careful way this is put actually leads to two criteria. The first is that all the truths mentioned above are self-evidently certain; they have the evidence of reason. This is a psychological criterion in that the evidence of such self-evident principles is such that only a madman would not accept them.[67] We are psychologically incapable of doubting them, and for good reason: The general and evident truths that the Academics accept "sont écrites & imprimées dans tous les espirits."[68] They constitute the natural, eternal light from God and are accepted by all men of good sense. They are recognizably certain in themselves, also, and in this we have a second criterion of truth. This is the logical criterion that a proposition is true if it is inconceivable that its contradictory could be true. Hence, for the discovery of truths beyond these that are immediately self-evident, the principle of contradiction is necessary.[69]

There is a third, sensible criterion of truth, which even the Pyrrhonians recognize. All the knowledge we have of pain, pleasure, sweetness, bitterness, light, darkness, red, green, heat, cold, and the other sensible qualities is not denied to be true by the Academics. With the Pyrrhonians, they take "pour leur *Criterium*, la perception ou façon-d'être connuë par elle-même."

These interior sensible qualities are perfectly comprehensible because they are known in themselves "par conscience." No one denies that they are what they are.[70]

Do we then have among these three criteria of truth, a criterion for determining the truth of propositions about the essences of external things? Foucher's caution about mathematical truths shows us that we do not. He says that the evidence we have that $2 + 2 = 4$ is such that the mind could not desire anything more evident and invarible; however, for all we know, such truth may be only for propositions in the mind and might not apply to judgments about the external world.[71] We can easily prove that we have many truths that are certain because our reason leads infallibly to necessary truths. If it did not, there would be no constant truths. However, we do have constant truths; hence our reason must be trustworthy. If this is not enough, one need only consider that he cannot will such truths to be otherwise.[72] However, when we judge that these truths apply to the external world, we make a claim that goes beyond evident knowledge; and for this new judgment we have no criterion of truth. This is apparent in Foucher's answer to the objection that mathematical truths are contested:

> On ne les conteste que pour les choses qui sont hors de nostre esprit & *à parte rei*, pour ce qui regarde la conception de ces veritez, elle est incontestable. Il est certain que les deux costez d'un triangle pris ensemble, composent un ligne plus grande que le troisième de ces costez separement, soit qu'il y ait des lignes & des triangles hors de nous, soit qu'il n'y en ait point, d'ailleurs les Academiciens ne pretendoient pas trouver, en matiere de Philosophie, des veritez plus certenes que celle de Geometrie, & je declarie que je m'en contenterois.[73]

The third criterion, that of sensible knowledge, offers at least a purchase on the external world. Foucher is quite explicit in saying that we cannot know the natures of external things, either by the internal ideas discussed above or by the senses:

> non sens ne sçauroient être les juges de la verité des choses qui sont hors de nous; parce que nous ne connoissons point ces choses *elles-mêmes*. Du moins par les sens nous n'en connoissons que les apparences & nous ne sçaurions sçavoir se ces apparences nous les representant telles qu'elles sont, parce que nous ne sçauriens les comparer avec les realitez de ces choses que nous ne concevons pas, il en est de même que si nous ne pouvoins voir l'original de quelques portrats; il nous seroit impossible de juger des défauts de ces portraits ne les pouvant comparer avec leurs originaux.[74]

He continues that we do not have direct knowledge of external things through the senses, car si ces choses nous estoient ainsi connuës, elles-seroiet en nous, & ne seroient pas hors de nous, ce qui seroit contradictoire. En effet la connoissance étant une action immanente, il faut que le terme de cette action soit dans la faculté ou substance qui connoît, autrement la connoissance seroit une action au dehors ce qui ne se peut; car ce seroit connoissance & ce ne seroit pas connoissance.[75]

It is impossible to know the essences of external things for by our nature we can know only things in our minds. Aristotle and the other ancient philosophers recognized this, Foucher says, and that is why they were obliged to discuss ideas or phantoms in conceiving of external things. It is even more apparent that what we sense immediately are only phenomenal appearances that are in the substance of our mind. Plato, Sextus Empiricus, Descartes, Rohault, Arnauld, Nicole, and Desgabets all agree in this with Foucher and the Academics.[76]

However, even though we cannot know external things in themselves by the senses, we can know that they exist as the causes of our sensations. And we can distinguish them from one another if they (1) cause some modification in us, (2) which we can know, and (3) which is more related to one particular external thing than to any other.

Cela posé, je dis qu'il est impossible de connoître les choses exterieures en elles-mêmes; c'est à dire de premiere veuë, d'où il s'ensuit manifestement que la premiere chose que je connois par les sens sont les resultats de l'action des objets exterierrus, & non pas ces mêmes objets ou leurs realitez, parce que ces realitez estant hors de nous, ne sçauroient être connueës immediatement en elles mêmes, étant impossible que nôtre âme sort d'elle-même pour aller dans ces objets, & que ces objets se rendent presens à nôtre âme, à moins que de luy devenir interieurs, acquel cas, ils deviendroient des façons d'être de nôtre âme, & ne seroient pas connus tels qu'ils seroient étant entrez en nous. Tant il est vray que la connoissance est immanente, & n'embrasse rien d'exterieur immediatement.[77]

Because ideas are also "façons-d'être" of our soul, it is manifest also that they do not give us direct knowledge of external things in themselves, nor any knowledge of external natures at all. It "est impossible de concevoir ces choses en elles-mêmes vû qu'elles somt hors de nous."[78] What we know "ne sont que des façons-d'être ou des modifications de notre propre substance." Finally, "il est impossible que les choses soient veritablement tout ce qu'elles paroissent être."[79] Foucher's development of this consequence against Malebranche is treated in Chapter 5.

Therefore, although Foucher does have knowledge, he has no criterion for determining whether or not these truths in the mind also apply to the external world. That such a criterion could ever be found seems to be denied by the very conditions of knowing; about external things we seem condemned to know no more than that they exist as causes of our diverse sensations. Nevertheless, Foucher says that it is the task of the philosopher to continue the search.

Despite the fact that we cannot have certain knowledge of external things, we can have a kind of "connoissances artificielles" that we ourselves have formed from sense experience.[80] This artificial knowledge might be true, and it certainly is useful. Foucher appeals to it in answer to the objection that stress on Academic purity is useless, for no one has yet found any truth in natural philosophy. Just as we cannot be certain that it is impossible to find, Foucher says, it is also not certain that no one has yet found it. Academic principles have furthered the new science of the seventeenth century, being important in the development of telescopes, microscopes, algebra, the laws of the equilibrium of liquids, and the art of navigation. Granted that the new science provides less than certain knowledge, we must admit that it has progressed only by conformity to rules very similar to those of the Academics. Foucher believes that Academic logic is much wider spread than many people think.[81] Mathematical knowledge in particular is quite useful, for with nothing but mathematics we can "expliquer toute la Physique, parce que l'univers estant une grand Machine, on en peut reduire tous les mouvemens & tous le ressorts aux lois de la Mechanique, *in pondere, numero, & mensura.*"[82] Only a dogmatic Cartesian would insist that this speculation about the causes of our sensations is certain knowledge. What the Academics say is that these mathematical applications to physics are of the highest probability. It is not infallible knowledge, but neither is it confused nor subject to ordinary doubt.

> Ce n'est pas qu'ils crûssent que nous pouvons juger des choses exterieures, en les comparant avec les idées que nous en avons, car il faudroit pour cela connoistre ces choses en elles-mêmes & immediatement; auquel cas nous n'aurions pas besoin d'idées pour les representer: mais c'est que nous pouvons sçavoir ce qu'il nous est permis d'attribuer à ces choses & ce qu'on ne leur doit point attribuer. Quoy que nous ne puissoins connoistre immediatement les triangles qui sont hors de nous, nous pouvons neanmoins estre assurez, que s'il y en a, leurs angles ne valent que deux droits: je veux que nostre conclusion en cela, ne soit qu'hypotetique, neanmoins elle est certene.[83]

That is, as mathematics it is certain knowledge; as physics it is hypothetical. Foucher is certainly correct that if there are triangles in the external world, then they have the properties of triangles. However, it is easy to understand how such hypothetical certainty is unsatisfactory to the dogmatist. At the peak of Foucher's investigations of the external world he still does not know whether it contains a triangle.

This does not mean that Foucher is in favor of depending upon probability in philosophy. He continues to seek certain foundations. What he means to do is to expose the major defect of dogmatic philosophers: They become too enamored of their prejudices. The Academics will admit that some of the dogmatists' principles are probable, but it is a gross mistake to take probabilities as certain truths. A true system of knowledge cannot be built upon probabilities.[84]

Foucher goes on to derive more truths from his principles than anyone might think possible. They parallel those of the Cartesian system, and while there is an element of grotesque virtuosity in the performance, it is undoubtedly serious. If from nothing else, this is evident from the fact that a careful examination shows that all these truths are about existence, but not about essences. First, our soul is known before all other things. This is because we know immediately only modifications of our soul, so if we know anything, we know our soul. This knowledge, however, is only of the soul's properties and not of its essence. The soul is a thinking being, but we do not know what this being is. However, the Academics can easily prove the spirituality and unity of the soul. That is, there must be an indivisible subject of all our thoughts, sensations and judgments. It would be impossible to construct a thinking being from insensible and separable parts; therefore, the soul is a spiritual unity. Plotinus very well pointed out that for the comprehension of the diversity of sensation, there must be a unitary point—the soul—of comparison. From the unity and indivisibility of the soul immediately follows its immortality, for what cannot be broken up into parts is immortal. Foucher admits that the various modifications of the soul succeed one another and pass away, but their transitory reality necessarily depends on the substance in which they inhere. Incidentally Foucher proves that we cannot know the essence of matter. If we knew matter immediately, then, as Plato says, we could not prove the immortality of the soul nor the existence of God.[85] However, Foucher says, we have just proved the immortality of the soul and will prove the existence of God in the next paragraph. It should be noted that the Academics, by not claiming that the essence of matter is extension, can admit with little embarrassment the real interaction of minds and bodies that everyone experiences taking place. That no one has been able to explain this interaction might be evidence that the essences of mind and matter are not yet known.[86]

The Academic demonstration of the existence of God depends upon the necessity of a Creator of substance. In particular, all extension presupposes thought; all the movements, figure, union, generation, corruption, composition, and dissolution of bodies that cause our sensations cannot exist without the prior thought of an Understanding that gives body being. The Academics, along with Plato, recognize this. Hence, the existence and reality of substance in the universe is proof of the existence of God. A unique eternal Understanding is implied; hence, the unity of God is proved. And, because thought is required for existence, the continual production of created things is proved, for they would cease to exist if God ceased to conceive them. The freedom of man and the providence of God easily follow on Academic principles from the recognition that we can suspend our judgment on doubtful questions. And although we do not know the essences of external things, God does.[87] Finally, Academic principles are most fitted to lead one to Christianity, for they exhort us to search for the truth; it is a most reasonable truth to accept Divine Faith.

Because the *Dissertations* are meant in part to be examinations of Descartes's principles, it is well to complete this chapter by giving Foucher's evaluation. I describe above some similarities and differences between their systems. They agree that the senses are not a source of knowledge of essences. The similarity between Foucher's five Academic rules and Descartes's rules of method is quite apparent. Foucher says its is obvious why the Academics and the Cartesians agree in method: Descartes took his rules from the Academics.[88] Where Descartes went wrong, Foucher says, is in following the first Academic law while failing to follow the third. He should not have affirmed "que tout ce qui est clairement enfermé dans nos idées, est contenu dans les choses que ces idées nous represent." Foucher does not understand "comment nos façons-d'être nous peuvent representer des choses differentes de nous-memes." In the Cartesian system, Foucher says,

> il faut premierement sçavoir si nos façons-d'être nous peuvent repre-senter quelque chose de different de nous-mêmes, & quoy qu'on appelle les façons-d'être des idées, il ne n'ensuit pas pour cela qu'elles soient representatives des choses exterieures.[89]

Descartes certainly begs the question here.[90] We cannot know whether ideas are similar to things; but even more,

> de vouloir que des choses ou idées qui n'ont ni étenduës, ni figures, representent neanmoins de certaines étenduës determinées & de cer-taines figures! pour moy je pense que si cela n'est absurde & impossible du moins cela n'est pas si évident qu'on n'en puisse douter.[91]

Foucher's development of these objections against Malebranche is given in Chapter 5.

The *cogito* is obviously not the first principle, Foucher insists, because we must know that everything that thinks also exists, and that everything must either be or not be to establish the *cogito*.[92] Foucher does agree with Descartes that our proper being consists in thought[93] but, as I show above, by this he means not that we know the essence of the thinking being but only that it has properties that are thoughts. The real dogmatism of Descartes comes in his assertion that we know the essences of mind and body. Because of this claim, Foucher says, Descartes cannot explain the real interaction between mind and body that Foucher allows simply by admitting that he does not know their essences. Foucher also differs from Descartes on the idea of infinity and infinite divisibility and, as is shown above, in his proof of the existence of God.[94]

chapter 4

Late Seventeenth-Century Cartesian Metaphysics and Criticisms of it

1 A MODEL LATE SEVENTEENTH-CENTURY CARTESIAN METAPHYSICAL SYSTEM

In this chapter I characterize the Cartesian metaphysical system. Orthodox Cartesians attempt to adhere to this basic position. La Forge, Rohault, Régis, Le Grand, and in most respects Desgabets and Arnauld are or attempt to be orthodox Cartesians. Malebranche, as he himself stresses, is not an orthodox Cartesian.

The last grand expositor of the Cartesian system is Antoine Le Grand, who in 1694 published *An Entire Body of Philosophy*. The characterization of the late seventeenth-century Cartesian metaphysical system given below follows Le Grand's exposition more closely than others, but it also incorporates elements from those of La Forge, Rohault, Régis, Desgabets, Arnauld, and Malebranche.[95] None of these Cartesians professes a system that is in all details like the one I present here, nor do I imply that any one of them does. What I provide is an ideally complete Cartesian system. My guide and rationale for drawing from the Cartesians such a model Cartesianism is the polemical writing of Simon Foucher.[96] His series of attacks upon Cartesianism (of which the second is his criticism of Malebranche of 1675, *Critique de la recherche de la verité*) give clearly the most important arguments against Cartesian metaphysics. The system outlined below, while more complete than some and less detailed than other expositions of Cartesian metaphysics, has the merit of including all those elements that play a role in the controversies that rocked Cartesianism. It provides a background against which I can analyze the problems that arise because of conflicts between ontological and epistemological principles.

The late seventeenth-century Cartesian metaphysical system within which Foucher discovers problems can be characterized as follows. Every existing thing is either a substance or a property of a substance. Substances exist in themselves independently either as uncreated or as created; properties exist only dependently in created substances as their modifications. The universe consists of three substances, one uncreated and two created. God is an infinite substance Who creates finite mind and finite matter. Mind is

unextended active *thinking*. Matter is unthinking passive *extension*. The two
created substances differ in essence, and because their essences *are* their being
as existents, they differ ontologically. There is no real difference between a
substance and its essence. That is, mind *is not* a substance informed or
essentially characterized by thinking; thinking *is* the substance of mind.
Matter is not a substance informed or essentially characterized by extension;
extension *is* the substance of matter. This stresses the point that there is
nothing in finite essence or being in common between mind and matter; even
though they are alike in genesis and exist as finite substances created by God,
they are entirely different in essence. This distinction between mind and
matter is completely clear and distinct.

Matter is modified by the properties of size, shape, and motion or rest.
These are the only properties a material thing can have. Mind is modified by
will and intellect and by passions, volitions, sensations, and ideas. Ideas
represent objects external to the mind; sensations do not. These are the only
properties a mental thing can have.

This organization of substances and their modifications was thought in the
seventeenth century to be Descartes's primary contribution to the revolution
in philosophy. Desgabets, for example, says that the insight that leads to the
distinction between material and mental properties shows that Descartes is
the greatest philosopher since Aristotle.[97] The popular seventeenth-century
understanding of Scholastic philosophy exhibited by many Cartesians is that
Scholastics believe that there are properties in material things similar to
sensations.[98] Descartes rehearses the traditional sceptical arguments based
on the variation of sensations, stressing the paradoxes that arise from the
attribution of sensible properties to material things. Cartesians consider it to
be a blow against both Scholasticism and scepticism to demonstrate that
sensible properties *as* sensed are modifications not of a material but of a
mental substance.

Man is a substantial union of mind and matter, the soul acting as the form
of the human body. Some Cartesians classify man as a fourth substance, a
finite compound fused by God. In this elaboration the essence of man is the
union itself, or finite human will.[99] Thus, despite their essential difference—
by God's will—mind and matter interact. Ideas and sensations—
modifications of mind—are caused by matter in this interaction. In the case
of ideas, whether they simply rise from the mind (having been innate) or are
provided or illuminated by God on the occasion of the interaction, or
whether the action of matter on mind contributes directly to the content of
the idea (and in this way objectively causes it) are points of contention. In
any event, interaction is usually sufficient for, and is often necessary to, the
occurrence of ideas. Ideas of immaterial things can arise, of course, without
interaction. Sometimes the human will (with or without interaction) forms

volitions that cause motions in matter; this is the reverse of the process by which motions in matter cause ideas and sensations. Passions also arise with or without interaction between mind and matter.

The mechanics of sensation and of perception are easily explained. The human body is so constructed that it has five kinds of sense organs that are connected to the brain by the nerves. When bodies of various kinds impinge upon these organs, motion is communicated from them through the nerves to the pineal gland, which is the central organ in the brain. The motions thereby caused in the pineal gland are uniformly distinctive dependent upon the various properties of the material bodies and the sense organs affected. Because space is extended, and extension is matter, the material universe is a *plenum* in which subtle matter is everywhere. To cause sensations, therefore, material bodies do not always have to strike the sense organs themselves; they can also act upon them through a material medium in the way, for example, that pulses of air put into motion by a vibrating body strike the eardrums. Hence, although the Cartesians disagree with Gassendi's assertion that a material species must travel from the material thing to the sense organ, they do agree that unmediated action cannot occur over a distance. And because distance is for the Cartesians nothing more than extension or matter, the very notion of an empty distance—and thus of action over it—is inconceivable.

The pineal gland is the unifying organ of common sense; also it is the mind's seat in the body. The occurrence of the distinctive motions in the pineal gland causes the mind to form sensations and ideas that are naturally and uniformly resultant from these motions. Conversely, certain volitions from the mind can cause other distinctive motions in the pineal gland that result in the movement of the human body. This far we can understand: There is a uniform causal interaction between body and mind mediated by the pineal gland. We can understand all the mechanics on the material side and we can learn which ideas and sensations are naturally connected with which motions. We experience the interaction. We cannot, however, understand how the interaction takes place, *how* body acts on mind, or mind on body. It is a fact that God has united mind and body in man, so that interaction between body and mind takes place; we experience this interaction all the time; we can know no more.

The Cartesian way of ideas and the distinction between primary and secondary qualities is implicit in the sharp dualism of the created world. Ideas are representational modifications of the mind. Through some of these mental modifications the mind knows material things. There is no other way of knowing than by having ideas, for this is the nature of the mind. Sensations are also modifications of the mind, but they are not representative; one does not have a sensation *of* a thing, although material things do cause sensations. Sensations serve only as signs by which a man is advised as to whether his body should pursue or avoid material things in the interests of its own preservation. The Scholastics mistakenly attributed to material things sensible or secondary qualities similar to sensations. It is apparent that this is impossible when one considers that the modifications of mind are as utterly different from the modifications of matter as are the two substances from one another. There can be no essential resemblance between the two created, finite substances: Mind is active thinking; matter is inert extension. This is Cartesian ontology.

A basic principle of Cartesian epistemology is that knowledge depends on direct acquaintance. The mind is directly acquainted only with its own modifications, so only ideas and sensations are known directly. The Cartesians are thus committed to a representative theory of mediate knowledge of material things. This is because they conceive of the relation of direct acquaintance only in terms of the relation between a substance and its own modifications. Therefore, all knowledge of mental substance (that is, beyond direct intuitive knowledge of one's own existence), of material substance, and of the modifications of material substance is by way of ideas. These ideas are mental modifications whose nature it is to represent their objects. Descartes himself believes that his greatest contribution to philosophy is the discovery of the criterion for true ideas, that is, clearness and distinctness; many Cartesians take this criterion to be the rule that establishes the truth of Cartesianism.

Finally, the Cartesians hold two likeness principles. The first is that an idea must be caused by something that has as much or more formal or eminent reality as the idea has objective reality. This principle is meant to explain both how ideas can be caused and how ideas can represent their objects. It derives from the basic axiom that something cannot come from nothing. This implies that there must be at least as much or more perfection in the cause as in the effect. Foucher takes "perfection" in this principle to mean "essential likeness" and thereby assumes that a basic principle of Cartesianism is that the cause must be like the effect to the extent that it is cause of the effect, or conversely, that the effect cannot be unlike the cause to the extent that it is effect of the cause. Besides this *causal likeness principle*, there is also a closely (but not necessarily) related epistemological principle embodied in the Cartesian dictum that the objective reality of an idea cannot exceed the formal or eminent reality of its cause. The *epistemological likeness principle* is that the knower must in some essential way be like the known, or, conversely, that the known must in some essential way be like the knower. Thus ideas obviously can be known, for an idea is essentially the mind modified, that is, an idea is a property of the mind. The mind is directly acquainted only with its own properties, however, so these ideas mediate knowledge of external things. It follows that ideas must be in some way essentially like their objects in order to represent these objects so that the mind can know them. Conversely, the principle that a representative idea must be essentially like its object implies that the mind of which these ideas are properties must also be in that same essential way like the mediately known objects.

The causal and epistemological likeness principles are important also in Scholasticism and are popularly expressed as like causes like, or like can be caused only by like, and as like knows like, or like can be known only by like. Foucher takes them for granted, and less obviously so does Malebranche. They form the basis for Foucher's objections to Cartesianism; he shows that the likeness principles cannot be satisfied in Cartesianism. He does this on the assumption that the Cartesians will want to retain these principles, and his assumption is justified (as is the inclusion of these principles in this model Cartesianism) by the fact that some of the Cartesians attempt to show how the principles can be retained, while others give them up only after a searching appraisal of what is important in Cartesian metaphysics as a whole.

The important principles of the model late seventeenth-century Cartesian metaphysical system sketched above are given below. Note that this listing of Cartesian principles is not meant to be complete; also, they are phrased here not necessarily in their most general form but in a form most appropriate for the arguments that follow.

Cartesian metaphysics is comprised of five ontological principles:

    A. God is an uncreated substance.
    B. There is a dualism of two created substances that differ in essence: mind is *thinking*; matter is *extension*.
    C. Volitions, passions, sensations, and ideas are the (only) properties, that is, modifications, of mind.
    D. Size, shape, and motion or rest are the (only) properties, that is, modifications, of matter.
    E. There is an all-inclusive ontological type-distinction between substance and property: substance is essentially independent; properties, that is, modifications, are dependent upon substance.

There are three causal principles:

    F. There is causal interaction between mind and matter.
    G. Ideas and sensations are caused by the interaction of matter and mind.
    H. There must be essential likeness between a cause and its effect.

And there are five epistemological principles:

    I. Ideas represent objects external to the mind.
    J. Sensations do not represent objects external to the mind.

K. There must be essential likeness between an idea and its object.
L. Direct acquaintance is necessary for knowledge.
M. Objects external to the mind are known only mediately by way of representative ideas.

The arrival of the Cartesians at such a system can be traced along many lines. The most obvious is that leading from methodic doubt to the *cogito* in Descartes's *Meditations*. Having only the *cogito* and the simple knowledge of existence it provides, sheer lack of clutter allows the Cartesians, so they believe, to recognize with certainty the essences and properties of mind and matter. Another line leads from a set of self-evident principles of which the first is that nothing can have no properties. Volitions, passions, sensations, and ideas appear to Cartesians necessarily to be properties of one substance, while size, shape, and motion or rest seem necessarily to be properties of a different substance. They are also influenced by reasoning concerning mathematics and physics. Mathematical thinking can lead to belief in the permanence of quantitative properties at the expense of qualitative properties in the conception of material things. And like Galileo, Cartesians do find that the real properties of material things are those that can be described in strict quantitative terms. Such a belief can either lead to or confirm the denial that qualitative properties really belong to material things. Cartesians find further evidence in experience, as does Gassendi, for denying the materiality of color, heat, and the other sensory qualities; their variations in the same thing are legion. Sceptics use such variations to show that knowledge of material things is uncertain. Cartesians, however, accuse sceptic and Scholastic alike of basing their arguments on naive childhood beliefs; it is a mistake to believe that the sensory qualities belong to material things. Such qualities are nothing more than sensations, modifications of the mind, caused by changes in the real, quantitative properties of material things. Most of the variations of sensory qualities are the result not of changes of real material properties but rather of varying conditions of the medium (such as light) or of changing relations between the perceiver (or his sense organs) and material things. By making the distinction between primary and secondary qualities—primary qualities being real properties of bodies, of which we have ideas, secondary qualities being only sensations, which are properties of the mind—Cartesians explain errors deriving from sensory variations and thus remove one basis for scepticism about our knowledge of material things. The sceptics are right and the Scholastics deceived, for knowledge of material things is not sensory but ideational. Sensations in themselves are what they are, and they lead to deception only if they are mistakenly judged either to belong to or to represent material things. With application, one can learn which modifications of material things cause the different sensations and their variations in various circumstances. Sensations are designed by God as nondiscursive natural signs that we can respond to immediately in action for the preservation of our bodies. Hence it is that lines of reasoning from psychological, metaphysical, logical, mathematical, physical, and sceptical considerations converge upon a system that implies the Cartesian way of ideas and the distinction between primary and secondary qualities.

Sufficient background has now been provided for examination of the epistemological conflicts that led to the downfall of Cartesianism in the late seventeenth century. The Scholastic way of knowing depends on a likeness between what is known (basically the form of the object) and the intelligible species through which or by which it is known. Whether this process involves representation of or sharing of essential form, both the comprehensibility of and the validity of the knowledge relationship are derived from the apparently self-evident explanatory force of a statement of resemblance or similarity between the intelligible species and what is known. The Cartesian distinction between the essentially different substances, mind and matter, means that ideas, which are modifications of the knowing mind, can be in no way like the known material things. Cartesians, then, cannot appeal to resemblance to explain how ideas represent material things. They are forced to recognize this by being reminded of the ontological similarity between ideas and sensations. If sensations, because they are modifications of mind, cannot resemble purported modifications of matter (secondary qualities), then neither can ideas, which are also modifications of mind, resemble real modifications of matter (primary qualities). Thus Cartesians have to resolve the dilemma that neither or both ideas and sensations represent. They cannot give up the distinction between ideas and sensations nor the closely related distinction between primary and secondary qualities, for these are major principles of Cartesianism that distinguish it from Scholasticism and support the new deductive mathematical physics.

I now state Foucher's objections to Cartesian metaphysics in summary form. Then, in Chapter 5, I examine in detail Foucher's polemic with Malebranche to determine to what extent his criticisms apply also to Malebranche's metaphysics. The attempts of nonoccasionalist Cartesians to fill the gaps in Cartesianism pointed out by Foucher are evaluated in Chapter 6. Finally, in Chapter 7, the roots of Foucher's objections are exposed and an analysis is given of the failure of Malebranche and the Cartesians to meet Foucher's objections.

2 FOUCHER'S MAJOR CRITICISMS OF CARTESIAN METAPHYSICS

Foucher makes four basic criticisms of Cartesian metaphysics.[100] First, he denies that causal interaction between mind and matter is possible on

Cartesian principles. If mind and matter differ in essence, then there can be no essential likeness or similarity between the two substances. Because essential likeness is necessary for causal interaction between substances—so that they can engage one another—it follows that no interaction is possible between mind and matter as defined by the Cartesians.

This leads Foucher to his second criticism: Cartesians evidently do not really know the essences of mind and matter. It seems obvious to Foucher that interaction does take place between mind and matter. It is further obvious to him that the causal likeness principle is self-evident. Consequently, the Cartesians must be wrong in their characterization of mind and matter as two substances differing in essence. The implication is that if they interact—as they do in fact—then they must have some likeness in essence. Foucher points out that the Cartesians admit the interaction but deny the likeness, thus contradicting themselves.

The third criticism is based on the ontological similarity between sensations and ideas, both of which are said by the Cartesians to be modifications of the mind. Both, also, are caused by the interaction of material things with the mind. However, ideas are said to represent objects external to the mind, whereas sensations do not and cannot. However, Foucher insists, if ideas are mental modifications representative of material things that cause them, why do not sensations, which are also modifications of mind, likewise represent the material things that cause them? In both cases, it is the same material things that are the causes, and if the cause has anything to do with the representative nature of the effect—which to Foucher seems implied—then sensations as well as ideas surely could or should be representative. On the other hand, Foucher asks, if sensations do not and cannot represent material things, then how is it that ideas do? Nothing in the causal situation distinguishes ideas from sensations, and ontologically both are modifications of mind. Hence, there is no reason for asserting that whatever is characteristic or a possible function of the one is not also characteristic or a possible function of the other. Foucher finds it obvious that ideas and sensations are essentially similar in being modifications of the mind; he finds it arbitrary to distinguish ideas as representative from sensations, which are not.

In his third criticism, Foucher depends upon the link between the causal and the epistemological likeness principles that seems to be expressed in the Cartesian dictum that the cause of an idea must have at least as much or more formal and/or eminent reality as the idea has objective reality. He apparently reasons that ideas can represent the objects that cause them only on the ground that in causing an idea an object causes that idea to have an objective reality similar to the formal and/or eminent reality of the object. And prior to and essential to the establishment of this epistemological relationship, there must be likeness between the object and the mind if there is to be a causal relationship between them. The Cartesians, therefore, evidently depend on some sort of likeness between mind and material object, and because of this likeness the object can cause the idea and also causes the idea to represent the object. So why is the sensation, which is also caused by the object in the same way at the same time, not likewise caused by the object to represent it? Foucher concludes that if an object cannot cause a sensation to represent it, then it must also be incapable of causing an idea to represent it.

The fourth criticism is deeper than the third; indeed, it goes to the heart of the matter. In Cartesian ontology, mind and matter are substances that differ in essence. Foucher takes this difference to be ontological; it implies that there can be no similarity between mind and matter, nor any likeness between modifications of mind and modifications of matter. And if there is no resemblance, Foucher claims, there can be no representation. Ideas cannot *represent* material things or material modifications, because ideas are mental modifications that can in no way *resemble* material things or material modifications.

Foucher here assumes that the required likeness between an idea and its object is ontological likeness. If mind and matter are essentially dissimilar, if *thinking* is completely different from *extension*, then no idea can be like matter. Foucher's criticism is that the Cartesian ontological dualism of created substances precludes adherence to the epistemological likeness principle. One cannot know material things by way of ideas on Cartesian principles.

Thus, just as the first two criticisms are based on an unqualified acceptance of the causal likeness principle, Foucher's fourth criticism is based on acceptance of the epistemological likeness principle. Foucher's four criticisms, with reference to the Cartesian principles outlined above, can be summarized as follows:

1. *F* cannot be true, because of *B*, which precludes the possibility of *H*, upon which *F* depends.
2. *B* cannot be true, because *F* and *H* are true, and *B* leads to *I*.
3. *C* and *G* give evidence not for the distinction made in *I* and *J* but rather for the denial of this distinction.
4. Because of *B*, *K* cannot be fulfilled; therefore, *I* is impossible.

Foucher's criticisms were believed to be destructive of Cartesian metaphysics. In particular, the two criticisms concerning ideas—3 and 4—were repeated by du Hamel, Bayle, and Huet.[101] Although Foucher's books were not widely read, Huet's were. And Bayle's *Dictionnaire* was a sourcebook for many philosophers, including Locke, Berkeley, and Hume. Berkeley and Hume subsequently used Foucher's criticisms to dispute Locke's distinction between primary and secondary qualities.

It seems obvious that we do have knowledge of material things. Cartesian ontological dualism is thought to lead necessarily to an epistemology that makes it impossible to explain—with reference to the likeness principles— how we have knowledge of material things. Hence, Cartesian metaphysics is denounced as false. Foucher traces the Cartesians' difficulties ultimately to their dogmatic assertion that they know the essences of mind and matter. Obviously they do not, he claims, for the metaphysical system built upon such assumed knowledge of the dissimilarity of the essences of these two substances leads to absurd conclusions.[102]

Therefore, to put it bluntly, Foucher insists that something has to go. And in fact, all the attempted solutions to the problems Foucher poses involve either denying the likeness principles or altering the ontological principles of Cartesianism.

There are at least five lines of development destined to meet difficulties arising in Cartesianism. These lines are through Malebranche, through a number of orthodox (nonoccasionalist) Cartesians, through Locke, through Spinoza, and through Leibniz. The next two chapters contain characterizations and analyses of the solutions of Cartesian problems offered by Malebranche (Chapter 5) and the orthodox Cartesians (Chapter 6). I thus show what these philosophers believe is essential to Cartesianism. Then in Chapter 7 I give brief consideration to the question of whether Foucher's criticisms apply to Descartes's philosophy as contrasted to Cartesianism. I show that the difficulties detected by Foucher are inherent in the foundations of Cartesianism.

With this perspective, I sketch the post-Cartesian development of the Cartesian way of ideas through Locke, Berkeley, and Hume in Chapter 8. Locke can be seen as still struggling to repair Cartesian metaphysics, but his repairs contribute as much to its final collapse as do the criticisms—drawn from Foucher—made by Berkeley and Hume.

The possible solutions of Spinoza and Leibniz are outside the direct line of this study and thus are but briefly mentioned. However, because of Leibniz's important relations with Foucher, his solution is treated at length in Chapter 9.

chapter 5

The Controversy Concerning Ideas between Malebranche and Foucher

1 FOUCHER'S READING OF THE FIRST VOLUME OF THE FIRST EDITION OF MALEBRANCHE'S *RECHERCHE*

The first volume of the first edition of *De la recherche de la vérité où l'on traite de la nature de l'esprit de l'homme, et de l'usage qu'il en doit faire pour éviter l'erreur des sciences*, by Nicolas Malebranche, appeared in 1674.[103] No volume number is given, and the only indication that the three books it contains do not constitute a complete work is a one-sentence paragraph in Chapter 4 of Book 1 that lists six topics to be treated; the volume closes with the word "FIN." It is not surprising, then, to find Simon Foucher publishing his short *Critique de la recherche de la verité où l'on examine en même-tems une partie des principes de Mr Descartes* in 1675[104] under the impression that he was examining a complete work. He was soon apprised of his oversight. Malebranche responded in the preface to the second volume of the *Recherche* with one of the nastiest printed attacks in the history of philosophy (Descartes's opinion of Pere Bourdin is comparable but was not meant for the public), which is crowned with the now famous line: "Quand on Critique un Libre, il me semble qu'il faut au moins l'avoir lû."[105]

The following short exposition of the theory of ideas found in the first volume of Malebranche's *Recherche* is developed from the assumption that Foucher did read it. Several other expositions of Malebranche's theory of ideas are available, but they are based on the complete edition of the *Recherche*, which contains numerous revisions and clarifications, some of which are meant to counter Foucher's objections or to keep readers from misunderstanding as Foucher supposedly does. The exposition in this chapter, however, is based on how Foucher must have read the first volume of the first edition. From his objections in the *Critique* and his responses to Malebranche's reply, it is evident that Foucher detects two theories of ideas in the first volume of the *Recherche*, the second of which he takes to be a spurious expression of piety not suited to philosophical discourse. Foucher's important argument concerning primary and secondary qualities is made against the theory he finds most strongly developed, a Cartesian theory that Malebranche disowns in the preface to the second volume. It can be contended that the first volume of the *Recherche* shows the development of Malebranche's theory of ideas seen in God from the orthodox Cartesian view; this is implicitly argued for in the following. Here it is shown that Foucher must have interpreted the *Recherche* in this way. He finds the Cartesian view thoroughly covered in the first volume and has good reason for believing that it is Malebranche's. He is shocked when Malebranche announces that the Cartesian theory is not his own. Foucher can see Malebranche's sketch of the vision in God only as a grasping at theological straws by one who has grappled unsuccessfully with the problems of the Cartesian way. Hence, in his *Reponse pour la critique à la preface du second volume de la recherche de la verité, où l'on examine le sentiment de M. Descartes touchant les idées* of 1676, Foucher merely stresses one aspect of his argument to meet Malebranche's parry; he does not alter it. Nor do Malebranche's revisions and clarifications cause Foucher to change his argument in later critiques. Foucher believes that the theory of the vision in God makes ideas themselves even more mysterious and difficult to know than are material things on the orthodox Cartesian view.

In the first volume of the first edition of the *Recherche*, Malebranche points out that the human soul has two major faculties: understanding and will. I confine my exposition to the understanding. The understanding is "la capacité de recevoir différentes idées & différentes modifications dans l'esprit." It "est entierement passive, & ne renferme aucune action."

> D'où il faut conclure que c'est l'entendement seul qui aperçoit, puisqu'il n'y a que lui qui reçoive les idées des objets; car c'est une même chose à l'âme d'apercevoir un objet ou de recevoir l'idée qui le represente. C'est aussi l'entendement qui apercoit les modifications de l'âme, puisque j'entends, par ce mot *entendement* cette faculté passive de l'âme par laquelle elle reçoit toutes les différentes modifications dont elle est capable; & que c'est la même chose à l'âme de recevoir la maniere d'être qu'on appelle la douleur, que d'apercevoir la douleur; puisqu'elle ne peut recevoir la douleur d'autre maniere qu'en l'apercevant.[106]

From this it can be concluded that

> c'est l'entendement qui imagine les objets absens, & qui sent ceux qui sont present; & que le *sens & l'imagination* ne sont que l'entendement, appercevant les objets par les organes du corps.[107]

Because the understanding is passive—that is, it does not originate its perceptions but is only the capacity for them to occur in the mind—it is obvious that the understanding does not judge in perception. Besides knowing, sensing, and imagining, the understanding also remembers and has passions.

Idea is both a general and a specific term for Malebranche:

les idées de l'âme sont de deux sortes en prenant le nom d'idée en general, pour tout ce que l'esprit aperçoit immediatement. Les premieres nous representent quelque chose hors de nous, comme celle d'un quarré, d'un triangle, etc. & les secondes ne nous representent que ce qui se passe dans nous comme nos sensations, la douleur, le plaisir, etc. Car on fera voir dans la suite que ces dernieres idées ne sont rien autre chose qu'une maniere d'estre de l'esprit; & c'est pour cela que je les appellarai de *modifications* de l'esprit.[108]

Ideas of this second sort, which are nonrepresentative and nothing more than modifications of the spirit, are usually called sensations. Ideas of the first sort, those that represent external objects, are usually referred to simply as ideas or "pure perceptions." In simple perception, these ideas are of simple things; in connection with judgments, the ideas the understanding knows are of relations among things; and in reasoning, what is known are ideas of relations among relations.

There are four things that might be confused in having a sensation: (1) the impressing motion (material action) of the material thing; (2) the impressed motion (material passion) of the sense organs that are agitated, this agitation being communicated along the nerves to the brain; (3) the passively received modification (mental passion) of the soul, which is the sensation properly speaking; (4) the active judgment (mental action) that what is sensed is both in the material sense organ and in the material thing. The mistaken notion that there are sensible qualities in material things arises because this judgment is so prompt and habitual that it is taken to be a simple sensation, which in turn is taken naively to present the object as it is. There is no causal relation between sensations (3) and the motions (1) and (2) of material things (including the sense organs and the brain) except that God has willed that they are parallel. This means that there need not necessarily (except for God's willing it) be a material thing present or in motion for one to have a sensation. This skeptical possibility aside, material things are (the only things) perceivable in sensation, for they are (the only things) capable of making impressions upon the sense organs.

C'est ainsi qu'elle voit des plaines & des rochers présens à ses yeux, qu'elle connaît la dureté du fer, & la pointe d'une épée & choses semblables; & ces sortes de perceptions s'appellent *sentimens*.[109]

Our senses never deceive us. "Quand on voit, par exemple, de la lumière, il est trés-certain que l'on voit de la lumière." Error arises when we judge that what we sense is outside the soul. One must follow this rule:

De ne juger jamais par les sens de la vérité absolue des choses; ni de ce qu'elles sont en elles-mêmes, mais seulement du rapport qu'elles ont avec nôtre corps, parce qu'en

effet ils ne nous sont point donnez pour connoître la vérité des choses en
elles-mêmes, mais seulement pour la conservation de nôtre corps.[110]

Light, color, heat, cold, pleasure, and pain are definitely modifications of
the soul. As for other sensations of material things,

> nos yeux nous trompent généralement en tout ce qu'ils nous
> représentent, dans la grandeur des corps, dans leur figure & dans leurs
> mouvemens, dans la lumière & dans les couleurs, qui sont les seules
> choses que nous voyons . . . toutes ces choses ne sont point telles qu'elles
> nous paroissent.[111]

The things we see and the distinctions of size, figure, and movement that
we can make by our senses are proportional to the size of our bodies. Reason
tells us that there are worlds within worlds upon fleas. We cannot comprehend such a manifold extension in all its infinity, let alone perceive it in
sensation.

> Nôtre vûë ne nous représente donc point l'étenduë, selon qu'elle est en
> elle-même; mais seulement ce qu'elle est par rapport à nôtre corps; &
> parce que la moitié d'un mite n'a pas un rapport considérable à nôtre
> corps, & que cela ne peut ni le conserver ni le détruire, nôtre vûë nous
> le cache entiérement.[112]

Not only is visible extension proportional to our bodies, but because of the
differences of men's eyes every man sees a different extension, one that is
proportional to his body alone. This is quite adequate, for "L'exactitude & la
justesse ne sont point essentielles aux connaissances sensibles, qui ne doivent
servir qu'à la conservation de la vie."[113]

Although we cannot know by sensations the absolute size, figure, or
motion of any material thing, we can know the relations among things. We
can know even of the relations among the infinite number of extensions that
are sensed; that is, we can reason that there are probably parasites on fleas
that seem about the same size to the fleas as do fleas to us.

> Il est donc constant que les jugemens que nous faisons touchant
> l'étenduë, les figures, & les mouvemens de corps, renferment donc
> quelque vérité: mais il n'en est pas de même de ceux, que nous faisons
> touchant la lumière, couleurs, & toutes les autres qualitez sensibles, car
> la vérité ne s'y recontre jamais.[114]

Hence, when, in sensing, a person is precipitated into the judgment that a
falling rock has the size, figure, and motion he sees, his judgment is not
completely incorrect. He does know its size, figure, and motion relative to the

size, figure, and motion of his own body. And although these things as seen are inaccurate so far as knowledge of the absolute size, figure, and motion of these bodies with relation to the true extension is concerned, there is a regular relationship between what one sees and the absolute properties; the proportions still hold. However, our judgments that material things are of a certain color, or have any of the other sensible qualities, are completely wrong. There is no corresponding set of colors, odors, and so on belonging to material things as there is a world of real extension corresponding to the extension we see.

Just as the sensation is the faculty for perceiving material things when they are present and causing an image in the brain, the imagination is the soul's faculty for perceiving material things when they are absent:

> elle se les représente en s'en formant des images dans le cerveau. C'est de cette manière qu'on imagine toutes sortes de figures, un cercle, un triangle, un visage, un cheval, des villes & des campagnes, soit qu'on les ait déjà vûës ou non. Ces sortes de perceptions s'appellent *imaginations*, parce que l'âme se représente ces objets en s'en formant des images dans le cerveau.[115]

It follows that one cannot imagine spiritual things "parce qu'on ne peut pas se former des images des choses spirituelles."

The third faculty of the soul is the pure understanding.

> Elle aperçoit par *l'entendement pur* les choses spirituelles, les universelles, les notions communes, l'idée de la perfection, celle d'un être infiniment parfait, & toutes ses pensées, comme ses inclinations naturelles, ses passions & ses perceptions. Elle aperçoit même par l'entendement pur les choses matérielles, l'étenduë avec ses propriétez; car il n'y a que l'entendement pur qui puisse apercevoir un cercle, & un quarré parfait, une figure de mille côtez, & choses semblables. Ces sortes de perceptions s'appellent *pures intellections*, ou *pures perceptions*, parce que l'esprit ne se forme point d'images corporelles dans le cerveau pour se représenter toutes ces choses.[116]

The pure understanding, then, is "la faculté qu'a l'esprit de connaître les objets de dehors, sans en former d'images corporelles dans le cerveau."[117]

The soul perceives two sorts of things, one kind in the soul and the other kind outside the soul.

> Celles qui sont dans l'ame sont ses propres pensées, c'est-a-dire toutes ses différentes modifications, car par ces mots, *pensée, manière de penser*, ou *modification de l'âme*, j'entends généralement toutes les choses, qui ne peuvent être dans l'âme sans qu'elle les aperçoive: comme sont ses propres sensations, ses imaginations, ses pures intellections, ou simple-

ment ses conceptions, ses passions mêmes, & inclinations naturelles . . .
que l'âme mesme d'une telle, ou telle façon . . . elle n'a pas besoin d'idée
pour les apercevoir.[118]

In summary, one does not need an idea to perceive an idea. Things outside
the soul can be perceived only by means of ideas; these things are either
material or spiritual. Malebranche is certain that no one will dispute that we
know them by way of ideas.

> Je crois que tout le monde tombe d'accord que nous n'apperçevons point
> les choses qui sont hors de nous par elles-mesmes, mais seulement par les
> idées que nous en avons . . . l'objet immédiat de nôtre esprit, lorsqu'il
> voit le Soleil, n'est pas le Soleil, mais quelque chose qui est intimement
> unie à nôtre âme; & c'est ce que j'appele *idée*. Ainsi par ce mot *idée*, je
> n'entends ici autre chose que ce qui est l'objet immédiat, ou le plus
> proche de l'esprit, quant le aperçoit quelque chose.[119]

Although an idea is necessary if an external thing is to be perceived, it is
not necessary for anything external to be present for one to have an idea.
When we conceive the idea of a square, for example, we can at the same time
imagine it, "c'est-à-dire l'apercevoir en nous en traçant une image dans le
cerveau."

> L'image d'un quarré par example, que l'imagination trace dans le
> cerveau, n'est juste & bien fait que par la conformité qu'elle a avec l'idée
> d'un quarré que nous concevons par la pure intellection. C'est cette idée
> qui regle cette image. C'est l'esprit qui conduit l'imagination, & qui
> l'oblige de regarder de tems en tems, si l'image qu'elle peint est une
> figure de quatre lignes droites & égales, dont les angles soient exacte-
> ment droits: en un mot si ce qu'on image est semblable à ce qu'on
> conçoit.[120]

In reading this passage, Foucher must take it to mean that the idea is
similar to the material image in the brain. That is, he must take "regle" in
the above passage in the sense of to regulate by being a material model. He
might then wonder whether Malebranche means that the idea is like the
material image, which in turn is like the material thing. He would certainly
detect some confusion here. A few pages later Malebranche says that
"l'image que le Soleil imprime dans le cerveau ne ressemble point à l'idée
que l'âme en a."[121] If Foucher interprets the previous passage as I suggest,
he cannot avoid finding a contradiction here. Malebranche adds that "toutes
les sensations & toutes les passions de l'âme ne représentent rien hors d'elle,
qui leur ressemble, & que ce ne sont que des modifications dont un esprit est
capable."[122]

Foucher perhaps found this extremely confusing, but more probably, he took it as evidence that Malebranche was confused. The many Cartesian elements in the work led Foucher to interpret Malebranche's theory of ideas as Cartesian. Malebranche speaks of pure intellections and conceptions as modifications of the soul, and he speaks of the idea of a square as something conceived in the mind. Ideas are most intimately united to our souls. Hence, ideas, like sensations, cannot resemble material things, for ideas are modifications of an immaterial substance. This is the source of Foucher's first major objection. How can ideas be singled out as representative of material objects when sensations are not? He finds his second objection in Malebranche's (on Foucher's interpretation) confusion. Malebranche says that ideas resemble material images in the brain, which in turn resemble material things. How, Foucher asks, is this possible? How—on the one hand—can an idea be a model for a material image traced by imagination in the brain? On the other hand, how can we know a material thing by an idea that cannot resemble it? Even if "idée" in "C'est cette idée qui regle cette image" were interpreted as rules or as directions for the construction of an image, Foucher would no doubt say that the problem of how one could check or compare what is conceived in the instructions with the resulting mental image still remains. Such comparison would seem to require real likeness between the "regle," the idea, and the object, a likeness that is comprehensible only when "regle" is taken to mean material model rather than rules or directions for the construction of an image.

What can be done with such a mix-up? Foucher sees Malebranche doing the only reasonable thing. Malebranche drops it and begins a new chapter.

In discussing sensations and imaginations, Malebranche says that they are nothing more than modifications of the soul, meaning, as Foucher reads it, that they are nonrepresentative. Then follows a passage that Foucher must see as anomalous, for it contradicts the presentation of pure ideas as modifications of the soul:

> les idées simples des objets de la pure intellection . . . bien que présentes à l'esprit ne le touchent ni ne le modifient pas . . . toutes les idées abstraites ne modifient point l'âme . . . toutes les sensations la modifient.[123]

This is the key passage Foucher must discount to interpret Malebranche's way of ideas as Cartesian. And, as shown above, there are later passages that seem to make it clear that ideas are intimately united with the soul (and hence touch it) and also are modifications of it.

Now, however, Malebranche follows up this anomalous passage. We see all things in God. God is the place of ideas: "il est absolument nècessaire que Dieu ait en lui-même idées de toutes les choses, qu'il crées, puisqu'autrement il n'auroit pas pû les produire."[124] Is this because they are necessary as

models? Are they modifications of God? This is not clear. What is clear is
that we have a new theory in which ideas are not modifications of man's soul,
which, to Foucher, seems based on nothing more than a pious phrase
conjured up to screen the debacle of the Cartesian way of ideas. Now
Malebranche says merely that when we perceive material things, God causes
us to have sensations (He does not have them Himself), and at the same
time:

> Pour l'idée qui se trouve jointe avec le sentiment, elle est en Dieu, & nous
> la voyons parce qu'il lui plaît de nous la découvrir: & Dieu joint la
> sensation à l'idée alors que les objets sont présens, afin que nous le
> croyions ainsi, & que nous entrions dans les sentimens, où nous devons
> estre par rapport à eux.[125]

God is the intelligible world and in Him is the general idea of extension
that "suffit pour faire connaître toutes les proprietez, dont l'étenduë est
capable."[126] This idea of extension is perhaps also the idea of infinity, for
"toutes ces idées particulieres [celles de l'esprit] ne sont que des participa-
tions de l'idée générale de l'infini." And perhaps it is also the idea of God, for
"il n'est pas possible que Dieu ait d'autre fin principale des ses actions que
lui même."

> Dieu ne peut donc faire un esprit pour connaître ses ouvrages, si ce n'est
> que cet esprit voie en quelque façon Dieu en voyant ses ouvrages . . . nous
> ne voyons aucune chose que par la connaissance naturelle que nous
> avons de Dieu. Toutes les idées particulières que nous avons des
> créatures, ne sont que des déterminations générales de l'idée du
> Créateur.[127]

The particular ideas we have of material things then, are determinations,
particularizations, or limitations of the idea of extension, of the idea of
infinity, and of the idea of God. The idea of extension is in God and may or
may not be the same as the idea of infinity; the idea of God also must be in
God and may or may not be the same as the idea of infinity.

Foucher, then, sees two theories of ideas in the first volume of the first
edition of the *Recherche*. The first is Cartesian: Pure ideas and sensations are
modifications of the soul, modifications that cannot resemble material things;
nevertheless, the ideas are said to represent material things, and to resemble
material images in the brain. Malebranche cannot extricate himself from this
tangle, so Foucher believes. Hence the second theory of ideas is offered: Ideas
are not modifications of the soul; they are in God, Who allows us to see them
when appropriate; through them we know material things. Malebranche
offers no further explanation of how ideas are in God nor of the relation they
have to our souls when we know them. Foucher certainly sees the need for an

alternate to the Cartesian theory of ideas, but he takes the notion of seeing ideas in God as nothing more on Malebranche's part than a pious afterthought. As I show above, Foucher, or any other contemporary, needs little more than the expectation that he will find the Cartesian theory of ideas in Malebranche to discover that Malebranche holds it to be philosophically (as opposed to theologically) important. Malebranche later develops the vision-in-God theory to some extent, but as Foucher himself (and later Arnauld) points out, it is less explanatory than, and is also subject to the same or even graver difficulties as, the defective Cartesian theory.

We see here in Foucher's eyes (and I would argue that it has been demonstrated) the development of Malebranche's major deviation from Descartes—his theory of ideas. This first expression of Malebranche's theory of ideas shows quite plainly the traces of its Cartesian origin. In grasping these traces, Foucher presents his critique of the Cartesian way of ideas. And when he later grants that Malebranche is making a major effort to break away from the Cartesian theory and thus avoid the troubles to which it is subject, Foucher never forgets the new theory's parenthood and claims that the offspring is heir to a tendency to suffer from the sire's ailments.

2 FOUCHER'S CRITICISMS OF MALEBRANCHE'S WAY OF IDEAS

In 1673, Foucher had a small number of copies of his *Dissertations sur la recherche de la verité, ou sur la logique des academiciens* printed in Dijon. In it he speaks of the need for workers in "la recherche de la verite." This perhaps gave him some grounds for believing that Malebranche's *Recherche* of 1674 was in response to the call in the *Logique* of 1673, although (as remarked above) Malebranche's title is not an uncommon one. Whether or not he seriously believed that Malebranche was inspired by the *Logique*, Foucher states that his *Critique de la recherche*, like his prior *Logique* and Malebranche's *Recherche*, is conceived as an aid in the search for truth. By pointing out some of the errors made by Descartes and Malebranche, Foucher believes that he can advance the search for certainty. The principles he uses in doing so are such as no man of good sense will deny; they are the laws of the Academic philosophers, which are as follows:

1. *Ne se conduire que par Demonstration en matière de Philosophie.*
2. *Ne point agiter les questions que nous voions bien ne pouvoir decider.*
3. *Avoüer que l'on sçait pas, ce que l'on ignore effectivement.*
4. *Distinguer les choses que l'on sçait de celles que l'on ne sçait pas.*
5. *Chercher toûjours des connoissances nouvelles.*[128]

Foucher points out that in the search for knowledge, first principles should be inquired into because they are necessary for founding true demonstrations.[129] His is the only way of avoiding error in judgment. Malebranche, however, who says he is going to show how to avoid error, does not examine first principles.[130] Malebranche violates the first rule in the search for truth; he assumes that he has already found it. His system is based on fourteen assumptions, all of which can be challenged. Foucher treats them in turn. The first seven assumptions are, in somewhat abbreviated form, as follows:

1. The soul of man is a simple indivisible substance without parts that is neither material nor extended.
2. There are two kinds of truth: necessary and contingent.
3. The mysteries of faith can be appealed to in philosophy.
4. Pure intellection is not accompanied by brain traces.
5. We have two kinds of ideas: those (ideas) that represent what is outside us and those (sensations) that represent only what is within us.
6. Our ideas need not resemble the objects they represent.
7. Extension, figures, and motions have real existence independent of our mind.[131]

Foucher's major objections to what he believes in Malebranche's theory of ideas are contained in his remarks on assumptions 5, 6, and 7.

Assumption 5 is that we have two kinds of ideas: those (ideas) that represent what is outside us and those (sensations) that represent what is within us. Foucher says that Malebranche recognizes that both kinds are immediately and truly known. Because they appear to us equally as modifications of the soul, it would be difficult to distinguish ideas from sensations. Surely both or neither of them must represent external things. Further, because according to Malebranche the soul has nothing in it similar to matter or extension, Foucher cannot see how it can represent anything except its own unextended ideas.[132] He says that "ces Idées . . . ne nous representent que les effects, que les Objets exterieurs produisent en Nous & non pas ce qu'ils sont en eux-même."[133] He believes that Malebranche recognizes this difficulty and perhaps has offered the vision in God to remedy it. But the only argument Malebranche offers for establishing his new theory is that all other hypotheses of how we know external things are false, so the theory of the vision in God is true. Foucher says this is not a good argument.[134] The notion of seeing all things in God is true in a broad, theological sense, of course, and is a fine and pious sentiment. But, Foucher points out in his comments on assumption 3, such theological remarks have no place in serious philosophical discussions and should be reserved for sermons.[135]

Assumption 6 is that our ideas need not resemble the objects they represent. If this is true, Foucher says first, then there are no grounds for asserting that our sensations are completely unrepresentative of what causes them; they, too, might be representative, for if resemblance is not required, any idea or sensation could represent anything. What is more, they might all represent the same object. Foucher claims that Malebranche takes this view from Descartes, who may not have meditated on it very much because he needs it to preserve the notion of matter, which is essential to his physics.[136] But, above all, Foucher finds that nonresembling representative ideas are incomprehensible:

> On n'entend autre chose par *representer*, si-non rendre une chose *presente*, ou faire le même effect qui si elle agissoit actuellement, ou du-moins en fare un *semblable*, autrement on ne sçait ce qu'on veut dire par ce mot.[137]

Even if ideas have effects on our souls similar to those material things have, the ideas still cannot represent these material things, for we do not know what the things are in themselves and so cannot compare them with ideas; besides, Malebranche admits that the effects are not similar to the things that cause them. Foucher points out that Malebranche at least does not fall into the error of thinking that we can know external things by images in the brain. Our ideas resemble neither these material images nor the external things.[138]

As for the Cartesian appeal to the fact that "arbre" represents a tree without resembling it, Foucher says this argument rests on a double equivocation. In the first place, it is not the word that is supposed to be representative in this case but the idea to which the word gives rise. And in the second place, the idea itself is representative not of the tree but only of the effect the tree causes in our soul. The word cannot represent the tree itself, for we have no idea of the tree itself. The only way that words can be said to represent things is that we can be trained to have the same ideas upon the occurrence of words as we would upon the presence of things. But even then, if we could know exterior things in themselves, then we might find that our ideas are no more similar to things than words are to ideas. There is no way of checking this. This is the final absurdity in suggesting that ideas can be representative of things they do not resemble. There is no way of knowing how nonresembling ideas represent external things, nor that they represent them accurately, nor even at all. It necessarily follows either that our ideas do not represent things in themselves or that our ideas represent things in themselves by resembling them. Because the latter is impossible, the former must be true.[139] Foucher closes his discussion by stating that everyone is well assured that we cannot know things in themselves.

Assumption 7 is that the extension, figures, and motions that we see have real existence outside our minds. Foucher complains that Malebranche fails to prove that judgments we make about these properties have more truth than judgments we make about light, color, and the other sensible qualities. Descartes assumes the same thing. Foucher says Cartesians base this assumption on the fact that we have ideas of thinking and extension, two things that seem to have nothing in common. Thinking seems to be what the soul is, so Cartesians take extension to be matter. However, Foucher says, we can doubt (1) that our ideas of thinking contain nothing of extension, such as movements, efforts, and figures; (2) that the same subject cannot support both thinking and extension, at least at different times; and (3) that our ideas of thinking and extension are always modifications of our soul, to which there is nothing similar outside us.[140]

Foucher recalls a discussion he had on knowledge of external material things with Rohault in 1667. Rohault supported Descartes's opinion that sensations are produced in our soul as mere passions similar to nothing in material objects. Foucher asked that if this is the case, then why is it not concluded that the extension known by the senses is also nothing more than a "Façon-d'estre de Nostre Ame" similar to nothing in material things? Rohault's reply was that we do not know extension by the senses. Foucher was very surprised by this answer, for it is evident that we know light and color by the senses; thus when one sees a red square, for example, one sees at the same time its color, figure, and extension. It is even the case that extension is known by two senses, those of sight and touch. Even Malebranche, Foucher insists, agrees that we know (sensible) extension by the senses. For Foucher, it is as obvious that we know extension by the senses as that there is light at noon. However, he restrained his surprise long enough to ask Rohault how we do know extension, if not by the senses. Rohault replied that we know extension by reason. One observes, for example, that objects touch him at different points and thus concludes that he is extended. Foucher points out that either this means that the soul is extended—which has been denied—or it begs the question. Unless one knows already that different sensations are caused from different places, he cannot conclude from feeling them at different places on his body that their causes are extended.[141] One just cannot distinguish ideas from sensations:

> Car toutes nos Sensations n'estant autres Choses que des Experiences de plusieurs Façons-d'Estre dont Nostre Ame est capable. Nous ne connoissons veritablement par les Sens que Ce que les Objets produisent en Nous, d'où il s'ensuit qui si on avoüe que Nous connoissons de l'Estendüe & des Figures par le Sens aussi bien que de la Lumiere & des Couleurs, il faudra conclure necessairement que cette Estendüe & ces Figures ne sont pas moins en Nous que cette Lumiere & ces Couleurs.
>
> Et quand on voudroit accorder ce Privilege à l'Estendüe qu'elle seroit dans Nostre Ame & dans les Objets exterieurs, au-lieu que les Couleurs ne seroient que dans Nostre Ame: ce seroit tousiours avoüer que la perception que Nous en aurions par les Sens Nous la seroit reconnoister

pour un Façon-d'Estre de Nostre Ame, ce qui d'estruiroit encore le
Systême de Monsieur DESCARTES, outre que de soustenir que l'Ame
& la Matière sont capables d'une même Façon-d'estre, ce seroit avanser
une chose encore plus opposée aux Principes de ce Philosophe que celle
que l'on voudroit éviter par cette Réponse.[142]

In summary, Foucher objects that Malebranchean ideas cannot be distinguished as representative from sensations that cannot be representative for
both are modifications of the soul; both or neither must be representative.
And because the soul is spiritual, none of its modifications can represent
material things, which are extended: neither sensations nor ideas—which are
unextended—can resemble material things. The criticisms are of the Cartesian way of ideas which, for good reasons, Foucher believes is central in
Malebranche's system. He criticizes Malebranche's theory of vision in God
here only by denying assumption 3, that the mysteries of faith can be
appealed to in philosophy. Foucher expresses, however, the criticism he later
stresses against the vision in God: if "to represent" does not mean "to
resemble," it is unintelligible.

3 MALEBRANCHE'S RESPONSE TO FOUCHER AND THE FAILURE OF MALEBRANCHE'S WAY OF IDEAS

Foucher did not have to wait long for Malebranche's reply.

Malebranche's response to Foucher's *Critique* appears in the second volume of the *Recherche* (1675) as "Preface Pour servir de Réponse à la critique
de premier Volume." Malebranche is most incensed about Foucher's assumption that the first volume contains a method; he quotes the sentence
outlining the six parts of the work and points out that only the first three
parts are included in the first volume. As for the assumptions Foucher
accuses him of holding, Malebranche says that they are all incidental
remarks, statements taken from examples, or responses to objections.
Foucher attributes these opinions to him out of failure to comprehend the
text. After making it abundantly clear that he does not believe that it is
worthwhile to answer Foucher's objections about what is called his assumption 1, Malebranche does answer them, and he then prints what Foucher has
to say about 2 and 3 in columns side by side with his own replies. He says
that he would continue through the whole *Critique* in such fashion if he
thought anyone was interested. However, it can easily be seen that Foucher
"n'a presque jamais pris mon sens & qu'il n'a aucune idée de mon dessein."[143]
Because of this, Malebranche does not believe that any reasonable person
would be interested. Hence, he closes with a few words concerning the rest of
the assumptions Foucher accuses him of making. He believes that his thorough

refutation of Foucher's first three criticisms shows "ce qu'on dit penser des autres auxquels je n'ai répondu qu'en deux mots."[144] Because it is my contention that Foucher does offer important objections to Malebranche's way of ideas, I examine carefully the few words Malebranche does have on assumptions 5, 6, and 7. It is worth seeing why he does not think arguments against Foucher's claims are necessary.

Malebranche says of assumption 5 that Foucher attributes to him:

> Il m'impose dans son cinquième Chapitre plusieurs sentimens, que je n'ai pas. Il n'est point vrai que *je reconnaisse que toutes nos idées ne sont que des façons-d'être de nôtre âme.* J'ay fait au contraire dans le troisième Livre qu'il critique, un chapitre exprès pour prouver que cette opinion est insoûtenable. Quand on Critique un Livre, il me semble qu'il faut au moins l'avoir lû. Il n'est point encore vrai, *que je reconnaisse, que les idées que nous recevons par les sens, ne nous représentent que les effets que les objets extérieurs produisent en nous*: j'ai dit le contraire en plusieurs endroits, dans le Chapitre quinzième du premier Livre & ailleurs.[145]

Malebranche evidently did not read Foucher's *Critique* with very much care for in Chapter 15 of Book 1 of his *Recherche*, Malebranche discusses the changes that take place in the retinal nerves during the perception of light.[146] It is not these effects that Foucher is talking about, but the sensations themselves as we experience them. As for the "chapitre exprès," Malebranche must be referring to Chapter 6 of Book 3: *Que nous voyons toutes choses en Dieu*. Here he says that in the perception of a sensible thing there are two elements: "*sentiment* et *idée* pure." "Le sentiment est une modification de nôtre âme." But "l'idée qui se trouve jointe avec le sentiment, elle est en Dieu."[147] Foucher comments in the *Critique* on this chapter by praising Malebranche's piety, but he insists that such a remark cannot be a philosophical principle. He goes on to say that even if ideas were in God, this still would not solve the problem of how we can know material things. God is, if anything, more immaterial than our own souls. Ideas in Him would presumably also be immaterial, so we are still faced with all the problems of nonresembling representative ideas.[148] Even more, Malebranche's pious remark cannot be taken seriously for the following reason:

> Il faut qu'il resulte quelque Façon-d'Estre dans nostre Ame, pour qüe nous ayons de la Connoissance: parce que la Connoissance, comme on a coûtume de le dire, est une Action *immanente*, ou si l'on veut c'est une simple Passion, & cela suppose encore plus évidemmēt quelque Effet dans la Substance qui connoist, . . . les Idées sont absolument necessaires pour la Connoissance: Car soit que ce soit un Action ou un Passion, il faut necessairement qu'elle aye quelque Terme, & c'est ce qu'on appelle ordinairement *Idée, Verbe*, ou *parolle de l'Esprit*.[149]

What one knows when knowing are ideas, every one of which is a "Façon-d'Estre" of the soul. Such ideas arise in the soul upon movements of the body because of the union of body and soul. It is utterly impossible for the soul to know something that is not its own modification. The notion of seeing things in God is as naive as the natural prejudice that we need only open our eyes to see external objects.[150] Malebranche himself knows that we see not external things but only our own sensations. Hence, Foucher cannot believe that Malebranche could make the naive mistake of offering ideas in God, which would be as exterior—and hence as unknowable in themselves—as are the external things they supposedly make known.

Malebranche attempts to subdue Foucher's doubts in this matter with his remarks concerning assumption 6. Foucher assures us, Malebranche says, *"que je me fonde sur ce que Monsieur Descartes a resolu touchant cette question. Cependant l'opinion de Monsieur Descartes est entierement differente de la mienne."*[151] Thus is Foucher finally told point blank what, as Gouthier remarks, is "à peine perceptible dans la *Recherche: une philosophie nouvelle est née, qui prétend être autre chose que celle de Descartes."*[152]

Concerning assumption 7, Malebranche says that it was not his place yet to prove anything about extension; he was combatting only "les erreurs des sens au regard des qualitez sensibles." As for the problem of nonresembling representative ideas, Malebranche says, "Je ne sçais pas comment il s'avise après *sept ans* de se plaindre d'une réponse de Monsieur Rohault. Il falloit le pousser lors qu'il étoit vivant."[153] If Foucher had complained while Rohault was living, Malebranche is sure that Rohault could have solved the problem with only "deux ou trois paroles." Malebranche has nothing to say about it himself, however.

Foucher was not long in responding to this preface. A letter from René Ouvrard to Nicaise of 24 September 1675 describes the impatience with which Foucher awaited the publication of the second volume of the *Recherche*. Ouvrard remarks that he would hesitate to visit Foucher now, for "Je m'imagine qu'il ne voit voler devant ses yeux que des fantômes, des atôms et des idées, et qu'il n'y a point de machine dans M. Descartes dont il ne remue tous les ressorts."[154] Ouvrard sees no good in such critiques, but it is interesting to note that he considers what might be expected to be a violent attack upon Malebranche as an attack upon Descartes. Evidently Foucher was given the benefit of an advance copy, for the official date of publication of the second volume of the *Recherche* is 28 September 1675. The publication date of the first volume is 2 May 1674.[155] The permission for the *Critique* is dated 10 December 1674. Foucher thus had six months to write and publish the *Critique*. The *Réponse pour la critique à la preface du second volume de la recherche* took even less time; the permission is dated 31 December 1675, which means that Foucher had only three months to get it ready after the appearance of the second volume of the *Recherche*. This was perhaps not too difficult, however, for Foucher repeats in the *Réponse* much that is in the *Critique*. The title makes one wonder how much Foucher was impressed by Malebranche's announcement that his is a new system of philosophy different from that of Descartes; Foucher's complete title includes the phrase, *où l'on examine le sentiment de M. Descartes touchant les idées.*

Foucher begins the *Réponse* by remarking that Malebranche should have answered the *Critique* wholly or not at all. Further, Foucher wants to stress that the *Critique* is meant to be a guide to errors made by many authors in the search for truth and is not meant to be a personal attack on Malebranche; the *Recherche* is only a touchstone. Foucher says that he does not mean that the assumptions cited are to be taken as Malebranche's complete method. However, any attempt to avoid error involves some method, and Foucher still believes that method should be one of the first things treated.[156]

Foucher proceeds as though Malebranche were a slow student. He carefully explains that all phantasms, sensations, and ideas are simple appearances, which are nothing more than "nostre âme, disposées d'une telle, ou d'une telle maniere." He points out again that no proof has been given that our senses do not deceive us with respect to extension, figure, and movement as they do with color, light, heat, and other sensible qualities. The total difference the Cartesians stress between soul and body means that ideas— modifications of the soul—cannot possibly resemble extended things. Hence, it is impossible for such ideas to represent extended things.[157]

However, Foucher retracts his attribution of assumption 5 to Malebranche because Malebranche says that ideas are not "*façons d'estre de nostre âme*." Foucher says that it is easy to see how he made the mistake. In Chapter 1 of the *Recherche*, Malebranche says that ideas and sentiments are to our souls as figure and configurations are to matter. Then Malebranche goes on to say that ideas are not modifications; Foucher thought this was merely to distinguish them as two "*façons-d'estre*" of the soul in analogy to the way Malebranche distinguishes between figures and configurations as two "*façons-d'estre*" of the body. Malebranche further says (in Book 3, Part 2, Chapter 1) that modifications are within us, so Foucher concluded that ideas are within us. Even granting Malebranche his correction that ideas are not modifications of the soul, and laying aside the question of how such entities can correctly be called ideas, Foucher points out that Malebranche still says of them: (1) they are spiritual, (2) they are not substances, and (3) they are received in our soul. Foucher cannot see why this is not contradictory, for these spiritual things can be only modifications of some substance; if they are received in the soul, then it is difficult to understand how they are not modifications of it. There is nothing else that they can be.[158]

As for assumption 6, Descartes wants extended things to be represented by ideas, which do not resemble these things; Malebranche cannot deny that he also purports to have nonresembling representative ideas, for example, in Book 3, Chapter 4. Malebranche replies to this only that Foucher does not understand; Foucher says Malebranche should instead have tried to explain. As for assumption 7, Malebranche makes no attempt at all to explain why our senses do not deceive us about extension as they do about other sensible qualities. Even though Foucher noticed the problem first in Rohault's exposition, its present locus is in Malebranche's system.[159]

Foucher points out that if ideas are not "façons-d'estre" of our soul, they cannot be known immediately, for then they would be external things.[160] However, there is an easy proof that they are not external. An idea is something that is known by itself without representation. The only things that can be known by themselves are modifications of our soul. Hence, it is contradictory to say that ideas can exist outside our soul; if they could, then they would not be knowable in themselves. Foucher's argument suggests that if one needs an external idea to know an external thing, then one would need an infinite regress of intermediary external ideas to know external ideas. Foucher concludes his task of clarifying the concept of ideas by remarking that Malebranche in the *Recherche* is the only person he ever heard of who says that ideas are not "façons-d'estre de l'âme." If Malebranche's vision-in-God system of ideas is not entirely incomprehensible, it is at least the most obscure Foucher has ever heard of.[161]

By 1685, Malebranche and Foucher were having occasional meetings. How can we visualize these encounters? No understanding seems to have arisen from them on either side. Perhaps we can see the two, scurrying away from one another in their robes, each refreshed and lightened—or frustrated and annoyed—by their tête-à-tête, each in wonder at the obtuse other. Foucher expresses his belief that Malebranche's system of ideas is incomprehensible even after a personal interview on the subject. He reports to Leibniz that it seems to him that Malebranche's "opinion des idées qui ne point façons-d'estre de l'âme, est insoustenable."[162] After ten years of occasional meetings, Foucher reports again in a letter of 28 April 1695 in almost the same words. However, he now stresses that Malebranche's theory is dangerous as well as unintelligible.

> Le Père Malebranche a assurement l'esprit bon et penetrant, mais il est embarrassé dans son systeme des idées, qui ne sont pas des façons-d'estre de nostre âme et sont hors de nous, et quand on luy demande comment il faut concevoir que nous ayons des perceptions de ces idées, qu'il veut estre hors de nous, il repond qu'il ne comprend pas comment cela se fait et qu'il ne pense pas qu'on le puisse jamais comprendre; mais il entre par là dans un profound pyrrhonisme.[163]

Foucher believes that to say that we cannot know how we know is close to saying that we cannot know, which is the extreme of dogmatic scepticism.

Foucher firmly believed that he had an influence on Malebranche's thought. In his letter of 8 December 1684, Foucher tells Leibniz that what led him to undertake the *Critique* was the fact that he had published his *Logique* more than a year before Malebranche published the *Recherche*.[164] When the third volume of the *Recherche* appeared, Foucher wrote to Leibniz (12 August 1678) that Malebranche now agrees with many things in the *Critique*, notably:

> (1) en ce qu'il veut que nous ne connoissions pas par les sens qu'il y a des corps hors de nous, (2) en ce qu'il avoue dans un chapitre particulier que nous n'avions point d'idée claire de la nature de nostre âme.

Foucher pointedly adds, "Cela estant, jugez, Monsieur, des consequences qu'on en peut tirer contre sa philosophie."[165] One conclusion Foucher does not draw is that it cannot be proved that there is something outside of us; he argues only that it cannot be proved that its essence is that of Cartesian matter. In his letter of 26 April 1679, Foucher again mentions to Leibniz that Malebranche's third volume is different from the first two in that "il paroist estre un peu Academicien."[166]

If Malebranche became more cautious in his use of the term "idée," he certainly never became Academic enough to doubt his theory. Foucher is particularly struck by the fact that Malebranche now admits that "nous n'avons point d'idée de la nature de nostre âme."[167] That the nature of the soul is known to be spiritual is the first unproved assumption of which Foucher accused Malebranche. He believes that Malebranche's whole defective theory of ideas derives from this assumption.[168] Because Foucher believes that the merits of a philosophical system can be determined by examining the theory of ideas it incorporates, he stresses the importance of not beginning with an unproven assumption that will determine a perhaps erroneous theory of ideas. From the first, the Cartesian distinction of thought from extension makes knowledge of the external world by ideas impossible. Because Foucher believes that we can know only by way of ideas, and that ideas are "façons d'estre" of our souls, the possibility of knowing the external world is destroyed if one assumes that its essence is extension and that thinking cannot contain anything of extension. The Cartesians' mistake is in believing that they know the essences of spirit and matter. Foucher says that we do not know these essences, and further that determining the answer to such a question is one of the last things one should do in constructing a philosophical system—not one of the first, as it is with the Cartesians. Descartes sees that extension seems to be different from thinking, so he jumps to the conclusion that thinking is the essence of the soul and that extension is the essence of the body. What he should do is suspend judgment until he examines the consequences of such assumptions. Foucher says that Descartes never meditated deeply on his notion of idea, for he perhaps suspected that he would have to give up his whole system if he did. It is not, after all, established that all extension is material nor that there cannot be some extension in our ideas.[169] Experience should not be denied; there is extension in our thoughts because we sense it. The problem is to determine what the essences of mind and matter are, given this fact. To deny this fact and to substitute ideas that supposedly represent extended things without resembling them is to go from the obvious to the absurd. Why deny the fact that we sense extension just as we sense color? Why arbitrarily divide the sensible qualities? Why—as Malebranche does—make ideas into external things, which are as impossible to apprehend directly as are extended things for the Cartesians? To do so is to make it impossible to know external things, and this, for Foucher, is to fall into dogmatic scepticism.

Foucher cannot break away from the belief that the soul must be united in some way with what is known. For the Scholastics, knower and known share the form of the thing known. Both Foucher and Malebranche say that the soul cannot go out to intercept external things directly. Foucher takes this to mean that the essences of external things cannot be known for certain, because all we can know directly are modifications of the soul. Whatever can be known is in the soul and therefore is not external. The only possible way out, Foucher says, is that somehow material substance and soul substance are similar. Because we do not know the essence of either, this is entirely possible. Malebranche clings to the Cartesian assertion that we know the essences of soul and body, claims Foucher, but Malebranche also tries to adapt the Scholastic way of knowing external things. He makes ideas external, but he still says that they are knowable in themselves, and that in knowing them our soul is united with them. Thus, in the vision in God, ideas are somehow united to our soul and yet exist external to our soul in God. This is contradictory. And even if it is a sharing of ideas by God with our soul, as in the Scholastic account—which if not contradictory is at least mysterious—ideas are shared not by knower and known but only by knower and God. And again, we may know *ideas* because of their union with our soul, but the problem still remains of how they make us know external material things. In us and in God ideas must be spiritual, so they cannot resemble the Cartesian material world. In offering such a solution, Malebranche cannot have seen clearly the real problem his system poses here—the need to define a new relation of representation between ideas and things that does not depend on resemblance.

Foucher believes that Malebranche is on the right track. He says he is writing not against Malebranche but to help him, for Malebranche does not attack the Academics and even agrees with most of their principles.[170] And Foucher hails as a milestone Malebranche's eventual statement that we have no idea of the soul. This leaves the door open for a reevaluation of essences and the bridging in new knowledge of the gap left by Cartesian dualism. Nevertheless, the solution Malebranche offers to the difficulties of the Cartesian way of ideas suffers from the same inadequacies as does the orthodox way. In making this clear, Foucher shows that as long as the Cartesian dualism is retained, any way of ideas based upon it will fail as a way of knowing. Malebranche may mean to deny that representation must be resemblance, but Foucher takes him to place ideas aside as something other than modifications of the soul in large part to avoid the objection that *façons d'estre de nostre âme* cannot be like material things. If they are neither mental nor material, neither substance nor modification, what, then, are they? In a Cartesian world—and Foucher cannot ever see Malebranche as outside this world—even Platonic essences are totally spiritual and thus completely unlike material things. Foucher points out that Malebranche never explains how representation can take place without resemblance between what represents and what is represented. Malebranche's explanation that one knows material things by ideas outside the mind itself needs explanation.

If ideas *in* the mind cannot give us knowledge of external things, how can ideas *outside* the mind give us such knowledge? Leaving aside the question of whether external ideas resemble external things, if external ideas are required to know external material things then, *as external*, might not these ideas themselves require intermediaries to be known? This would lead to an infinite regress of external ideas. Thus, Foucher believes, the Malebranchean way of external ideas is even more chimerical than the abandoned Cartesian way. Malebranche simply adds complications, doubling defects while removing none.

On Cartesian grounds, all we can know directly are modifications of the mind, and (Foucher says) anything that does not resemble these mental modifications cannot be represented by them. This excludes not only material things and material modifications, but also Malebranche's external ideas. The principle that resemblance is necessary for representation seems sufficient to Foucher for rejecting both the Cartesian way of ideas and Malebranche's way of ideas.

Foucher's criticisms are directed at vulnerable points in Malebranche's system. Malebranche did not, and evidently could not, answer these criticisms satisfactorily. Foucher believes that the major theory of ideas in the first volume of the *Recherche* is Cartesian, and that Malebranche introduces the theory of the vision in God only after encountering the difficulties of the Cartesian view in the actual composition of this first volume. Detailed analysis shows that Foucher is justified in this belief.

Malebranche's occasionalism is in part a response to the problems beset-
ting Cartesian dualism with respect to interaction between mind and body.
Foucher believes that occasionalism is contrary to the experienced fact of
interaction (and that Malebranche develops it because of his uncritical,
dogmatic adherence to the Cartesian ontological dualism), but he concentrates his criticisms upon Malebranche's way of ideas. I show above how
Foucher must have interpreted the first volume of the first edition of
Malebranche's *Recherche* not merely to vindicate Foucher but also to present
what would be a plausible reading by any late seventeenth-century philosopher versed in Cartesianism. Ideas must be modifications of the mind, for
everything must be either mental or material and either a substance or a
modification. When Foucher finally sees that Malebranche posits ideas as
entities outside the Cartesian ontological framework, he decides that Malebranche is simply talking pious nonsense. Foucher dismisses the theory as an
exhibition of religious enthusiasm and goes on to criticize the Cartesian way
of ideas, which many of Malebranche's remarks seem to support. As I show
in Chapter 8, Berkeley has a similar difficulty in attempting to introduce an
entity outside Cartesian ontology, and it is not until Hume that the linkage of
substance and modification is broken. Orthodox Cartesians try to solve their
problems within the Cartesian framework—as I agree with Foucher that
Malebranche is trying to do in the first volume of his *Recherche*—and it is to a
consideration of these orthodox (nonoccasionalist) Cartesian attempts that I
now turn.

chapter 6

The Orthodox (Nonoccasionalist) Cartesian Way of Ideas

Malebranche gives up the notion that interaction occurs between mind and body. Like Foucher, numerous Cartesians think that this interaction is obvious and thus retain it in their expositions of Cartesianism. I call these philosophers who do not offer occasionalist solutions to Cartesian problems orthodox Cartesians, although I do not insist upon the term "orthodox." As a matter of fact, these philosophers do consider themselves to be orthodox expositors of Cartesianism in contrast to someone like Malebranche, who goes so far as to assert that he is not a strict Cartesian. However, the orthodox Cartesians do not retain all the principles that seem to underlie Cartesianism, and they add some principles Descartes does not propose. They do retain the strict ontological dualism between mind and matter and thus can explain interaction only by dispensing with the causal likeness principle. Concurrently, to contend that mind can know matter, which is utterly different from it, they also deny the epistemological likeness principle.

1 ROBERT DESGABETS: THE ORTHODOX CARTESIAN SUGGESTION OF NONRESEMBLING REPRESENTATIVE IDEAS

Robert Desgabets (1605?–1678) was a Benedictine whose only publications are an exposition of Descartes's explanation of transubstantiation, and a purported defense of Malebranche against Foucher.[171] His unpublished writings include 240 folio pages conceived as a supplement to the philosophy of Descartes.[172] In his polemic with Foucher, Desgabets does not so much defend Malebranche as give what he considers to be an orthodox exposition of Cartesianism. He accuses Foucher of regressing to Scholasticism in his attempt to compress the distinction between sensations and ideas, pointing out that both scepticism and Scholasticism derive from attributing sensible qualities to material things. Desgabets does not, however, belittle the severity of the problems Foucher raises with attention to the distinctions between mind and matter, between mental and material modifications, and between ideas and sensations, that are basic to Cartesianism. But to maintain these distinctions, Desgabets dispenses with the likeness principles. He sees that if the causal and epistemological likeness principles are retained as primary in Cartesianism, then neither is interaction between body and mind nor knowledge of body by mind possible. Desgabets thus says simply that interaction is obvious, and that the knowledge relationship is dependent upon intentional resemblance of ideas to things known. However, Foucher finds that this relation is—for Desgabets—neither intentional in the Scholastic sense nor resemblance in any ordinary sense. Thus, Desgabets actually has no explanation; he merely presents the mind's causal interaction with, and knowledge of, the material world as two of God's mysteries.

Desgabets says that unnecessary problems are generated because Descartes overextends the method of doubt. The natural light gives us intuitive knowledge of the natures of the soul, of the body, and of their union. The essence of the soul is thinking; we are immediately aware of this upon having any thoughts. But we are equally aware of the essence of the body, which is extension. And in every thought that we have is contained the intuition that the thought is a modification of the mind and is caused by an entirely different substance—body; no one ever mistook the one for the other. Further, all experience contains the intuition that soul and body are completely united in interaction. Descartes, then, should not—and in actuality cannot—cast doubt on the existence of body. In doing so, he denies the further intuitive truth that is evident to anyone who meditates upon his own thoughts. It is impossible not to know "que la chose a laquelle on pense est telle en elle-même hors la pensée, qu'elle est représentée par la pensée."[173] The logically first truth, and the base of all sciences, is the following:

> Toutes nos idées ou conceptions simples ont toujours hors de l'entendement un objet réel, qui est tell en lui-même qu'il est représenté par la pensée, et qui contient le degré d'étre qu'on y aperçoit.[174]

Our knowledge of the existence of the external world, then, rests not upon Divine Veracity but upon the principle that our ideas give us certain knowledge of the world. We know this with intuitive certainty; nothing is more clear and distinct than this intuitive principle of the truth of ideas, which Desgabets insists is—rather than the *cogito*—the foundation of Cartesianism.

As for the distinction between sensations and ideas, Desgabets says that it is absolutely necessary if one is to remove error from the natural sciences. Once one realizes that only ideas of figure, position, size, and motion of material things are representative, and that sensations represent nothing external, then one sees that the Scholastics have no reason to postulate occult powers, and that the sceptics have no variation of properties from which to construct paradoxes.[175]

In the *Critique de la critique*, Desgabets accuses Foucher of not being concerned with the search for truth. Foucher engages only in destructive criticism.[176] Foucher ignores the clear intuitive knowledge we have of the essences of mind and matter. He further ignores the intuitive certainty that ideas always resemble their objects truly.[177] As for the interaction between body and soul, it is enough to remark that God is responsible for it.[178]

Desgabets admits that both ideas and sensations are caused by the action of material bodies upon the mind, but he says that this is no reason why both ideas and sensations should be representative.[179] It is a fact that ideas are and sensations are not representative. As for representations, it is indubitable that some sort of resemblance is necessary if an idea is to represent a material thing, but Desgabets denies that this need be a resemblance in essence or substance as Foucher demands. Rather, it is "ressemblance intentionnelle & non pas entitative."[180] He explains that

> la ressemblance intentionnelle ou de representation est tout d'un autre genre que la réele, & que quelque parfaite qu'elle soit on n'en peut tirer aucune consequence à un ressemblance d'estre ou de nature.[181]

Foucher argues that our ideas cannot represent material things, because they do not resemble them, but Desgabets says that ideas need not "really" resemble their objects. Ideas represent their objects in that ideas make objects known.[182] He says that everyone is aware that we think directly, immediately, and truly of the things of which we think; we seldom think of ideas.[183]

Desgabets further detects an insidious danger in Foucher's argument concerning the equality of sensations and ideas. This argument leads Foucher to claim that because secondary qualities are modifications of the soul, so also must primary qualities be modifications of the soul. That is, secondary qualities are nothing more than sensations; so also must primary qualities be nothing more than ideas. Both ideas and sensations are merely mental modifications. When Foucher claims that nothing mental can (resemble or) represent anything material, he would seem to be on the slope toward idealism. But Desgabets fears worse than this. Foucher says that our knowledge of the natures of body and soul is obscure.[184] In suggesting that our ideas of extended things are nothing more than modifications of the soul, this Academic is suggesting that there is no distinction between body and soul, that they are perhaps at base the same substance, and (Desgabets fears alas!) this substance is material.[185] He sees in Foucher's objections to nonresembling representative ideas not only a persistence of a notion of representation deriving from the Scholastic belief that our sensations resemble real sensible qualities in external things, but also even more an argument calculated subtly to convince one that the soul is material. That is, the notion that an idea must resemble to represent, coupled with the indubitable intuitive truth that our ideas represent their objects as they really are, would inevitably lead to the conclusion that the soul is material like the objects our ideas represent.

Foucher, in denying the distinction between sensations and ideas, puts primary and secondary qualities (as do the Scholastics) in the same— possibly material—substance. Desgabets, by clearly stating the *difference* between sensations and ideas—that sensations do not give us knowledge of the properties of external things, whereas ideas make these properties known without resembling them—still admits with Foucher that both ideas and sensations are mental modifications. But by insisting upon the notion of nonresembling representation, Desgabets claims that he preserves the profound distinction between body and soul, true philosophy, and (incidently) religion.

Desgabets believes that Malebranche, like Foucher, is bound to the principle that likeness is necessary for representation. He takes Malebranche's ideas to be images that resemble their objects. He believes that Malebranche conceives pure intellection to be a process in which the soul observes spiritual images that resemble the material images traced in the brain. Malebranche takes an idea to be a "milieu objectif" in which one sees the object in the way that one sees a man when looking at a portrait; Desgabets has correctly, he claims, shown that an idea is only a "milieu formel," that is, a thought, which makes the thing known without resembling it.[186] He agrees with Foucher that the theory of the vision in God is merely an expression of piety, dangerous when misunderstood.[187] However, Desgabets believes that he has—unlike either the sceptical Foucher or the pious Malebranche—provided an adequate Cartesian way of ideas, the way of nonresembling representative ideas.

2   FOUCHER'S REPLY TO DESGABETS

Foucher immediately prepared a reply to Desgabets, although it took him four years to find a publisher who would undertake a book that is the response to the critique of the critique of the *Recherche*. Foucher begins by asking the strongest of sceptical questions: What is the criterion of the criterion of certainty? Men of good faith, Desgabets says, intuitively know that their ideas truly represent things outside them. But, Foucher asks, cannot even men of good faith be deceived? How is one certain that intuition is nondeceptive? Certainly the many who believe that sensible qualities are in external things do so in good faith. Perhaps Desgabets himself is deceived in his intuitive truths.[188]

Further, Desgabets's general rule for the sciences—that our ideas represent objects as they are—is based on the assumption that the criterion of truth has been established; no arguments are given for this.[189] Beyond that, even though Desgabets says that the rule holds only for simple ideas, it is still the case that not even all simple ideas represent their objects truly. Desgabets's rule gives no criterion for distinguishing true from false ideas. Who is to say that one who has a simple idea of a red square is wrong in believing that redness is a (secondary) quality of the square? And who is to say that the insane do not see objects having the (primary) qualities they describe? All ideas are true in that they are what they are, Foucher agrees, but Desgabets fails to give a criterion for determining when ideas are true of the external world. *The* criterion of truth is still to be found.[190]

Foucher is also puzzled about how Desgabets distinguishes ideas from sensations. It is agreed that the sensible or secondary qualities are modifications of our soul; yet many men still believe that material things are colored. And all men still *see* things as both colored and extended. Desgabets says God would be a deceiver if there were not a world of extension outside us. But why would God be any more a deceiver if there were no extended world than He is because there is no colored world? Foucher cannot believe that it is not obvious to everyone that wherever colors and the other sensible qualities are, there also are extension and figure. Ideas of extension, then, are as much sensible qualities as are sensations of color.[191] One can conclude from our sensations and ideas that they have an external cause, but from these effects alone we can determine nothing about what this cause is in itself, call it body or call it soul. Desgabets is making an incredible claim when he asserts that God would be a deceiver if ideas were not of their objects, for the distinction between ideas and sensations is arbitrary.[192] If Foucher recognizes a danger in his contention that we do not know clearly the essences of mind and matter, it is only that impatient dogmatists—like Desgabets—may thereby be led to make assertions about them on insufficient evidence. Foucher certainly is not advocating materialism, for he does not have enough evidence to make any positive claims about the essences of mind and matter.

As for Desgabets's nonresembling representative ideas, Foucher repeats that he still cannot comprehend how an idea can represent without being like the object it represents.[193] Foucher points to the ontological similarity of ideas and sensations in that both are modifications of the soul. Desgabets's difference between them—that ideas represent and sensations do not—must be based on something nonessential that surmounts their equal ontological status. But Desgabets does not explain the basis of this differentiation. To state clearly that ideas make things known without resembling is no more than to repeat the Cartesian problem without solving it.[194] What must be done is to explicate this strange relation of making down, without resembling. Desgabets seems to be suggesting some notion of intentional species when he speaks of "ressemblance intentionnelle," yet he gives no explication at all of this sense of intentional. And in saying that he considers this sort of resemblance to be "tout" d'un autre genre que la réele", he admits that his sense of resemblance is not *ressemblance* at all. In fact, "ressemblance intentionalle" seems to be nothing more than a phrase equivalent to nonresembling representation. It is easy to understand what one means when one says that a portrait represents a man; Foucher would like Desgabets's sense of representation to be explained as clearly.[195]

Desgabets offers the basic orthodox Cartesian answer to Foucher's objections. Causal interaction between mind and matter takes place because God decrees it. Representation of material objects by ideas is nonrepresentative. Desgabets attempts to explain this sort of representation by speaking of intentional resemblance, but he offers no explanation of what this sort of resemblance can amount to. At one point he says that, after all, we see things, not ideas;[196] and for this he has sometimes been considered to be a precursor of Thomas Reid. Despite his use of the term, however, Desgabets does nothing at all toward developing an intentional realism, and throughout he stresses the need of representative ideas, even if he cannot explain how they represent.

I now examine the answers of further orthodox Cartesians, and Foucher's replies to them. In general, they constitute a repetition of the debate with Desgabets, and for that reason I consider them only briefly. The one new element is that explanation by appeal to the mysterious power of God is extended from covering the domain of causal interaction to cover also the domain of knowing. It is claimed that nonresembling representation need not be explained, for God assures it. The orthodox Cartesians abandon the likeness principles in order to retain strict dualism and interactionism, but they can conceive of no metaphysical principles to repair the breaches in their system; they are driven to dependence upon the God in the Cartesian machine.

Louis de La Forge, Jacques Rohault, Pierre-Sylvain Régis, Antione Le Grand, and Antoine Arnauld all are orthodox Cartesians in that each retains the strict dualism between mind and matter and concludes that ideas are representative without resembling their objects. La Forge was a physiologist, Rohault an experimental physicist, Régis a virtuoso lecturer and demonstrator, Le Grand a widely read expositor, and Arnauld a distinguished theologian and philosopher. By examining their writings, I show the full force of Foucher's criticisms, and how such criticisms, striking to the heart of Cartesian metaphysics, hastened the downfall of Cartesianism.

3   LOUIS DE LA FORGE: THE ORTHODOX CARTESIAN
DEPENDENCE UPON GOD

Louis de La Forge (1605?–1679?) collaborated with Clerselier in publishing Descartes's *Traitté de l'homme*, and in 1666 he published his own *Traitté de l'âme humaine*.[197] La Forge stresses the contradictory nature of Scholastic species, which are neither material nor immaterial, pointing out that in their immaterial aspect they cannot be emitted from a material thing, and that in their material aspect they cannot be received by the immaterial soul. The species, or images, become in Cartesian terms nothing more than the various motions of material things, sense organs, nerves, and animal spirits operative in the Cartesian perceptual mechanism.[198] These material motions do not resemble mental modifications.

The Scholastics believe, La Forge says, that resemblance is necessary for representation because they confuse material images (the material motions) with ideas, because men have a natural prejudice to believe that sensible qualities exist in external things, and finally because the principle that nothing is in the understanding that has not first been in the senses leads to the mistaken belief that ideas must be like material things just as sensations are thought to be. Representation, for the Scholastics, means resemblance. To point out the inadequacy of this notion, La Forge says that in such a case mirrors must be said to know.

La Forge stresses that what is known directly and in itself is always a modification of the mind.[199] He states that it would be a contradiction to say that ideas resemble material things,[200] but we *do* know material things by way of ideas.[201] How? La Forge's answer more or less amounts to defining his terms. Ideas are said to be in themselves *"des formes, modes, ou des façons de pensées de l'Esprit, par la perception immédiate desquelles nous apercevons les choses qu'elles nous représentent."*[202]

La Forge continues:

> Ie sçay bien qu'on ne manquera pas de me demander icy, comment il est possible que des choses Spirituelles, telles que sont nos idées ou les formes de nos pensées, nous puissent faire concevoir le Corps & ses propriétéz, avec lesquels elles n'ont aucun rapport ny ressemblance. Cela n'est pas sans difficulté; mais néanmoins vous devez pas douter de ce qui je vient dedire, principalement si vous prenez garde a duex choses. La premiere, que l'Esprit estant une chose qui pense, sa nature est nécessairement telle qu'il peut par ses propres pensées se représenter toutes choses à luy mesme; la second, que notre Esprit est *divinae quasi particula mentis*. Or cet Esprit Infiny qui connoiste toutes choses par luy mesme, ne pourroit pas connoistre les Corps, s'il estoit impossible que sa pensée, toute Spirituelle qu'elle est, les lui put représenter.[203]

Hence, it is the nature of ideas to represent without resembling, it is the nature of our spirit to know material things by its ideas, and that is the way God knows, too. It seems superfluous to add that nothing is impossible for God: He, Who is no deceiver, has made us this way.[204]

God also assures the union between body and soul, thus establishing causal interaction. And since representation cannot be based upon resemblance, La Forge bases the natural symbolism of ideas that represent material things on the causal relation. However, the Scholastics also say that material objects cause us to have ideas that make these objects known. And the Scholastics go on to explain how the representation is effected, as La Forge—depending on God—does not. La Forge also leaves to God the problem of how substances unlike one another can causally interact; he is reported to have been, at least in conversation, a complete occasionalist upon this point.[205]

However one solves the problem of causal interaction, the problem of representation remains. In defining an idea as that immediate object of perception through which we know external things, La Forge may be claiming that ideas have a primitive intentionality that needs no further explanation. It would seem, even, to be superfluous to point it out, for the only argument that can be given for it is that ideas are representative, and this should be obvious to everyone. More subtly, an intentional idea so transparent that we do not notice it, but rather observe through it the external objects it represents, would seem to be effectively invisible. The difficulty with such intentionality—and it is a difficulty La Forge sees[206]—is that it makes ideas themselves unnecessary. If all they do is mediate a knowledge of external things, if what we think about are material things and not ideas, as Desgabets says, then why are ideas needed at all? If one can see things directly, an analogy might run, why look at them in a mirror, or more to the point, through a windowpane? Such an elimination of ideas is, of course, impossible for La Forge because what Cartesians perceive are ideas and not material things. Representation can no more be *transparency* than it can be resemblance.

Foucher does not comment on La Forge's exposition, but he obviously would have demanded again an explanation of nonresembling representation. La Forge abandons the likeness principles but has only God to fill the gaps. He is followed by Rohault in his dependence upon the explanatory force of God's hidden ways.

4   JACQUES ROHAULT: THE DENIAL OF THE CAUSAL LIKENESS PRINCIPLE

Jacques Rohault (1620–1672) was a leader in Cartesian affairs in France.[207] He gave lectures in experimental physics that made him a famous man, and Foucher probably made his acquaintance at these lectures. Rohault's *Traité de physique*, published in 1671, was a standard text for nearly fifty years. Samuel Clarke thought it so good that rather than writing a Newtonian text he translated Rohault's *Traité* into Latin, correcting it by adding footnotes from Newton. Then John Clarke translated the Latin text into English.[208]

As an experimental physicist, Rohault stresses mechanical explanations. Careful thought about matter informs us that its essence is extension and that its essential properties are divisibility, figure, and impenetrability.[209] Hence, the real elements from which all things are made are small figured bodies. By actions of these bodies upon our sense organs there arise in our minds sensations and ideas by which we distinguish external bodies one from another. No further explanation is given of how this process takes place other than that it is the nature of our soul as formed by God to be so affected in causal interaction with the body.[210]

The Scholastic mistake of thinking that sensations resemble sensible qualities in external things comes from their belief that "it would be impossible for luminous or coloured Bodies to cause those Sensations in us which we feel, if there were not in them something very like what they cause us to feel, for, say they, nothing can give what it has not."[211] Rohault says that the simplest reflection will show this principle to be faulty. One need only consider the pain we feel when we are pricked with a needle to see that the needle can cause an effect that is nothing at all like anything in the needle. The misleading notion of intentional species that resemble their objects derives from a Scholastic interpretation of Aristotle's theory of vision. This is that things impress images upon the air, which images continue to be impressed through the medium until they are impressed upon the eye, where the soul observes them. As an explanation of how this takes place, Scholastics say that it occurs in the same way that an image is reflected in a mirror. Rohault first says that Aristotle is not to be taken literally here. Then he says that it is harder to explain reflected images than direct images, so the mirror analogy can be no explanation. Finally, he appeals to experience. He assumes that at their source images would be as large as their objects, and that they would diminish in size in direct proportion to the distance they are from the eye. This would mean that we could not see images of things within a few yards of us, for these images would be too large. But we do see large things that are close to us, so the Scholastic theory of intentional species is absurd.[212]

Rohault's objection here seems to be based on a misunderstanding of the Scholastic position. His own theory of perception is that outlined above in Chapter 2: Material things are impressed upon the sense organs, from which distinctive motions are transmitted along the nerves to the pineal gland; this causes in the mind sensations and ideas, which are immaterial effects that do not resemble their material causes. Ideas represent "the *Place, Situation, Distance, Magnitude, Figure, Number,* and *the Motion or Rest* of such Objects," but sensations do not.[213]

Foucher asks Rohault (perhaps at one of Rohault's lectures) his standard question of why it is that extension is not in the mind if color is. Rohault first replies that we do not know extension by the senses. Foucher proceeds to show that if we know color by the senses, then we must know extension by the senses also. Rohault disagrees; in response to Foucher's question of how then we do know extension, he says that we know extension by reasoning from sensation of touch on different parts of the body. This either begs the question or implies that the soul is extended. Assuming that Rohault wishes neither of these consequences, Foucher expands upon the contention that extension too is a sensible quality. He believes that Rohault really means to say that the ideas—Foucher says sensations—of extension resemble primary qualities of bodies, whereas other sensations do not.[214] Foucher believes that in maintaining this distinction, Rohault implies that soul and body are capable of the same "façon-d'estre," and this destroys the Cartesian dualism.

Foucher could not have been impressed by Rohault's argument that material things can cause mental modifications that do not resemble their causes. This is just the point Foucher himself stresses in claiming that we can reason from the occurrence of ideas and sensations to the existence of some cause but can say nothing of the essence of this cause. If the essence of anything is known here, it is the essence of sensations and ideas, not the essence of material or mental substance. Descartes himself says that we know directly only our ideas. Rohault would not have to appeal to the mysterious power of God to explain the interaction between mind and matter if he knew their true essences, for knowledge of how this interaction takes place would necessarily follow from knowledge of their essences.

Rohault says that there is no reason for assuming that ideas (effects) resemble anything in the objects that cause them any more than do sensations.[215] Ideas need not resemble their objects to represent them. But, Foucher insists, if Rohault truly understands a nonresembling representative relationship between ideas and their objects, he would not have to use—as he does—the unphilosophical recourse of insisting that ideas make their objects known without resembling them because that is the role assigned to them by God. Régis, the next orthodox Cartesian treated, clearly recognizes the necessity of explicating a new representative relation in which ideas make their objects known but do not resemble them.

5 PIERRE-SYLVAIN RÉGIS: THE DEPENDENCE UPON INEXPLICABLE CAUSAL RELATIONS

Pierre-Sylvain Régis (1632–1707) was converted to Cartesianism by Rohault and followed in his footsteps to become a highly successful lecturer and writer on Cartesian physics.[216] He comes to realize that nonresembling representative ideas are a necessary part of the Cartesian system, and like Rohault before him, he finds the causal and epistemological likeness principles to be in conflict with the more basic principles of the Cartesian dualism. Consequently, he examines in detail how causal interaction and knowing can take place between two substances. His conclusion is that whereas interaction between bodies can be explained by reason in the order of nature, interaction and knowing between spirit and body are events in the order of grace that can be "explained" (that is, accepted) only by faith.

Ontologically, Régis recognizes only two kinds of substances that differ in essence: spiritual substance and material substance. God is not a substance, for He takes no modification. Among twelve self-evident metaphysical principles that are the the foundation of all certitude in metaphysics, logic, physics, and ethics,[217] four concerning the ontological framework of Cartesianism are quite important to the present interpretation of Cartesian difficulties:

1. *Que tout mode présuppose une substance dans laquelle il existe.*
2. *Que les modes sont tellement attachez à la substance dont ils sont modes, qu'il est impossible qu'ils deviennent jamais les modes d'une autre substance.*
3. *Que tout ce que existe, est une substance ou un mode.*
4. *Que les essences des choses sont indivisibles, & qu'on n'y peut rien ajoûter ni diminuer sans les détruire.*[218]

From these four principles, several important conclusions follow for orthodox Cartesianism. Because mind and matter differ completely in essence (and their essences are clearly and distinctly known), nothing can be added to either of them that is like the other. And of key importance is the axiom that whatever exists is either a substance or a modification. Ideas can be *only* modifications of the mind; any attempt to make them into something outside the all-inclusive ontological framework of substance and modification, as Malebranche (and later Berkeley) does, is ruled out from the start. The final conclusion is that ideas for Régis must necessarily be modifications of the mind that represent material objects without resembling them.

In further principles, Régis stresses that we know only by way of ideas:

5. *Que je ne connois les choses que sont hors de moy que par des idées, & les choses dont je n'ay point d'idées, sont à l'égard de ma connoissance, comme si elles n'estoient pas du tout.*

He bases the representative relation (as does La Forge) on the causal relationship between material objects and their ideas:

6. *Que toutes les idées, quant à la propriété de représenter, dépendent de leurs objets comme de leurs causes exemplaires.*

7. *Que la cause exemplaire des idées doit contenir formellement toutes les perfections que les idées representent.*[219]

Régis reports that sensations do not represent external things but only guide us in actions of self-interest, whereas ideas truly represent their objects.

In explicating principle 6, that their objects are exemplary causes of ideas, Régis compares ideas to paintings. He does not do this in order to suggest that ideas are images;[220] the comparison is made to stress a broad causal analogy. Both paintings and ideas are representative beings. Just as in painting there is the painter, the model, the brush strokes, and the canvas, so also in the production of ideas; God is the first efficient cause, the material things are the exemplary causes, and the soul is the material cause.[221] But here, unlike the cause of the painting where both model and canvas are extended, the material thing is extended while the soul is an unextended "material cause." Régis's analogy serves only to accentuate the fact that there can be no resemblance between an idea and its extended exemplary cause. Although he stresses as a self-evident principle that the exemplary causes of ideas must contain "formellement toutes les perfections que les idées représentent," Régis does not go on—as do the Scholastics—to explain by reason how, as a part of the order of nature, ideas represent these perfections.

Régis says that knowing external objects by way of nonresembling representative ideas, and causal interaction between spirit and body, are not to be explained by reason in the order of nature at all. Such events belong to the order of grace and are to be "explained" only in the sense that they are to be accepted on faith. Régis's extended interpretation of the facts of the Cartesian dualism is as follows. Man is an accidental union of spirit and body, and only in this union is a spirit a *soul*. That such union is possible is of the essence of neither spirit nor body, and it pertains only by the grace of God. While in this union, the *soul* always has the idea of extension. Particular brain movements always give rise to particular sensations and ideas of objects affecting the brain. All the *soul's* ideas, even of God, depend upon brain movements. Pleasure and pain lead men to love or to hate and thus to pursue or to flee objects of ideas for self-preservation. After separation of spirit and body—that is, after death—spirit has no longer the idea of extension, imagination, nor memory of nor power over the material world. Spirit then can know and love only itself and God.[222]

This is Régis's "explanation" of events that belong to the order of grace. It is a description of events that are inexplicable by reason, but that do occur, and that can be accepted only on faith. Even the "reasonable" statement that spirit has the idea of extension only when in union with body is not offered as an explanation by reason, for we still do not know *why* this should be the case, nor *how* unextended spirit has the idea of extension. If anyone wonders how sensations and ideas are caused when material objects act on bodies united to spirits and how ideas represent material objects, Régis's reply is that we cannot know these things—not simply because our knowledge is limited, but because the question itself rests on the mistaken assumption that one can explain these things by reason. The consequences of the union of spirit and body belong not to the order of grace. What one knows about them is that they occur, and that their "explanation" rests on faith, not on reason. Régis believes, then, that there is no conflict between reason and faith, because the independent principles of each apply only to the nonoverlapping orders of nature and of grace. Scholastics and Cartesians alike have a tendency to attempt to explain events in the order of grace with the principles of reason, and events in the order of nature with the principles of faith, but neither is possible.[223]

Beyond the fact that they try to explain matters of grace with reason, Régis traces the Scholastics' mistake of attributing sensible qualities to material things to the fact that sensations and ideas have a common cause in these material things. When one says, for example, "je vois cet homme," one is led to think mistakenly that his sensations are of a material thing as it is. However, material things are never sensed. What actually occurs in such situations is that one sees colors (that is, has sensations of color) and at the same time has ideas of a certain figure. Considered separately, ideas and sensations are seen for what they are. The Scholastic mistake comes from not considering ideas as such, but as including in their conception the judgment that sensible qualities (because sensations are caused by the same objects at the same times as ideas) belong to the objects of which one is concurrently having ideas.[224]

Jean Du Hamel attacks Régis's exposition concerning ideas by pointing out that Régis's use of the painting analogy is grossly misleading, for the major purpose of the analogy should be to show not how an idea is caused but how it represents its object.[225] Du Hamel gets the impression that Régis is saying that Cartesian ideas must be like their objects without being like them; and of course this is contradictory.[226] At least the Scholastic explanation of resembling species makes it intelligible how we know things, Du Hamel says. Even if this explanation may be incorrect in detail, it is correct in stressing that resemblance is necessary for representation. Hence, Du Hamel dismisses as unintelligible the notion that ideas can represent without resembling. (Of course, Régis's point simply is that it is unintelligible.) Du Hamel reiterates Foucher's objections and then develops a sceptical argument that Foucher brought up against Malebranche. We can never know for certain that our ideas represent material things unless we can compare them with these things. But on Cartesian principles we can know only ideas directly, and material things only through the mediation of ideas. Hence, this comparison is impossible. Even if it is the case that external things cause our ideas, we can still never compare the cause with the effect. Régis even claims that we can tell the difference between substances by examining our ideas, for example, of thinking and extension. But this is clearly impossible because our ideas are strictly modes of thinking, which can be compared only with other modes of thinking, that is, with other ideas. On Cartesian principles one can never know directly either body or soul; so one can never be certain that one has knowledge of external things. Du Hamel concludes that all this shows Cartesianism to be absurd, for obviously we do know external things.[227]

In replying to Du Hamel, Régis explicitly rejects what he takes to be the Scholastic likeness principles. He expands this rejection by stating that ideas are neither formal nor objective images of their objects. Since Du Hamel insists that the Cartesians explain the notion of representation that allows them to judge of external objects by internal, nonresembling ideas, Régis offers the following: (1) It is the case that we know things only by ideas; (2) our ideas do not resemble their objects; therefore, (3) ideas represent by making their objects known. That is all. It is the nature of ideas to make things known, and it is the nature of our soul to know. To ask for any explanation further would be like asking how light makes us see, that is, have sensations of brightness and color. The point is that sensations and ideas are known in themselves as what they are.[228]

But, of course, in shifting the problem, Régis raises another difficulty. It *is* an embarrassment for the Cartesians to explain how light—that is, the motion or "pression" of particles of matter, or ultimately motions in the pineal gland—can cause sensations, which are modifications of the soul. Ideas are caused the same way, and even if one could bridge the causal gap, the question still remains of how it is that ideas represent their objects. All Régis can say is that in knowing ideas, we know them in themselves, and part of what we know is that ideas represent their objects. (Concurrently, in knowing sensations in themselves, part of what we know is that they do not represent objects.) There is no explanation by reason of these experienced facts. Régis says that all we can do is accept them on faith.

Du Hamel has the final word. He repeats Régis's answer to the request for an exact explanation of nonresembling representation: It is the nature of ideas to make things known, and it is the nature of the soul to know things by way of ideas. This, sighs Du Hamel, is a remarkable discovery, for which all schools no doubt will be eternally grateful to the Cartesians. It is, however, hardly a proper principle on which to base a system of philosophy.[229]

I now consider another Cartesian, who does give an explanation. Antoine Le Grand tries to show how nonresembling ideas can make their objects known by acting as signs.

6 ANTOINE LE GRAND: IDEAS AS NATURE'S SIGNS

Antoine Le Grand (1620?–1699) published in 1694 *An Entire Body of Philosophy*, in which he reduces the Cartesian system to a "Scholastic" scheme; that is, he presents a Cartesian scheme of hierarchical concepts for understanding the world.[230] This work is the last major exposition of Cartesianism, and along with the publication of the last enlarged edition of Malebranche's *Recherche* in 1712 (actually completed in 1699) it heralds the close of the Cartesian era.

Le Grand, like Arnauld, develops more than do the other orthodox Cartesians the notion that ideas have a double aspect. He says that:

> in the *Idea* or notion of a Thing two things are to be consider'd: *First*, That it is a *Modus* inherent in the *Mind*, from whence it proceeds: The *other*, That is shews or represents something. The former of these proceeds from the *Mind*, as its effective Principle; the latter from the *Object*, or thing apprehended, as from its Exemplary cause.[231]

The representative aspect of an idea is expressible in words as a proposition that reports the results of simple apprehension; it is not a judgment. All ideas represent possible existents, and error can arise only through judgment that they represent things that actually exist.[232]

Le Grand makes it clear that although ideas are spoken of as "Images of things,"[233] this is in no way a picture imagery. It is a conceptual imagery, that is, an understanding of the essence of things, for:

> the Ideas . . . which we have of Things . . . are *Conceptions*, or rather the Things themselves conceived and understood by the *Mind*; by which Intellection things are said to be Objectively in the *Intellect*.[234]

We can, for example, have no pictures of God nor of spiritual things, but we can have ideas of them. And although material things can be pictured in their own realm, it is impossible to picture them with a nonextended substance such as the mind.[235]

Le Grand explains nonresembling representation by ideas of material things merely by characterizing the more inclusive relation of substitution. He says that:

> *Relation* is nothing else, but a Mode of our Understanding, comparing one thing with others, because of some Properties or Acts that are found in them.

The relation of substitution is a comparative relation such as "that which intervenes betwixt the Sign, and that which is signified by it; the Measure and the thing Measured: the Image and the Original."[236]

Substitution of an image for the original cannot generate a relation in which a thing is made known without being resembled, however, for all agree that images must resemble their objects. And a basic principle of measurement is that only commensurables—entities like one another in some way—can be measured against one another. A material expanse thus cannot be measured with—or represented by—a spiritual thing.

The relation of making known must be that between sign and what is signified. But in saying this, Le Grand does as do the other orthodox Cartesians. He states the problem, offering this statement as a solution. That is, the sign has nothing to do with making what is signified known. Once the thing is known, Foucher would agree, a sign can be established or recognized for it, and this sign need not resemble its object. But original knowledge—which is what is in question—cannot be attained by way of a sign. One might agree that an idea is a sign of a cause, but in itself the idea gives no notion of what the cause is. For a Cartesian, there is no possibility of comparing signs (ideas) with what is signified (material objects), no relation "of some Properties or Acts that are found in them" to allow one to recognize that this is a sign of that. Natural signs do exist—lightning is the sign of thunder—but in such a case both lightning and thunder have been observed. But ideas must ever be (upon Cartesian principles) signs of the same sort as are mysterious comets, the portent of which is unknown. The Cartesians know the signs (ideas) but never what they are signs of. To learn that ideas are the signs of certain particular material things, one would have to observe the signs and the things in conjunction. But by the very nature of the case, all that is ever observed are the signs, never the signified.

Le Grand's major causal axioms also make it difficult to characterize the relation. "A Cause cannot give that which it hath not" is matched with "No

Effect exceeds the virtue of its Cause."[237] From these principles one could argue that ideas cannot be the effects of material causes, for ideas are completely unlike material things. In fact, because of this complete unlikeness, it would seem to be impossible for the two to be in any relation whatsoever, let alone in a causal relation.

Le Grand says that the essential differences between sensations and ideas is that ideas are understandings, whereas sensations are not. Ideas can also be general; sensations are always particular.[238]

The representative aspect of ideas is separated as propositional by Le Grand from the ontological aspect of ideas, which is their being as modes of mental substance. He makes this distinction explicit in saying that besides ordinary ideas there are also:

> Propositions of *Eternal Truth*, which are not understood as Existing things, or the Modes of things; but as Eternal Truths abiding in our Understanding: As, *That which is, whilst it is, cannot be nothing: I am, because I think: what is once done, cannot be undone*; which are therefore called *Common Notions*, because they are so simple and clear, that they cannot but be perceived by all Men. Neither must it be look'd upon as an Absurdity, that we call any thing *Eternal* and *Immutable*, besides GOD; because we do not speak here of Existing things, but only of Notions and Axioms which are in our Mind.[239]

These notions and axioms enjoy a peculiar status in the Cartesian ontological framework. In Le Grand's classification of everything in the world, each thing represented is either a substance or a modification of a substance.[240] However, axioms and notions are not "Existing things" but are only "in our Mind" and ultimately in God's mind. Le Grand might have gone on to say that the representative aspect of all ideas is only in the mind, while their other aspect is their existence as modifications of the mind. (These modifications, by the way, he consistently conceives of as acts or actions of mind in consequence of their being modifications of an active thinking substance.) But having suggested an element (as does Malebranche) that has no place in the Cartesian ontological framework, Le Grand finds no way of classifying it. In his diatribe against Scholastic intentional species, which some Peripatetics say are neither material nor spiritual, Le Grand ridicules the notion that they can have any role in the perceptual process. More likely they are nothing at all. He forgets himself so far as to ask (supposing they are not material), "how can they represent *Extended Beings*, without *Extension* themselves?"[241] As a matter of fact, Le Grand holds that ideas, which are modifications of the mind, *do* represent extended things without being extended themselves. The Scholastic prejudice, says Le Grand, that the cause must be like the effect is as absurd as to reason that the earth must be a fiddler because it produces fiddlers. Ideas and sensations need not be like the motions that produce them, nor need ideas be like the material things they represent.[242]

As for explaining nonresembling representation, Le Grand says that just as we assign significance to words, "Why may not *Nature* as well appoint a Sign" that has no resemblance to what it represents?[243] That is, nothing can be transferred from material things to ideas, and no idea can be a similitude of material things, but God could so arrange it that material things do cause ideas that represent these material things. These ideas would be innate in the mind, arising due to the occurrence of certain motions in the pineal gland. Thus Le Grand, the last great expositor of Cartesianism, follows the other orthodox Cartesians in resting nonresembling representation upon the will of God. God can and does support such representation, but no explanation is forthcoming as to how He does it. Le Grand suggests the possibility that ideas are outside the Cartesian ontological framework completely (and thus these ideas are perhaps not susceptible to the objections here raised), but he reserves this status for Eternal Truths, which are said to be in the mind. Ultimately they reside, without being, in the mind of God. According to Le Grand's own principles, if they have no being, they are nothing. And if they are in the mind of God with being, they could be there only as modifications.

I have now traced the development of the orthodox Cartesian way of ideas from Rohault to Le Grand. All these philosophers try to avoid sceptical criticisms of Cartesianism by denying the principles that likeness is required between cause and effect and between knower and known. None of them finds an intelligible substitute for these principles of explanation, so all of them conclude by calling upon God to support interaction and a representative relation, which are basically mysterious. Antoine Arnauld comes to the same general conclusion with his treatment of perceptions that are by nature representative. After looking at his position briefly, I examine the underlying causes and implications of the Cartesian failure to explicate a nonresembling sense of representation in Chapter 7.

7 ANTOINE ARNAULD: REPRESENTATIVE PERCEPTIONS

Antoine Arnauld (1612–1694), a famous Jansenist, wrote the "Objectiones Quartae" to Descartes's *Meditation*.[244] Despite the fact that the traditional argument that Descartes's establishment of the criterion for true ideas is circular appears in these objections and became known as "Arnauld's Circle," Arnauld's positive philosophical position is Cartesian. *La logique, ou l'art de penser* (which Arnauld wrote with Pierre Nicole) is derived from Descartes's *Regulae*; and in *Des vrayes et des fausses idées, contre ce qu'enseigne l'auteur de la recherche de la vérité,* Arnauld cites Descartes throughout as authority against Malebranche. It is in this dispute with Malebranche over the nature of ideas that Arnauld presents his own orthodox Cartesian position concerning the nature and role of ideas.[245]

In direct opposition to Malebranche, Arnauld says that ideas are modifications of thinking substance or spirit, and not separately existing *êtres reprêsentatifs.*

> Je prends aussi pour la même chose, l'idée d'un object & la perception d'un objet . . . il est certain qu'il y a des *idées* prises en ce sens, & que ces idées sont ou des attributs, ou des modifications de nôtre âme.[246]

Elsewhere, Arnauld says that besides "modifications de nôtre âme," the terms "mode," "maniere d'être de l'esprit," "pensée," "notion," "modalité de l'esprit," and "perception" are synonymous with the term "idée."[247] Arnauld generally speaks of these mental modifications as perceptions that are representative of their objects. He insists that "Penser, connôitre, apperçevoir, sont la même chose."[248] Obviously, such ideas cannot represent their objects by resembling them, for this would lead to the damnable conclusion that the mind is material.[249] Hence, Arnauld is scandalized to find Malebranche holding to two principles:

> *Que l'âme ne pouvoit appercevoir que les objets qui lui étoient présents, & que les corps ne lui pouvoient être présents que par de certains êtres représentifs, appellés idées ou especes, qui tenoient leur place, leur étant semblables, & qui, au lieu d'eux étoient unis intimément à l'âme.*[250]

These two propositions are contradictory in two ways: first, because the only things that can be intimately united to the soul are modifications of the soul, and these modifications cannot resemble material objects; second, because representative beings, which are not modifications of the soul and which resemble material objects, cannot be intimately united to the soul. Arnauld argues persuasively that in the early parts of the *Recherche* Malebranche takes ideas to be mental modifications and only later shifts to the notion that they are separate representative beings.[251] Because of this shift, Malebranche makes the mistake he does.

Arnauld traces the origin of Malebranche's nonmodal representative ideas to a confused childhood belief: Because we supposedly see in mirrors not objects themselves but only their images, we go on to think that we never see objects themselves but only their images. Because Malebranche adheres to the epistemological likeness principle, he must make these image-ideas into entities external to the mind. Arnauld's attack upon Malebranche is based upon the principle that only a modification of a substance can be united intimately with that substance. Because ideas are so united to minds, their representation of material objects cannot depend upon any resemblance to material objects. Arnauld believes that Malebranche holds to the epistemological likeness principle because of a mistaken analogy to corporeal images or signs in the material world. The way ideas represent, however, Arnauld contends, is unique to ideas:

> Quand on dit que nos idées & nos perceptions (car je prends cela pour le même chose) nous représentent les choses que nous concevons, & en sont les images, c'est dans tout un autre sens, que lorsqu'on dit, que les tableaux représentent leurs originaux & en sont les images, ou que les paroles, prononcées ou ecrites, sont les images de nos pensées. Car, au regard des idées, cela veut dire que les choses que nous concevons sont *objectivement* dans notre esprit & dans nos pensée. Or cette *maniere d'être objectivement dans l'esprit*, est si particuliere à la esprit & à la pensée, comme étant ce qui en fait particuliérement la nature, qu'en vain on chercheroit rien de semblable en tout ce qui n'est pas esprit & pensée. Et c'est comme j'ai déjà remarqué, ce par a brouillé toute cette matiere des *idées*, de ce qu'on a voulu expliquer, par des comparaisons prises de choses corporelles, la maniere dont les objets sont représentés par nos idées, quoiqu'il ne puisse y avoir sur cela aucan vrai rapport entre les corps & les esprits.[252]

Thus, there can be no explanation of the way ideas represent by analogy to the way pictures represent (by resembling) their objects. Arnauld says, in fact, that there is no explanation of how ideas represent at all. One should be satisfied to learn that it is the nature of spirit to think of material objects, that is, to have ideas or perceptions of them. One of his rules in the search after truth is not to seek for reasons beyond natures.[253] Like the other orthodox Cartesians, Arnauld believes it is enough to point out that God made thinking beings capable of thinking of material objects.

Ideas themselves have two essential relations: They are called ideas with respect to the relation they have to the soul they modify, and they are called perceptions with respect to the relation they have to the objects perceived.[254] Malebranche seems to believe, says Arnauld, that the two relations mean that there are two different entities: perceptions and separately existing representative ideas. This, Arnauld says, is not so. Perceptions themselves are representative of external objects through a relationship to those objects established by God. Arnauld specifies this relation only negatively and does not explain it (nor does he believe that he needs to). He says explicitly that the relation is not of the sort that exists between the signs of language and their objects, but it is fair to suggest that for Arnauld ideas or perceptions are some sort of indicative signs. Certainly he is open to this interpretation when he speaks of sensations. Malebranche agrees with Arnauld that sensations are modifications of the mind, and also that this does not mean that the mind is colored when it is having a sensation of color. Similarly, Arnauld insists, perceptions of squares need not be square.[255] Perceptions indicate their objects without being like them just as sensations indicate their objects without being like them. This is to say that perceptions or ideas are like signs. God assigns them to objects.

Malebranche's external ideas, which represent their objects by resembling them, are both unnecessary and redundant, for one would have to have perceptions of them if they did exist. Arnauld says it is better to face the fact that perceptions are of material objects directly. Nevertheless, Arnauld concludes that such perceptions are representative in essence.[256] By taking the representative relationship for granted as established by God without trying to explain it, Arnauld joins the ranks of the other orthodox Cartesians who fail to meet the crucial challenge—the demand for a philosophical explanation of nonresembling representative ideas.

chapter 7

An Analysis of the Cartesian Failures to Solve Problems Facing Cartesianism

Desgabets, La Forge, Rohault, Régis, Le Grand, and Arnauld are called orthodox Cartesians because they have the following in common:

1. They keep the strict Cartesian ontological dualism between the two created substances: mind, which has as its essence or *is* active unextended *thinking*; and matter, which has as its essence or *is* inert unthinking *extension*.[257]
2. They insist that causal interaction takes place between these two substances, resulting in ideas and sensations; ideas are representative of their material causes; sensations are not representative of their material causes.
3. They agree that whatever has being must be either a substance or a modification of a substance.

Obviously, ideas, which are modifications of active, unextended thinking, cannot resemble inert, unthinking extension or its modifications. Thus, it follows logically that support for the orthodox Cartesian claim that ideas represent material objects cannot be based upon a relation of resemblance. Similarly, it follows that if there is causal interaction between mind and matter, such interaction cannot depend upon any sort of engagement—on analogy of one gear with another—between like aspects of the two substances. In this way, the orthodox Cartesians find these threee principles to be inconsistent with the likeness principles. Therefore,

4. They reject the principles that likeness is necessary between cause and effect, and that likeness is necessary between what represents and what is represented.

Foucher's objections are based upon an acceptance of these likeness principles, and upon the conviction that in any conflict of principles, a reasonable philosopher will abandon most other principles before abandoning the likeness principles. Even in the face of statements from them to the contrary, Foucher still contends that the orthodox Cartesians cannot really mean to give up the likeness principles. These principles, Foucher insists, are basic to the explanations of the engagement between cause and effect and of the representative aspect of ideas. Foucher cannot understand how interaction between substances could be explained without there being some likeness between them. And representation seems to him to be so dependent upon resemblance that the two terms are practically synonymous. Therefore, the essential difference between mind and matter that the orthodox Cartesians profess precludes (according to Foucher) the possibility of interaction and representation, which everyone experiences. It seems much more reasonable to Foucher to suppose that the orthodox Cartesians do not really know the true essences of mind and matter. If mind and matter *do* differ in essence, then, Foucher says, a new relation of nonresembling representation must be made plausible. I have shown that no Cartesian managed to provide the long-demanded explication. Some of the inadequate attempts of the orthodox Cartesians to provide an explanation, and some of the reasons for the failures of these attempts, are considered in this chapter. Specifically, I examine the notions of ideas as natural signs, mechanical causation, external ideas, and direct acquaintance. I conclude that Cartesians have trouble with each of these notions because of their (implicit) dependence upon the likeness principles and the ontology of substance and modification.

1   IDEAS AS NATURAL SIGNS

The orthodox Cartesian notion of *idea* must be examined closely. The distinctions between the faculty of the intellect that makes it possible for the mind to have ideas and the operation of this faculty, and between each of them and the object of this operation (if there are such distinctions), are not always clear. What does seem clear (this is expressed most strongly in Le Grand and Arnauld) is that ideas, being modifications of an active mind, are actions of the mind in contrast to the passive modifications of inert matter. There are four recognizable aspects of such ideas. They represent objects to the mind; they are modifications of the mind; they differ from sensations; and they differ among themselves. The representative aspect could reasonably be thought to depend upon a causal relation between the represented object and the representing idea. Thus, the object could be considered to be both the exemplary and the efficient cause of the idea. But, if the object is a *material* object, it can be neither. A material object cannot be an exemplary cause in the sense of being a model, archetype, or pattern of a mental idea, because there is no likeness between them. A material object cannot be an efficient cause of an idea, because the essential difference between mind and matter precludes the possibility of any conceivable interaction between them. (As discussed below, the Cartesians are restricted to mechanical explanations of causation.) Nevertheless, the orthodox Cartesians are convinced that material objects somehow cause ideas, and that in doing so they cause those ideas to represent the said material objects. How this is done they do not explain.

Ideas differ one from another and they represent different objects. It might be thought, therefore, that the aspect by which they are distinguished one from another is the same as the aspect by which they represent different objects. This would reduce the actual aspects of ideas to three. However, this conclusion cannot be drawn. Sensations are equal to ideas in being modifications of the mind that differ among themselves, but the aspect that allows us to distinguish them one from another is not a representative aspect, for sensations do not represent. Hence, if in ideas we identify the representative aspect with the aspect that allows us to distinguish ideas one from another, then ideas can no longer be distinguished from sensations. If there is to be a reduction of kinds of aspects of an idea by finding or making two of them to be identical, these two cannot be the aspect by which ideas are distinguished one from another and the aspect by which ideas represent objects external to the mind. They can be only the aspect by which ideas represent an object external to the mind and the aspect by which ideas differ from sensations. In fact, this is just what the Cartesians say: Ideas differ from sensations by having a representative aspect; sensations differ from ideas by lacking a representative aspect. (That is, sensations have only three aspects: Sensations are modifications of the mind; sensations differ from ideas; and sensations differ among themselves.) Foucher's criticisms amount to pointing out that the orthodox Cartesians do not indicate what the representative aspect of ideas is. Foucher would reduce the aspects of both ideas and sensations to two. Both ideas and sensations are modifications of the mind that differ one from another, but ideas do not differ in any appreciable way from sensations. Because Foucher notices no *special* representative aspect, any representative aspect is that aspect by which ideas and sensations differ one from another (so both are representative), or neither ideas nor sensations have any representative aspect at all. (Sensations, of course, can be signs. I show immediately below that the interpretation of representative ideas as signs is inadequate because the relation of signification is externally, arbitrarily imposed, and is not based on any representative aspect internal to the sign.)

The orthodox Cartesians say that ideas represent their objects by making them known. They see that the representative aspect of ideas cannot be resemblance and therefore agree that the picture analogy is misleading. The analogy to the way signs represent their objects is a possible alternative explanation of *making known*. The first step they take toward explicating representation in the sense of making known, then, is by giving as examples signs such as words, mathematical symbols, and noises, all of which represent without resembling their objects. These signs represent both our ideas and external objects, yet resemble neither. Therefore, if the sign relation is understood, there should be no difficulty, say the orthodox Cartesians, in conceiving that ideas can represent without resembling. However, once the sign relationship *is* understood, it is seen to be of no help in explicating how ideas make their objects known, for ideas are not signs. The relation between a sign and what it signifies is arbitrary. The sign "sun" represents the idea we have of the sun because we can know the idea directly and arbitrarily assign this sign to it. On the sign analogy then, if the idea of the sun represents the real sun, we should have to know the sun apart from the idea in order to be able to assign the idea to it. But, of course, because material objects are known not directly but only by way of ideas, it is contradictory to suppose that we can know material objects prior to assigning ideas to them in the direct way that we know ideas prior to assigning words to the ideas.

The orthodox Cartesian reply to this objection is that *God* assigns non-resembling ideas as signs of external objects. Now, one wants to know of ideas that make their objects known, how it is that we know through them *which* external objects they represent, and how we know that they represent their objects *truly*. The picture analogy offers an answer to the first question. A picture-idea pictures its object. But concerning the second question, recall a classic sceptical objection to the picture analogy; one cannot determine how accurate a portrait is if one has never seen the model. Similarly, one cannot assert that picture-idea is an accurate representation of an object (or even that it is representative at all) unless one knows the object in some other way than by way of ideas. One must have knowledge independent of ideas of what the idea is meant to represent if one is to check the truth of an idea. *If* the orthodox Cartesians could accept the picture analogy (which they cannot because of the dualism), then they might answer that what the picture-idea represents is guaranteed accurate by a nondeceiving God. But because they cannot use the picture analogy, whether or not and how the represented object is made known through our knowing a nonresembling idea of exactly the questions at issue.

Consider again how it is that a sign signifies its objects. A sign signifies not through any special internal representative aspect (as does a picture-idea), but through an arbitrary external relation. Before knowing which idea a word represents in the sense of signifies (for example, a word representing the idea of an animal one has never seen), one must have known directly an idea that is at least similar to the one the word represents. (Obviously, the analogy here is only to words that *do* represent.) In the same way, if one is to know what his ideas represent, one must (on the sign analogy) have known directly an external object at least similar to the object the sign-idea represents. However, it is impossible on Cartesian principles to know *any* external object directly. Hence, although a nondeceiving God might assure us that sign-ideas are *signs*, this would not help us in knowing of which and what objects they are signs. We still would not know what the sign-ideas represent unless we knew the external objects directly. God's veracity would be of use here only if ideas resembled their objects, which is ruled out.

Another way of putting this point is that, on the picture analogy, ideas in themselves have sense, content, or connotation, as well as a referential or denotative aspect. On the sign analogy, ideas in themselves have only a neutral (sense-less) referential or denotative aspect. So if God assures us of the truth of a *picture*-idea, we can know what (its connotation) and that it denotes without ever encountering its object directly. But if God assures us of the truth of a *sign*-idea, we can know only that it denotes, and not what its object or connotation is. Again, in another vocabulary, God's assurance that a sign-idea has extension does not tell us anything about its intention.

This way of making the point also brings out a further inadequacy of the sign analogy. The Cartesians wish to speak of the truth, or accuracy of ideas; it is not usual to speak of a sign's being true to its object. Perhaps one could make sense of a truth of signs by speaking of systems of signs organized with formation rules and type-levels. God's assurance, then, would amount to guaranteeing that the relations holding among the signs are true of the relations holding among objects. But again, we would not know *what* the objects are in themselves; we would know only the relations among them. (And, as a matter of fact, such a system of isomorphism between the relations of a formal sign system and the relations holding among signified objects is really only a variant of the rejected picture theory.)

Hence, the conclusion must stand: While the picture analogy is ontologically incoherent, the sign or language analogy is epistemologically inadequate. For although it is perfectly true that we can signify ideas with words that do not resemble them, to state as an explanation of representation that we can signify external objects with ideas that do not resemble them is to miss the crucial point. The problem is not to show how something nonresembling (a word) can signify what can be known directly (an idea), but how something nonresembling (an idea) can represent what can *not* be known directly (an external object). What we have to be able to know is *what* a sign-idea represents. And, according to Cartesian principles, we cannot. The difficulty is precisely that external objects are *not* known directly as ideas are. It is thus a mistake to think that nonresembling ideas can make external objects known in the way that signs signify their objects, for the relation standing between a sign and its object holds only given that the object is previously and directly known. God presumably can know external objects directly and thus can assign nonresembling ideas as their signs. And He can tell us He has done so but, again, this is not to tell us *what* the idea-signs indicate. It seems clear then, that if external objects *are* known only by way of representative ideas and never directly as Cartesians claim, then these ideas cannot be sign-ideas, for signification cannot in this case be a relation of representation that makes sense to us. Thus, because sign-ideas are inadequate and picture-ideas are incoherent, the Cartesian theory of representative ideas remains unexplained and mysterious.

The basic objection is similar to that of Sextus Empiricus on indicative signs.[258] The orthodox Cartesian response is a theory like that of the (opaque) Stoic *lecton* theory: One knows that ideas make things known because one gets to know things by way of ideas.

In the end, the orthodox explanation of how nonresembling ideas resemble their objects amounts to the claim that there is a primitive, indefinable relation of representation between ideas and the objects they make known. It is a fact about the way God maintains the world that ideas make external objects known. If someone objects that just as a man born blind cannot be told with words what the sensation of color is, so it would seem that a man who can never know objects directly cannot learn from ideas what external objects are, the orthodox Cartesians might agree. Such making known by ideas seems impossible, and it certainly is inexplicable. Nevertheless it occurs, and it is guaranteed by God, Who is no deceiver. That mind knows body by nonresembling representative ideas is nothing short of miraculous. Foucher's last word in the controversy is the scornful reminder that expressions of faith in the infinite wisdom and incomprehensible ways of God cannot be substituted for metaphysical explanations.

The orthodox Cartesian explanation—or lack of it—leads to one final possibility. La Forge recognizes that nonresembling ideas that represent external objects in no way that we can understand may seem to be superfluous. Why could not God allow us to know external objects directly? Ideas then would be unnecessary or, if they were present, their representative aspect could be described as transparency. However, if the traditional way of mediate ideas is abandoned, and a theory of direct perception is substituted, then all the sceptical problems the Cartesian theory of ideas is meant to avoid return—as Thomas Reid was later to discover.

2   THE MECHANICAL NOTION OF CAUSATION

The orthodox Cartesians have a tendency to answer the question of how ideas represent material objects by making the statement that material objects obviously cause ideas, and for this reason ideas can represent them. Of course, then they must explain why caused sensations (secondary ideas) do not represent the material objects that cause them at the same time and in the same way that these material objects cause (primary) ideas. And even if it were enough to point out that ideas represent material objects because they are related to them as effect is to cause, causal interaction between mind and body stands in need of explanation. Such an explanation is not provided.

The only explanation of cause offered by the orthodox Cartesians is a sheerly mechanical one, based on the impact of bodies, in which the effect always resembles the cause. (The statement that God causes—that is, creates—all things is not considered to be a philosophical explanation. Kemp Smith points out how the Cartesians improperly try to save themselves with causation in the sense of creation.[259]) The traditional causal axioms imply the causal likeness principle, that the cause must be like the effect. Le Grand states them as follows:

> A *Cause* cannot give that which it hath not. No *Effect* exceeds the virtue of its *Cause*.[260]

In the material world, all changes are caused by the impact on figured particles of extension by other such particles that are in motion. If the bumping particle loses motion, the bumped particle gains it. If the shape of a particle is changed, there is compensation; a new indentation, for example, is matched either by a bulge on the other side or by internal spatial adjustments. Any seemingly new or different properties in the effect caused by the material thing are always explained as deriving from properties that must have existed imperceptibly in the cause or must be a direct consequence of the cause, explicable by mechanical laws of motion and impact.

Illustrations of this principle are numerous. One might not expect the phenomenon of magnetism, for example, to be explained in mechanical terms. The Scholastics appeal to occult powers to explain it, and observations of magnetism and similar phenomena are among the reasons that lead Leibniz to introduce forces into his New System. The Cartesian explanation of the phenomenon of magnetism, however, is a striking tour de force in its adherence to mechanical principles. It is postulated that there are imperceptible pores with screwlike paths in loadstones. These pathways exactly match the twist of some of the tiny particles that are being continuously whirled through the universe by subtle matter. When a matched combination is made of pore and particle, the particles spiral into and out of the ends of the loadstone with a violent spin, turning to the right from one end and to the left from the other. Now if ends that accommodate similar twists are put together, they repulse one another, for the twisted particles move on the same pathways and thus bump into one another head on. Ends that accommodate opposite twists, however, attract one another, for the outstreaming particles spin in opposite directions and so do not encounter one another. This means that the two opposite sets of outstreaming particles drive all the air out from between the opposite poles, and thus the surrounding air pushes them together. This attraction and repulsion is actually observed in experiments.

Ordinary iron is attracted by either end of a loadstone because the pores in iron are in a general state of disorder. By keeping a piece of iron in contact with a loadstone, the violent motion of the spinning particles aligns the pores in the iron, turning it into a magnet.[261]

Such examples abound in the writings of the orthodox Cartesians. Chemical changes are also explained mechanically. The digestion of food and the growth of animals are viewed as nothing more than the breaking down and rearrangement of particles. Experiments with a microscope seemed to confirm such theories. For example, the box-within-box theory of animal and plant generation seems to be both reasonable and mechanically possible to the Cartesians. Because matter is infinitely divisible, it is possible that all the trees that are ever to be the heredity of a single seed could easily be contained in miniature in that seed. Dissection shows that this is the case for the plant that is to grow immediately from the seed, so there is every reason to believe that with even more powerful microscopes one could discover seeds within seeds within seeds.

In all the mechanical explanations of events in the material world then, the effect is in some way like the cause. Any engagement of one thing with another—again on the analogy of one gear with another—depends upon likeness between the two things. All causal interaction is reducible to impact between material things, and all effects are seen to follow from their causes in a fashion that is ultimately as simple to understand as it is to understand how a seal makes an impression in wax.

The seal and wax example is significant. It is one of the more obvious examples used in applying the picture analogy to the way of ideas. In the Scholastic explanation of perception also, the effect must be like the cause. Both of these explanations (the picture analogy and the Scholastic) open the possibility of interpreting the soul as being material like the material things it knows. If seal and wax are material, then would not mind similarly impressed by a material thing have to be material? And if the form of a thing can be shared (something Malebranche as well as the Scholastics suggests), would not the mind that shares the form with a material thing have to be essentially like that material thing? I show above that the orthodox Cartesians are quite aware of the danger of materialism. This is one reason they stress the essential difference between mind and matter, and hence that ideas by which we know material things are not like the material things. And because these ideas are also said to be caused by material things, the Cartesians must stress that an effect need not be like its cause. The examples of causal interaction between unlike things, however, are limited. They reduce to the statement that the material world is an effect unlike God Who is its cause.[262] Therefore, because causal interaction between unlike things occurs in this one case, it is possible for ideas to be caused by matter that is unlike them. But even this appeal to God's causing the material world cannot support the possibility of causal *interaction* between mind and matter (although it might support occasionalism), for God's causal activity is creative. God causes the material world in the sense that He creates it; He does not interact with it. Even though we may not understand this creative activity, we do understand it well enough to know that the causal relation evidently obtaining between matter and mind is not of the sort in which one substance creates another. Hence although God's creative act is mysterious, the causal interaction between body and soul is even more mysterious. It is not natural, the orthodox Cartesian would agree, for an effect that is not the result of an act of creation to be unlike its cause, and to assert that it is would be to shake the foundations of mechanical physics. The only *understandable* explanation of causal interaction rests on the engagement made possible by the likeness between cause and effect.

Thus, the orthodox Cartesians must explain not only how nonresembling ideas can represent their objects, but also how these ideas can be caused by nonresembling causes. They can do neither on the only explanatory principles available: those of mechanical physics. Thus, they are reduced to asserting over and over again that representation and interaction *do* happen, and that such phenomena are inexplicable only in the sense that they do not require explanation: God has ordained that such interaction and representation be.

3 EXTERNAL IDEAS

Malebranche is represented in this study, as is usual, as deviating from the orthodox Cartesian position, although here not simply because he is an occasionalist. After all, to an outsider, the inexplicable interaction of the orthodox might not seem to differ significantly from Malebranche's position that it is only an appearance of interaction, particularly since in both cases God is the supporting agent. Malebranche's radical innovation is in his treatment of ideas. Concerning ideas he breaks not only with the Cartesian but also with the Scholastic ontological tradition.

Malebranche meets the problem about causal interaction by denying that there is interaction between mind and matter. This seems to be an immediate result of his joint adherence to both the ontological dualism and the causal likeness principle. It is because of the essential difference, or unlikeness, between mind and matter that Malebranche insists that they cannot interact. Even God, Who is certainly different from both matter and finite mind, can interact with both only if He is essentially mental, and because He contains matter eminently. The causal likeness principle thus seems to be preserved.[263] So while Malebranche objects to the orthodox solution on the grounds that mind and matter cannot interact, although God can interact with each of them, the orthodox Cartesians object to occasionalism on the grounds that if God can interact with substances completely different from Himself, He can surely make it so that mind and matter can interact despite their essential difference. It would require a breach of the causal likeness principle, but it would be, they feel, less deceptive than occasionalism.

Malebranche's serious break with Cartesianism comes over the all-inclusive ontological type-distinction between substance and modification. It is an unsuccessful break, primarily because he does not see fit to deny the causal and epistemological likeness principles, nor the principle that direct acquaintance is necessary for knowledge. His retention of the likeness principles is most evident in that he still insists that the cause of an idea must have as much or more formal or eminent reality as the idea has objective reality.

Malebranche realizes that on the dualistic Cartesian principle of the complete difference in essence between mind and matter, plus the likeness principles, it is impossible for Cartesian ideas to represent material objects. On these principles, no modification or action of the mind can *resemble* a material object; hence no idea (an idea being a mental modification) can represent a material object. Although Malebranche could deny that there is real interaction between mind and matter, explaining why it appears to us that there is such interaction, he could not very well deny that we have real knowledge of material objects, even though material objects are only the occasional causes of this knowledge. It would not do to explain that we only appear to have knowledge, for either that would be the same as having knowledge or it would not be an appearance of *having knowledge* at all. Therefore, Malebranche makes a bold move. He attempts to separate the idea from the modification or action of the mind. Malebranche says that ideas are *not* modifications of the mind, but are *in* God. God has to have ideas of the essences of material objects before He creates material objects, and by sharing these ideas with us, God allows us to have knowledge of material objects just as God Himself has knowledge of them.

Malebranche, particularly in his controversy with Arnauld, seems to believe that he has said enough simply by saying that ideas are not modifications of our minds, but are *in* God. One might grant that if ideas are *in* the mind of God as they are thought by Cartesians to be in our minds, that is, as modifications, then they would be mental, and we could possibly know them on Cartesian principles. We might know modifications of God's mind by having ideas that resemble and hence represent those in God's mind. But since God's ideas would be modifications of a presumably mental substance, one could ask how even *they* could resemble and hence represent *material* objects. Malebranche avoids this question by denying that ideas are modifications of God's mind. Not only are ideas not modifications of mind; ideas are not even mental!

Malebranche reaches this conclusion as follows. He stresses the distinctions between ideas, which represent, and sensations, which do not, explaining that the basis of this distinction lies in the fact that sensations are mental modifications whereas ideas are not. Obviously, mental modifications cannot represent (resemble) material objects, but ideas *do* represent material objects. But does this mean that ideas are material? Even though it is implied that ideas resemble (because they represent) material objects, Malebranche surely denies that they are material. He seems to be suggesting that ideas are neither substances nor modifications of substances. But what, then, are they? Malebranche retains the ontological type-distinction between substances and modifications of substances, but for a Cartesian this classification is all-inclusive. Whatever is, is either a substance or a modification of a substance. Malebranche must deny that the traditional ontological categories are complete. Ideas appear to be some kind of third representative entity that allows the mind to know material objects.

Such a third entity, however, looks very much like a third man. Malebranche cannot say that ideas are material, for the role of ideas is simply to permit the mind to know mediately material objects which cannot be known directly. Material ideas themselves cannot be known directly. (And if they could, why could not other material objects be known directly?) Also, if ideas were material, other mediate entities would have to be introduced to mediate knowledge of them. And so it seems for external ideas as well. If they are nonmental external entities, will it not be necessary to have some mediate entity for knowing them? If a bridge is needed to know external objects, which are unlike the mind, then has not Malebranche suggested a system in which external ideas are needed to mediate knowledge of external ideas ad infinitum?

It is assumed in the above paragraph that Malebranche's external ideas could help us attain knowledge of material objects. It is more traditional to argue that ideas that are neither mental nor material, and neither substance nor modification, cannot possibly represent material substances and modifications. Such ideas are unlike both mind and matter. This is the stumbling block Malebranche seems unable to avoid. He insists upon the epistemological likeness principle, this being his reason for denying that sensations are representative of material objects (because sensations are mental modifications) and for denying that ideas are mental modifications (because ideas are representative of material objects). Consequently, if external ideas are to represent material objects, it would seem that they must be like them in some way, but this they cannot be.

Malebranche faces these problems primarily by saying that it is the nature of ideas to represent. He remarks, as do the orthodox Cartesians, that some of the ways of God are mysterious. He recognizes that his external—third entity—ideas have no place in the Cartesian ontological framework; but rather than alter that framework, he tries to add to it by calling upon God to be the place of representative entities that have no place in a substantial God nor in an ontological structure that is still basically that of substances and their modifications.

4 DIRECT ACQUAINTANCE

Both Malebranche and the orthodox Cartesians adhere to the principle that direct acquaintance is necessary for knowledge. If it is impossible for the mind to be directly acquainted with material objects, then mediating representative ideas are necessary to account for our knowledge of these material objects. That it seems obvious to these philosophers that the mind cannot be directly acquainted with material objects derives from their explicit or implicit acceptance of the causal likeness principle. If the mind could be directly acquainted with material objects, mind and matter would be in immediate relation, which could come about only if they were enough alike to *engage* one another. This very engagement is disallowed because of the difference in essence between the two substances. The danger feared is not—as some later philosophers believe—that any contact between mind and matter would lead to subjectivism, but rather that direct acquaintance of mind with matter would imply that the mind is material. And materialism is the bastion of the blasphemist and the atheist. The strictness with which the distinction between mind and matter is kept, and the insistence that mind cannot be directly acquainted with matter, is based partially if not wholly on the horror of the likeness that would have to be admitted between mind and matter if they stood in any direct relationship.

Malebranche and the orthodox Cartesians also adhere explicitly or implicitly to the epistemological likeness principle, which means that the only things with which the mind can be directly acquainted are mental entities like itself. They all assert that these entities are ideas. But what about our knowledge of God and other minds, which are also mental? They too are known by way of representative ideas; and although there is no problem about the possibility of their being represented by ideas because they are not unlike them (except one that I discuss when treating Berkeley), it is puzzling why we cannot know them directly. The reason seems simple enough: *The only possible explication of direct acquaintance in the Cartesian system is that which makes it the same as the relation between a substance and its modifications.* Malebranche himself announces in the *Recherche* that he is sure that no one will disagree with him when he says that all that the mind knows directly is its own ideas.[264] He can depend upon this lack of disagreement simply because it seems obvious that the mind is directly acquainted with its own properties, which directly modify it. The intimate union between a substance and its modifications does service for the Cartesians in the guise of the mind being directly acquainted with its own ideas.

For Malebranche, sensations are modifications of the mind. The mind is directly acquainted with these sensations, but through this acquaintance the mind knows nothing more than the sensations themselves, for they are nonrepresentative. Malebranche recognizes that this relation of direct acquaintance is internal to the mind. In effect, it is nothing more than the relation of a substance to its own modifications.

Malebranche's external ideas are not modifications of the mind. Consequently, when he says that the mind is directly acquainted with *external*, he trades upon a notion of direct acquaintance that is no longer available to him. And he does not go on to give an explication of a new relationship of direct acquaintance, that is, one different from the direct acquaintance that depends upon (or is) the direct relation between a substance and its modifications. What Malebranche offers is the statement that God illuminates the ideas, allowing us to know them. Malebranche could possibly explicate *illumination* the way the Scholastics do, with the notion of sharing. But he does not do this, because he is quite aware of the problems it would raise. Instead, he treats illumination as a form of revelation, once more calling upon God to bolster with His mysterious power an inexplicable occurrence.

Malebranche is certainly trying to solve the problem of how we know external objects by way of ideas, by breaking out of the ontological pattern of substance and modification. But he succeeds (at least within the Cartesian framework he accepts) only in making it as difficult to understand how a mind can know external ideas as it is for the orthodox Cartesians to explain how a mind can know external material objects. For even if we should grant Malebranche's contention that external ideas represent external objects through these ideas being God's ideas, he does not explain how *we* could be directly acquainted with them and hence does not explain how we could know them. For Malebranche, the process of knowing external things is—as is the causal interaction between mind and matter—an abiding miracle.

There is a final problem connected with this notion of direct acquaintance that depends upon or is identical with the relation between a substance and its modifications. It raises once more the specter of thinking matter. For if mind is directly acquainted with its own modifications because they modify it, why could not matter be directly acquainted with its modifications? There are, of course, several answers to this. Matter is not active, and it does not think. Being acquainted with something is a form of thinking. But in giving these answers one may simply be begging the question. If direct acquaintance is grounded in the relation of a substance to its modifications, this relation is what is basic. And material things do have modifications. The only move at this point is to assert that the essential difference between mind and matter extends to the relation each has with its own modifications. The relation of a mental substance to its modifications is very different from the relation of a material substance to its modifications. The relation amounts to direct acquaintance between active minds and mental modifications (the Cartesians might say), but it does not amount to this for passive material things and material modifications.

Both the orthodox Cartesians and Malebranche fail to give satisfactory answers to the problems facing Cartesianism. Their failures lead to the downfall of Cartesianism, but their struggles herald the way to the development of new metaphysics rid of the shackles of an ontology of substance and modification.

The orthodox Cartesians abandon the likeness principles *because* they keep the Cartesian ontology. Existents, for them, can be only either substances or modifications of substances. It is evident to them that mind and matter differ in essence, and that matter is known by way of ideas, which are modifications of mind. Hence the principles that like can cause and be known only by like must be erroneous, for it simply *is* the case that there is causal interaction between mind and matter, and that mind knows matter without similarity. Hence, they abandon the likeness principles common to Scholasticism and Cartesianism, but they offer no substitute principles to ground Cartesian causality and epistemology other than the statement that God can make it so. I argue above that part of their inability stems from their implicit retention of the likeness principles.

Malebranche retains the likeness principles. He abandons causal interaction between mind and matter. His important innovation is the introduction of an entity external to the ontological pattern of substance and modification common to Scholasticism and Cartesianism. He does this by denying that for something to be *in* the mind, it must be a modification *of* the mind. Malebranche finds it necessary to take this step to preserve knowledge by way of representative ideas, for modifications of mind certainly cannot resemble and thus cannot represent material things. He still believes, however, that direct acquaintance is necessary for knowledge. Because he cannot attain direct acquaintance by appealing to the relation of a substance to its own modifications, he speaks of God's allowing us to know external ideas through the mystery of illumination. Further, having broken with the Cartesian ontological framework, he offers no explanation of what might be a new ontological structure. Instead, he does as the orthodox Cartesians do: He appeals again to the mysterious ways of God. It is to his credit that he sees that ideas external to (in the sense of not being modifications of) all minds are necessary to begin to solve the epistemological problems facing Cartesianism. But just as the orthodox Cartesians offer no new principles to take the place of the likeness principles that they find must be abandoned, so neither does Malebranche offer any new ontological explanations to establish a place for his new entity, the external idea.

Both the orthodox Cartesians and Malebranche are bound to the principles they supposedly abandon. They show this by resorting to God to repair their systems. The orthodox Cartesians can find it mysterious how mind can know matter, which is different from mind, only *by reference to* the likeness principles they purport to abandon. And Malebranche can find the real ontological status of ideas inexplicable only *with reference to* the ontology of substance and modification with which he seems to be breaking.

chapter 8

Post-Cartesian Developments of the Way of Ideas

1 MONISTIC SOLUTIONS TO CARTESIAN PROBLEMS

A monistic solution to the Cartesian problems is suggested in Descartes's own writings. Concerning the interaction between substances, mind and matter are alike for Descartes as substances created by God. And although he stresses that mind *is* thinking and that matter *is* extension, Descartes does not always identify substance with its essence. This could be construed as a denial of absolute dualism. Hence interaction could take place because of real ontological likeness between the two substances. This likeness might also serve to explain how ideas represent material things, except for the claim that sensations are not representative. Sensations would have just as much likeness to material things as would ideas, so the representative character of ideas cannot be this likeness alone if sensations are to be nonrepresentative. There is a possibility that Descartes could solve the epistemological problem by denying the epistemological likeness principle. He does sometimes say that ideas and sensations are innate. If they arise only upon the *occasion* of real interaction between mind and matter, there is no need to say that their representative character is *caused* by this interaction. Innate ideas could a priori (from God) have a representative character, while sensations do not. One could not object that both must represent because both are caused by interaction, for the representative character would *not* be caused by interaction. To this solution one might object that there is no clear notion of what this representative character might be, whereas if there were likeness between sensations (as well as between ideas) and material objects, this would be enough to establish that sensations (as well as ideas) can represent material objects. Descartes and the orthodox Cartesians (and Malebranche), however, would surely reject these moves toward an underlying substantial likeness between mind and matter for fear of materialism.

Spinoza—whose system is in large part a development of the implications of Cartesianism—can be seen as giving a monistic solution to Cartesian problems. He denies the ontological dualism. Mind and matter are for Spinoza nothing more than parallel modifications of one substance, God. Spinoza also denies interactionism. He could probably incorporate most of the other Cartesian principles, even interactionism, although it may be that

117

his definitions would alter their sense too radically for one to say that he keeps them as the Cartesian principles listed above.

Foucher argues that the solution lies in finding an essential similarity between mind and matter. He understands that the Cartesians will not give up their identification of substance with essence, so he does not see the possibility for this similarity in Cartesianism. Rather, he is much intrigued by Leibniz's notion that force is the essence of substance. In a correspondence with Leibniz that extends over twenty years (see Chapter 9), Foucher suggests that if force is the essence of substance, then one can explain therewith the interaction that obviously takes place between mind and matter. He believes that there can be a possibility of interaction in a plurality of substances only if they are all essentially the same. Leibniz, however, explains why it *seems* that interaction takes place, rather than how it is that it *does* take place, even though he suggests denying the ontological dualism.

Locke also admits the possibility of denying the dualism. He says that extension is only a modification of matter, and that thinking is only a modification of mind; we do not know the real essence of either substance. Consequently, it is possible that the two substances are enough like one another even to support similar modifications. Locke also claims that ideas do resemble, and thus represent, material modifications. This seems to be evidence that mental substance also resembles material substance. Of course, in such case, the problem of why sensations are nonrepresentative would remain.

Monistic solutions are in fact almost universally rejected by Cartesians and their opponents alike. There are a number of reasons for this, and it is well to consider them, for the dualism is the seat of the difficulties that infect Cartesian metaphysics. First, they all undoubtedly believe that dualism is an empirical fact. Second, without dualism, a system can hardly be called Cartesian. Descartes establishes it, and it certainly is important to most of his disciples that they carry the spirit if not the letter of the master. Third, less likely, but possible, Cartesians may have thought that in the face of problems, adjustments elsewhere in the system would lead to a more elegant system than the rejection of dualism would provide. Fourth, however, there is finally a historical reason that is perhaps sufficient for all. Spinoza develops a monism and is for it called an atheist. Whoever develops a monism is in danger of being accused of saying that God is material. Hence, although Foucher suggests a possibly monistic way out, he does not develop it. And Locke, arguing much as does Foucher, throws doubt upon the clearcut distinction between matter and mind. For saying that we do not know the real essences of mind and matter, and thus opening the possibility that they are similar enough for material and mental modifications to be properties of either mind or matter—if matter could be modified by ideas, then matter could think—Locke, also, is accused of being an atheist. It would not seem to be strictly necessary for those who intend to follow Descartes to deny all similarity between mind and matter, but as a matter of fact it is prudent of them to keep this distinction if possible.

2 JOHN LOCKE (1632–1704)

Despite the failure of Cartesianism as a metaphysical system, Cartesian principles guide post-Cartesian development. John Locke, for example, keeps a dualism of mind and matter, an ontology of substance and modification, and both likeness principles. He also incorporates into his system a variety of Scholastic elements, specifically, occult forces. His system can be seen as an attempt to make the Cartesian way of ideas intelligible—he read the Cartesians, probably including the debate between Malebranche and Foucher[265]—and in this sense the failure of his representationalism can be seen as sharing that of the Cartesian way of ideas.

For Locke, an idea is "whatsoever is the *object* of the understanding when a man thinks"; it is "whatever is meant by *phantasm, notion, species,* or *whatever it is which the mind can be employed about in thinking.*"[266] Ideas of material objects are of two sorts: Primary ideas resemble (or are images of) the qualities of bodies; secondary ideas do not resemble (or are not images of) the qualities of bodies. This distinction is coextensive with the Cartesian distinction between ideas and sensations.

Bodies actually have the primary qualities of solidity, extension, figure, motion or rest, and number; these qualities have the primary power to cause (primary) ideas, which ideas resemble (and hence represent) the qualities. Certain combinations of primary qualities are called secondary qualities, and they have the (secondary) power to cause sensations (secondary ideas), which do not resemble (and hence do not represent) anything in material objects. Sensible qualities in bodies, therefore, are nothing but primary qualities that in combination have the secondary powers to cause us to have sensations. Primary qualities are seen to belong to bodies because of their permanent presence in bodies; whatever alteration one can effect upon a body, it still will have primary qualities.[267] That we mistakenly attribute colors, for example, to material objects is due to the weakness of our senses. Powerful microscopes, Locke contends, would undoubtedly show us that the minute particles of which all things are made have only primary qualities.[268]

As in the Cartesian way, we are directly acquainted only with ideas. We know immediately only ideas (including, of course, sensations):

> Since the mind, in all its thoughts and reasonings, hath no other
> immediate object but its own ideas, which it alone does or can contem-
> plate, it is evident that our knowledge is only conversant about them.[269]

Thus, all our knowledge of external things is mediated by ideas.[270] About
external things we know that their modifications must be supported by a
substance. Our ideas are known to be modifications of spiritual substance.
Primary qualities and their powers are known to be modifications of material
substance. However, unlike the Cartesians, Locke says that the real essences
of spiritual and material substances are unknown. Thinking is merely a
modification of mind. Extension is merely a modification of matter.[271] Each
of these substances is "but a supposed I-know-not-what, to support those
ideas we call accidents."[272]

Sensations do not represent any real qualities in material things, but they
have a reality "in that steady correspondence they have with the distinct
constitutions of real beings." Locke goes on to state clearly the correspondence between external things and sensations that the Cartesians assume
when they say that the role of sensations is to guide us in our everyday
contacts with other bodies.

> Our *simple ideas* are all real, all agree to the reality of things: not that they
> are all of them the images or representations of what does exist; the
> contrary whereof, in all but [primary ideas of] the primary qualities of
> bodies, hath been already shown. But though whiteness and coldness are
> no more in snow than pain is; yet these [secondary] ideas [sensations] of
> whiteness and coldness, pain &c., being in us the effects of powers of
> things without us, ordained by our Maker to produce in us such
> sensations; they are real ideas in us, whereby we distinguish the qualities
> that are really in things themselves.[273]

It is significant that Locke states that this nonresembling correspondence
is not a case of representation.

Locke, as does Leibniz, recognizes that Cartesian mechanistic explanations of perception are adequate only from material objects to the pineal
gland but do not provide comprehensible grounds for explaining how material objects cause ideas and sensations. How do material movements in the
pineal gland cause ideas and sensations? Cartesian physics does not make it
possible to explain even how material objects can cause changes in one
another. So Locke introduces a third power that combinations of primary
qualities have, a tertiary power to rearrange the primary qualities of other
bodies. The result of this alteration is that the changed bodies then have
(because of the rearrangement of their primary qualities) new secondary
powers for causing sensations and new primary powers for causing ideas
different from the powers they formerly had. Besides primary qualities, then,

bodies have three sorts of powers: the power to cause ideas, which ideas resemble primary qualities; the power to cause sensations, which sensations correspond to but do not resemble combinations of primary qualities; and the power to rearrange primary qualities in other bodies.[274] These powers are obviously Scholastic occult forces. A Cartesian might very well say that they explain nothing. The power one body has to alter another is simply a Scholastic way of describing what takes place according to the laws of impact, something that is perfectly understandable in itself. The postulation of powers to cause sensations and ideas is nothing more than a misleading way (Cartesians might say) of admitting that although according to a physics of impact we can describe what takes place in the material world during perception, we do not know the mysterious ways of God, Who makes it so that these impacts cause sensations and ideas.

Locke's system raises numerous problems. Do we have ideas of powers? A Cartesian would say that we do not because we cannot, powers of material things being nothing that we can perceive. If there really are powers, Locke carelessly confuses them with perceived primary qualities or modifications. At best, according to his system, we can infer the existence of powers; but this may be based on nothing more than general adherence to the principle that all things—including ideas and sensations—must have a cause. Must one necessarily infer that because ideas represent, and because sensations correspond to (if they do) material objects, then these material objects have the power to cause ideas and sensations? Malebranche, at least, infers from the fact that ideas and sensations are totally unlike material objects, that they obviously cannot be caused by material objects. As for ideas that resemble and hence represent primary qualities, ideas like sensations are modifications of the mind. It is difficult to understand how something unextended could be an image of something extended. Such criticisms of Locke's way of ideas, similar to Foucher's criticisms of the Cartesian way, are actually made by Henry Lee and John Sergeant.[275]

It might be thought that with his recognition of the correspondence of sensations to material things, Locke presents a possible new sense of representation not dependent on resemblance that is open to, but is curiously ignored by, the orthodox Cartesians. For whatever reason the Cartesians ignore it, it still remains that sensations are nothing more than signs of material objects. As such (see Chapter 7) they cannot be expected to give knowledge of—to represent—material objects unless these material objects are known previously in some other way.

Locke obviously agrees that an idea must resemble its object in order to represent it. He also holds to the Cartesian dictum that direct acquaintance is necessary between knower and known and, like the orthodox Cartesians, he makes this relation coextensive with that of substance to modification.

Consequently, he is necessarily bound to knowledge only of ideas. He remarks, as does Leibniz, that if there are any external triangles, then they have the properties known in contemplating the idea of a triangle.[276] But he admits that one can never really be certain that our ideas are truly of their external objects if this can be ascertained only by comparing the object with the idea. Ultimately, Locke appeals to God, as do the orthodox Cartesians. God has ordained that our ideas represent external things (or at least their primary qualities) as they are in themselves. And there is a final admonition: Stop yearning for deeper knowledge of essences, for God has given us faculties adequate to the attainment of as much knowledge as our state requires.[277]

Putting aside other difficulties, could Locke's ideas resemble and hence represent primary qualities of material things? It seems possible, for Locke admits that he does not know the essences of mind and matter. If these two substances have similar essences, then resemblance between their modifications could be supported. Locke reports what seems to take place, which is that ideas do resemble material modifications; consequently, one might very well infer that mind and matter are similar substances. Locke is chastised for even suggesting this possibility. The monistic solution is not a popular one.

Whether Locke is trying to repair the Cartesian system or is trying simply to state the truth as he sees it, he lays himself open to attack from all sides. The Cartesians attack him for introducing occult qualities; the sceptics attack his notion of representative ideas; and the bigots attack him for opening the doors to materialism, scepticism, and atheism. Locke leads the Cartesian way of ideas to disaster. One reason for this probably lies in his incomplete digestion of continental metaphysics.

3   GEORGE BERKELEY (1685–1753)

George Berkeley's philosophy of ideas also can be viewed as an attempt to circumvent the problems inherent in Cartesianism. Berkeley's studies and earliest publications are contemporary with the last major publications of Cartesianism[278] and there is little doubt that he knows of the problems of Cartesianism and of Malebranche's solutions to them. He is specifically concerned to deprive the sceptics of the foothold they have in the theory of representative ideas.[279] Whether or not Berkeley develops his philosophy of ideas in an attempt to avoid the problems inherent in Cartesianism, it is illuminating to consider it as though he does.[280] A consideration of his system in the context of Cartesianism throws new light upon the epistemological roles and ontological status of Berkeley's ideas and notions.

What I argue is the following: Cartesian problems arise primarily through difficulties of characterizing the relationships between two substances that differ in essence. Berkeley, in denying that matter exists, abandons the Cartesian principles having to do with the ontological dualism (see Chapter 4). He thus, in one stroke, dispenses with the problems given rise to by the first and second of Foucher's criticisms outlined in Chapter 4. There are no problems concerning how two substances that differ in essence can causally interact, nor concerning how one can know the other, for there is only one kind of substance. Berkeley, however, evades the problems concerning the relationships of one substance to another different one, only to find problems concerning the relation between a substance and its modifications.

As derived from Cartesianism, Berkeley's position can be reached as follows: Berkeley utilizes Foucher's third and fourth criticisms against the Cartesian distinction between sensations and ideas to show that we cannot know material things.[281] He agrees with the principle that direct acquaintance is necessary for knowledge and then goes on to say that what we know is all that exists. Because we cannot know matter, it cannot exist. Berkeley thus denies ontological dualism and interactionism. Sensations and ideas are not ontologically different from one another, and neither of them is representative of things; sensations and ideas *are* things. By doing away with external matter and the representative ideas by way of which it is supposedly known, Berkeley undercuts much sceptical argument. We can be certain of our knowledge of ideas because we are directly acquainted with them and they are all—save minds and relations—there is to know.

Berkeley shows his adherence to the causal and epistemological likeness principles in two ways. First, he uses them in his attack upon matter and the theory of representative ideas. One of his principles is: "Nothing can give to another that which it hath not itself."[282] From this he reasons that where there is no likeness between two substances, there can be no causal interaction. Because the two Cartesian substances are utterly different, it is impossible for matter to cause ideas. Berkeley points out that because matter is inactive, it is contradictory even to say that there is interaction between bodies; and if matter is said to be inactive merely to distinguish it as contrary to mind, which is active, then even a special kind of material action would not permit matter to interact with mind. It is quite inconceivable, Berkeley says, that an unthinking thing could produce thought.[283]

Second, when considering the possibility that ideas might represent external objects, Berkeley insists that nothing can be like an idea but an idea.[284] From this he concludes that the only things ideas could represent are other ideas, because they resemble one another in being ideas. Representation is not the primary function of ideas, of course; it is only accidental upon their likeness to one another. Thus it would be wrong to characterize Berkeley as

Malebranche without matter, for then he would have representative ideas that have no material world to represent, and that are different from sensations.

Berkeley is also bound to the all-inclusive ontological type-distinction between substance and modification. He adheres to this pattern particularly in saying that ideas depend upon minds in that their being is being perceived by a mind.[285] *Ideas*, for Berkeley, *must be mental modifications*.

There are four direct arguments for establishing the claim that for Berkeley ideas must be mental modifications. First, and least impressive, for Locke and the Cartesians what is perceived by the mind are ideas, and for these philosophers ideas are modifications of the mind.

Second, Berkeley denies the ontological dualism, and in denying that anything is material he seems to be asserting that everything is mental. Of course he need not maintain that mental substances and mental modifications are all there is, but in ordinary ontological parlance this is all that would remain. If extension, for example, is not a modification of matter, but only an idea, one can plausibly suppose that as an idea it still has the characteristic of being a modification; minds, for Berkeley, are the only things of which it could be a modification.

Third, Berkeley uses Foucher's arguments for establishing that if sensations are in the mind, then so are ideas. Many philosophers say that sensations are modifications of the mind. If it is correct to say that Berkeley modeled his ideas on Malebranche's ideas (as is often suggested),[286] it is also the case that Berkeley compounded these Malebranchean ideas with sensations, and Malebranchean sensations are modifications of the mind. Berkeley is seldom interpreted as elevating sensations to ideas; he is usually interpreted as reducing ideas to sensations.[287]

Fourth, and most important, if Berkeley keeps the ontological type-distinction between substance and modification, then by posing ideas as mental modifications he has a ready and familiar ground for the relation of direct acquaintance of a mind with an idea. His lack of concern for how a mind can be directly acquainted with ideas can be explained by the fact that it is for him dependent on, or coextensive with, or the same as the familiar relation of direct support by a substance of its modifications.

However, in Principle 49, Berkeley contrasts being "in the mind . . . by way of *mode* or *attribute*" with being in the mind "by way of *idea*"; that is, he says explicitly that the qualities of extension and figure "are in the mind only as they are perceived by it, that is, not by *mode* or *attribute*, but only by way of *idea*."[288] If it is to be claimed that for Berkeley ideas *are* mental modifications, the claim can be established only by showing that he reasons as though they are, whatever he says to the contrary. There are five lines of evidence that Berkeley depends upon the relation between substance and modification in reasoning about ideas. First, Berkeley creates problems by denying that God has ideas of pain.[289] If the question were, Is God modified by pain? then Berkeley's denial is perfectly understandable. Because Berkeley's example is the idea of pain, and he equates having a pain with knowing (perceiving) a pain, this shows that he reasons about ideas as though they were modifications of the mind. If the dependence that ideas have upon being perceived were a *mere* causal dependence, then why not allow God to cause-perceive-know them? But if the dependence is that of modification upon substance, if the knowing relation is to be explicated with reference to the relation of substance to modification, then it *does* pose a problem to assert that God knows pain. This would mean that He is modified by pain.

Second, because both ideas and minds are mental, it would seem easy enough to assert that ideas resemble and thus can represent minds. But Berkeley explicitly denies this, and in doing so he understands something that is clear to Descartes, although somewhat unclear to Malebranche. In answering objections raised by Gassendi, Descartes says "y a plus de différence entre . . . des accidens & une substance, qu'il n'y entre deux substances."[290] Berkeley recognizes this in saying that ideas are passive, whereas minds are active.[291] Minds can cause ideas because both are mental, but because ideas are passive, they cannot represent active minds even if the ideas are mental like minds. This would pertain whether or not ideas are mental modifications. Even mental ideas that are not mental modifications could not represent minds if these ideas are passive. However, it seems reasonable to suppose that ideas are considered here by Berkeley as mental modifications. Their passiveness would be a reflection of their dependence upon the substance they modify, and their inability to represent minds would rest on the basic ontological difference between substance and modification.[292]

Third, relations are known only through notions. Certainly no idea that is itself a modification of the mind could resemble as such a relation between two entities. The very being of a mode resides in its dependence upon a substance. So if Berkeley thinks of ideas as related to the mind as modifications are to a substance, he would certainly find them inadequate (as he does) for representing relations.

Fourth, Berkeley says that we know our own minds because we are directly acquainted with their ideas (recall that modifications are often said to be nothing more than a substance modified), but that we know other minds through notions.[293] Could these notions be modifications of the mind? If they were active modifications, then they could indeed represent active minds by being like them. Other minds could act upon our minds to cause notions, so the causal likeness principle would be satisfied as well. But Berkeley is concerned to deny representationalism in order to escape scepticism; if he introduces representative notions he will open himself to sceptical attack, whether they are mental modifications or not. Suppose, then, that one interprets notions as mere occasions (mental modifications or not) for direct acquaintance with other minds. If this were so, then this direct acquaintance would be of a different sort than that between substantial minds and ideas that are mental modifications, for other minds certainly are not, for Berkeley, modifications of one's own mind. But Berkeley is no occasionalist. By ridding himself of matter, he allows for causal interaction between the substances that remain. Causal interaction between minds—at least between God's and others—is possible because of their likeness to one another. In any case, Berkeley says that notions are necessary for the mediate knowledge of other minds. It is clear why we cannot know other minds directly if we can be directly acquainted only with our own modifications. What other reason is there for restricting direct acquaintance to ideas, than the assumption that being directly acquainted with something makes it a part—a modification—of one's own self?[294]

Fifth, Berkeley has trouble with notions—with how we are directly acquainted with notions and with how they make known things with which we are not directly acquainted—*because* he does *not* reason about notions as though they are modifications of the mind. Berkeley's notions, modeled on Malebranche's ideas, which are external to the mind in the sense of not being modifications of the mind, are entities outside the ontological framework of substance and modification. For someone bound to reasoning within this framework, as Berkeley is, not only are such external entities ontologically unclassifiable, but also their role cannot help but be obscure. Berkeley has difficulty with his doctrine of notions because he has no ready explication of how one can be directly acquainted with something external to the mind. He cannot depend upon the familiar relation between substance and modification in clarifying the role of notions.

But Berkeley and many of his readers find the mind's knowledge of ideas unproblematic. This is because he conceives of the *having* or knowing or perceiving of an idea, or of an idea's being *in* the mind, as though the idea were a property of the mind; consequently, he can utilize the Cartesian relation of dependence between a modification and a substance to establish direct acquaintance of a mind with its ideas. The fact that he does not feel that an explanation is necessary for how the mind is directly acquainted with ideas is evidence that even though Berkeley explicitly denies that ideas are modifications of the mind, he reasons about them as though they are.

Berkeley, like Malebranche, can be seen as striving to break out of the Cartesian ontological pattern of substance and modification. Neither of these philosophers can make this break successfully because each is still dependent upon the explanatory force of the relation between substance and modification. The dependence indicated in the principle that *being perceived* is the essence of ideas, and *perceiving* is the essence of mind, appears in Berkeley's philosophy as the dependence of a modification upon the substance it modifies. Berkeley cannot perceive other minds because their essence is not being perceived—they are not modifications of the perceiver's mind. But Berkeley is certain that we do know other minds; so he introduces notions, which are *in* the mind or *had* by the mind without being modifications of the mind. But how can we be directly acquainted with these notions? And even if we can be, if notions are representative of minds, they must be like minds. And if we can be directly acquainted with something like minds, why not with minds themselves? Finally, if notions are representative of minds (whether or not they resemble them), all the sceptical problems left at the heels of Locke and the Cartesians would come to hound Berkeley.

Berkeley escapes the problems of positing causal and epistemological relations between two different substances, but he cannot escape the problems inherent in a dependence upon the relation between substance and modification. He strives to break out of this pattern, but he cannot do it. If Berkeley had taken ideas as external to—in the sense of not being modifications of—the mind, he could not have taken it for granted that we are directly acquainted with ideas; he would have had to explicate a sense of direct acquaintance that makes it different from a relation that is dependent upon or coextensive with if not identical to the relation of a substance to its modifications. That Berkeley is unable to give such an explication is evident in his treatment of notions, external entities whose epistemic role and ontological status remain problematic in Berkeley's system.

However Berkeley, following the lead of Malebranche, does continue the break with Cartesian ontology. Notions, like Malebranche's ideas, have no place in an all-inclusive ontology of substance and modification. But Berkeley fails to make the break cleancut, and it remains for Hume to dispense completely with the dualistic pattern of substance and modification,[295] just as Berkeley dispenses with the ontological dualism of different substances.

In a Cartesian context then, Berkeley's ideas are knowable because the mind is directly acquainted with its own modifications; his notions are problematic because they represent an attempt to escape the ontological pattern of substance and modification.

There is a question that I have not yet asked in this study that can appropriately be raised here. Can the question, What is an idea? be construed as an ontological question at all? Obviously ideas do have ontological status for all the philosophers here considered. All of these philosophers indicate that ideas have aspects other than the ontological, but the burden of this study is to show that the ontological status of ideas is crucial in determining their epistemic efficacy, for example, when a philosopher believes that likeness is necessary between an idea and what it represents. Attempts to escape the weight of ontological status for ideas are characterized as attempts to break out of the ontological pattern of substance and modification. Everything is either a substance or a modification. As long as this principle is adhered to, the way of ideas is doomed. One could say that ideas are nothing, or at least that they are not entities, or one could try to introduce a new ontological entity. But as Malebranche and Berkeley illustrate, it is difficult to characterize such an entity. There is another alternative. Everything might be of the same ontological status. Then if likeness is necessary for representation, everything could represent everything, for anything that is would be an idea; ideas are like ideas. David Hume might be seen as taking this expedient. I introduce Hume now, near the close of this study, not as a monist who reduces all ontological categories to one, but as a philosopher who breaks entirely with the ontological structure of substance and modification.

4   DAVID HUME (1711–1776)

David Hume, like Berkeley, comes to sceptical conclusions about Cartesian ontology after reading Bayle and Locke.[296] Not only does he deny the ontological dualism, but also he explicity denies the all-inclusive ontological type-distinction between substance and modification.[297] Foucher argues that Cartesians do not know the essence of mind and matter as they claim to; Malebranche argues that we have an idea of the essence of matter but not of mind; Locke argues that we cannot know the essence of either mind or matter; and Berkeley argues that we have a notion of the essence of mind but not of matter. Hume concludes that we have no idea, and thus no knowledge, of any substance at all.

Perceptions, that is, what is immediately perceived, are divided by Hume into impressions and ideas. Impressions have more force and vivacity than the ideas derived from them; every idea is initially preceded by an impression. Perceptions include everything Locke calls ideas and are the only objects we know. From this Berkelean conclusion that only objects we can immediately *know* to exist are impressions and ideas, Hume argues that impressions and ideas are the only objects that *do* exist. When we examine our idea of substance, for example, we find that it is not an idea of an independently existing entity at all, but only a compound idea of a collection of related perceptions. Our ideas of modes are similarly found to be not of dependent entities but of other collections of related ideas. No impression or idea in itself carries with it the notion that it is dependent as a modification upon some substance.[298] Humean compounded "substances" would anyway resemble traditional mind and matter very little. Like Berkeley, Hume dismisses Locke's notion of "material" substance as an empty I-know-not-what.[299] Hume, however, goes on to dismiss also the notion of "spiritual" substance, of which we also have no idea. Selves, like material objects, are nothing more than bundles of perceptions.[300]

Hume argues, as does Foucher, that the primary qualities are quite as sensible as the secondary. Thus, while he admits the usefulness of the distinction, he claims no superior reality for primary over secondary qualities. In fact, Hume insists that the Cartesian implication that secondary qualities are less real than primary qualities leads to "the most extravagant scepticism" about our knowledge of external things. Equally insidious is the notion that ideas are mediate entities in the process of knowing. Ideas, says Hume, do not make things other than themselves known. Even if they did, there would be no way to compare them with their so-called objects to check their accuracy.[301]

Hume retains the notion that representation is the same as or is dependent upon resemblance. Ideas can represent impressions because they resemble them.[302] One of his reasons for concluding that we have no idea of a substance is that no perception can resemble a substance. Resemblance is so basic in Hume's system that he takes it as a general rule that *"no relation of any kind can subsist without some degree of resemblance."*[303] All ideas are derived from and resemble impressions; therefore,

> as every idea is deriv'd from a preceding perception, 'tis impossible our idea of a perception, and that of an object or external existence can ever represent what are specifically different from each other.[304]

Such representation is impossible because, in Hume's terms, our idea "of an object or external existence" is nothing more than a complex idea of a collection of perceptions.[305]

Hume can be seen as making sense of the Cartesian way of ideas by retaining the epistemological likeness principle, but he does so only by abandoning the dualistic system that gives rise to the difficulties. Impressions are not external objects, nor do collections of them comprise external objects. But they are not internal either; they are all—together with ideas, which are in essence only weaker perceptions—that exists. There is no problem of the causal interaction of substances because there are no substances. There is no essential difficulty about representation, for all entities are of the same sort. Perceptions do not in themselves point beyond to anything they must inhere in or that must cause them; they are what they are, and we can know of nothing—and thus nothing exists—that transcends them. All the other philosophers considered here, even, emphatically, Foucher are searching for knowledge of the essences of substances. With Hume, the search for knowledge of qualities, powers, forms, forces, and essences or natures of substances founders at last. This is because nothing remains to which these terms can be applied; all that exists, for Hume, are impressions and ideas, which are perceived openly to be what they are and nothing more.

In the role of critic of the Cartesian metaphysical system, Hume agrees with Foucher that ideas and sensations are of the same kind, and that the relation of representation is or depends upon resemblance. But instead of finding new and certain knowledge of the essences of substances as Foucher hopes someone will, Hume instead denies the possibility of the knowledge and even of the existence of substances. And if the abandonment of the ontological pattern of substance and modification requires that new explanatory support be given for the relations of an idea's being in the mind and of a mind's being directly acquainted with an idea—because these relations can no longer depend upon the relation between a substance and its own modifications—Hume can be seen as offering for this explanatory role the relation of an idea to the collection of perceptions of which it is a member.

Hume thus completes the breakdown of Cartesian metaphysics.[306] He abandons the traditional all-inclusive ontological distinction between substance and modification that Descartes inherited from the Scholastics. In destroying the ontological structure that gives rise to Cartesian problems, however, Hume at the same time destroys the ground for the Cartesian explanation of the relation of a mind to its own ideas. If an idea is not a modification of a substantial mind, then what is it? The twentieth-century concern with the ontological status of such items as concepts and propositions, and of particulars and universals, is in part a legacy from the reactions to sceptical criticisms of Cartesianism in the late seventeenth century.

chapter 9

Leibniz and Foucher

Leibniz also considered the problems of Cartesian dualism. His New System was partially inspired by Foucher's objections to Cartesianism, and can be seen as providing a way to avoid Cartesian difficulties. Hence, I now present an interpretation of Leibniz's New System, with emphasis on his concern with first principles, certain knowledge, and the external world. This is done in the context of Foucher's criticisms of Leibniz. The chapter concludes with an examination of Leibniz's system in its role of solving Cartesian problems.

1 THE CORRESPONDENCE BETWEEN LEIBNIZ AND FOUCHER CONCERNING FIRST PRINCIPLES, CERTAIN KNOWLEDGE, AND THE EXTERNAL WORLD.

The correspondence between Leibniz and Foucher extends from 1676, the year Leibniz left Paris, to 1696, the year of Foucher's death.[307] Foucher sent Leibniz his works as they appeared (always with complaints about how hard it was to publish) which Leibniz read and commented upon. He valued Foucher's criticisms and sought them from him concerning his New System of philosophy. Extracts from the correspondence appear in the *Journal des sçavans* from 1692 to 1696,[308] in which Leibniz first places his New System before the public and Foucher provides its first critique to appear in print. Relations between the two men were most cordial throughout the twenty years.

In his *Nouveaux essais sur l'entendenment humain*, Leibniz remarks that he has discussed the existence of external things at length with Foucher.

> Or je luy fis connoistre que la verité des choses sensibles ne consistoit que dans la liaison des phenomenes, qui devoit avoir sa raison et que c'est qui les distingue des songes: mais que la verité de nostre existence et de la cause des phenomenes est d'une autre nature, parce qu'elle etablit des Substances, et que le Sceptiques gastoient ce qu'ils disent de bon, en le portant trop loin et en voulant même etendre leur doutes jusqu'aux experiences immediates, et jusques aux verités geometriques, ce que Mr. Foucher pourtant ne faisoit pas, et aux autres verités de raison, ce qu'il faisoit un peu trop.[309]

This remark seems to apply primarily to Leibniz's first letter to Foucher of 1676. Leibniz begins:

Je demeure d'accord avec vous qu'il est de consequence que nous examinions une bonne fois toutes nos suppositions, à fin d'etablir quelque chose de solide. Car je tiens que c'est alors qu'on entend parfaitement la chose dont il s'agit, quand on peut prover tout ce qu'on avance.

Leibniz takes Foucher to be concerned with discovering truths which will assure us that there is an external world. Foucher grants to Leibniz the "veritéz hypothetiques" which do not assure us about anything external, but only about what would be the case if there were something external similar to what the hypotheses are about. Hence, there is no disagreement between the two men about the internal truths of arithmetic, geometry, and many propositions of metaphysics, physics, and morals, "dont l'expression commode depend de definitions arbitraires choises, et dont la verité depend des axiomes que j'ay coustume d'appeler identiques."[310] Leibniz says he believes that all such hypothetical propositions should be entirely demonstrated and resolved to identities. He recognizes that this still does not give us truth about external things, so he proceeds to offer two proofs of the existence of something external. The possibility, impossibility, or necessity exhibited by each hypothetical proposition shows that it has a truth value which does not depend upon us. The essence of a circle, for example, and all other natures or essences and what we call eternal truths have an external cause of their constancy. This is the first proof in the order of knowledge. In the order of nature, the first proof of any existence is of ourselves from the fact that we think; but second, we realize that there is a variety in our thoughts, and that this variety does not come from ourselves, so there must be something external which causes the variety in our thoughts and sensations.[311]

However, Leibniz credits Foucher's Academic objections at this point. The soul in itself cannot cause the changes so there must be an outside reason for them, but from this only two things follow: 1) that there is a connection in our appearances which allows us to predict future appearances, and 2) that this connection must have a constant cause. "Mais de tout cela il ne s'ensuit pas à la rigueur qu'il y a de la matiere ou des corps, mais seulement qu'il y a quelque chose qui nous presente des apparences bien suivies."[312] All could be a dream caused by a demon. Hence, we do not know the essence of what is external. Leibniz suspects that it is impossible for us to penetrate to such truths, knowledge of which would approach "de la vision beatifique." Descartes's distinction between body and soul is thus well made, for although we cannot doubt that there is something external causing our thoughts and sensations, we can doubt that it is something so utterly different from the soul as matter is. As for the demon, there is no need to prove the existence of God as Descartes does to find a non-deceiving being, "puisqu'il est en nostre pouvoir de nous detromper dans beaucoup de choses, et au moins sur les plus importantes."[313]

The first letter we have from Foucher to Leibniz is of 1678, and it is not an answer to the above. Hence, I must make my remarks by drawing from what Foucher says elsewhere. It is first quite apparent that there is hardly any disagreement between Foucher and Leibniz. The proofs Leibniz offers for the existence of an external world are those Foucher admits in the *Apologie*. It is probable that Foucher never does deny the existence of *something* external. Leibniz's remarks about mathematical truths and the essence of body make it clear that he realizes that Foucher's real concern is with how we can be assured of truths about this extenal world which has been proved to exist. And in this first letter, Leibniz goes as far as Foucher ever did toward a statement that such knowledge is impossible for man. Leibniz does, later, however, venture an opinion, and it may be that those truths of reason which Foucher doubted "un peau trop" were the ones which Leibniz felt constraining him to offer his New System. Leibniz's optimistic epistemology is probably related to his unconcern about whether or not life is a dream, for even dreams are real and have external causes.[314] Foucher never mentions the demon and hardly recognizes such depths of doubt, perhaps because it is irreverent speculation.

Probably in 1685, Foucher sent Leibniz his *Réponse* to Desgabets and his volume of verse, *De la sagesse des anciens*.[315] Leibniz was enchanted, and replied that there was much of interest in the ancients, suggesting that Foucher compose a synthesis of all that is valuable in them. Leibniz thinks the Academic philosophy, "qui est la connoissance des foiblesses de nostre raison, est bonne pour les commencemens." And because we are always beginning in religion, Leibniz agrees that it is best there to submit reason to authority.

> Mais en matiere de connoissances humaines il faut tacher d'avancer, et quand même ce ne seroit qu'en establissant beaucoup de choses sur quelque peu de suppositions, cela ne laisseroit pas d'estre utile, car au moins nous sçaurons qu'il ne nous reste qu'a prouver ce peu de suppositions pour parvenir à une pleine demonstration, et en attendant, nous aurons au moins des verités hypothetiques, et nous sortirions de la confusion des disputes. C'est le methode des Geometres.[316]

We need only begin by putting in geometric order such assumptions as the principle of contradiction and that in all true propositions the predicate is in the subject. Then we would begin to end disputes by demonstrations.

> Il est même constant qu'on doit supposer certaines verités, ou renoncer à toute esperance de faire des demonstrations, car les preuves ne

sçauroient aller à l'infini. Il ne faut rien demander qui soit impossible autrement ce seroit témoigner qu'on ne recherche pas serieusement la verité.[317]

Leibniz says that it would be to abuse words to say that necessary propositions such as that two contradictories cannot be true, and that what implies a contradiction cannot be, were established by God's free decree. He quibbles that Foucher even supposes them in writing and reasoning.[318] The rest of this letter contains an outline of Leibniz's New System. If Foucher ever answered it, Leibniz never received the letter.[319] It is questionable what Foucher could have said to the above. Leibniz's "assumptions" are all either identical propositions or reducible to identical propositions. The first, upon which all demonstrations are to rest, is the principle of contradiction, which is Leibniz's logical criterion of truth. It is psychologically impossible to doubt the principle of contradiction. Foucher agrees to the validity of both of these criteria of truth. He does not ask that Leibniz's assumptions be proved by truths pushed back to infinity. He agrees to the *internal* truth of such deductive systems. Leibniz is merely showing his impatience. He is offering a criterion for proving something about the external world, while at the same time he recognizes its inadequacy. He says that because eternal truths have an external case, this cause must be like them, and then we can go on to deduce further truths about the external world. But Leibniz has already said that knowledge of the existence of an external cause allows us no speculation about the essence of that cause. It is just this leap he is steeling himself to make, urging Foucher to join him. Foucher steadfastly refuses to decide upon a question for which he sees insufficient evidence.

In the remainder of the correspondence, each reiterates his major points. Leibniz agrees that the laws of the Academics "sont celles de la veritable Logique," but that in practice one must build.[320] Foucher is pleased that Leibniz continues to agree that the essence of matter, that is, the external cause of our sensations, is not extension.[321] Foucher warns that all our conclusions are finite and our ideas are only "façons d'estre de nostre âme."[322] Leibniz returns that it is true that a few people should search for final proofs, but urges Foucher to make it clear that the Academics are not against advancement in science. The difficulties of Sextus Empiricus are not to be scorned, but practical progress can be made in science even when these difficulties are not resolved. Leibniz praises Foucher's *Apologie*, but he adds, somewhat ironically perhaps, that he wishes that to set a good example Foucher had given an examination and demonstration of some accepted axioms to commence the great search for truth.[323]

Leibniz agrees that some useful, internally consistent mathematical concepts are materially or externally false in that things could not exist which answer to them. There are no mathematical points, and so on. But of them,

Leibniz says, "il y a certains faussetés utiles pour trouver la verité."[324] The remark is equivocal. If Leibniz means the internal truths of mathematics, then what he says is obvious, but then these concepts are not (internally) "faussetés." And if he means that concepts which cannot be true about the external world can lead us to truths about the external world, he has at least not satisfied Foucher. Foucher responds by saying that the Academics doubt only "des propositions non demonstratives."

> Je consens que l'on démontre tant que l'on voudra les secondes veritez, en les reduisant dans leurs principes immediatement, mais cela n'empesche pas qu'il ne faille une fois pour le moins, aller depuis les derniers principes jusqu'aux premiers, et vice versa.[325]

The demonstration Foucher wants is one that shows that these "secondes veritez" apply to the external world, and this is just the point upon which Leibniz strongly doubts that any demonstration can ever be given. Foucher stops at that point; the "vice versa" in the last quotation is impossible because the reduction has not been given. Leibniz continues to cede the point. "Le meilleur seroit de reduire tout aux premieres verités," Leibniz says, "mais en attendant il sera tousjours bon de prendre les secondes qu'on attrape en chemin."[326] To this Foucher responds with the dogmas of the Academics, insisting that they do not doubt immediate experience and are not against progress in science based on sense experience. But one should be careful not to allow oneself to be led into dogmatism about the external world.[327] This is what Foucher is afraid that Leibniz has done in his New System.

2   LEIBNIZ'S NEW SYSTEM AND FOUCHER'S CRITICISMS OF IT

Foucher in a letter probably written in 1685 says that he would like to see a personal philosophy from Leibniz.[328] Leibniz responds in 1686 in the course of a long letter commenting on Foucher's *Réponse* to Desgabets. In agreeing with Foucher's doubt that body and spirit could interact, Leibniz offers his own view, which seems necessary to him:

> Je croy que toute substance individuelle exprime l'univers tout entier à sa maniere, et que son estat suivant est une suite (quoyque souvent libre) de son estat precedent, comme s'il n'y avoit que Dieu et Elle au monde; mais comme toutes les substances sont une production continuelle de souverain Estre, et expriment le même univers ou les mêmes phenomenes, elles s'entraccordent exactement, et cela nous fait dire que l'une agit sur l'autre, parce que l'une exprime plus distinctement que

l'autre la cause ou raison des changemens, à peu pres comme nous
attribuons le mouvement plus tost au voisseau qu'à toute le mer, et cela
avec raison.[329]

The external world can be explained mathematically and mechanistically,
of course, and this is how science should be done. But this does not mean that
the essence of matter is simply extension. There is no real interaction among
substances nor are there occasional causes:

> je soutiens une concomitance ou accord de ce qui arrive dans les
> substances differentes, Dieu ayant créé l'âme d'abord, en sorte que tout
> cela luy arrive ou naisse de son fonds, sans qu'elle ait besoin de s'accom-
> moder dans la suite au corps, non plus que le corps à l'âme. Chacun
> suivant ses loix, et l'un agissant librement, l'autre sans choix, se recontre
> l'un avec l'autre dans le mêmes phenomenes.[330]

Souls and matter, then, are in a pre-established harmony. The problem of
their interaction is solved by showing how it is that one can talk about their
interaction when in actuality there is none.

The New System is further developed in an extract of a letter to Foucher
published in the *Journal des sçavans* of 27 June 1695, entitled "Sistême nouveau
de la nature & de la communication des substances, aussi bien que de l'union
qu'il y a entre l'âme & le corps."[331] Leibniz tells how as a young man he was
a confirmed mechanist who scorned Scholastic faculties and forms. After
many years of meditation however, he found that the mechanical principle of
extended matter is not enough for explanatory purposes. One needs also a
metaphysical notion of force which can act as a principle of unity among
extended things; such force or power of action is something like a soul with
sentiment and appetite. It is a substantial form, but not such as is to be used
to explain particular problems in physics for which mechanical principles are
still sufficient. These primitive forms are the indivisible sources of activity.[332]
They are metaphysical points which by their unifying activity constitute the
only real substances, "et sans eux il n'y aurait rien de réel, puisque, sans les
véritables unités, il n'y aurait point de multitude."[333] Leibniz then goes on to
explain how God has created souls and bodies so that, with no interaction
whatsoever between souls and bodies, each is in perfect harmony in its
actions with all the others by following its own laws. And "c'est ce rapport
mutuel réglé par avance dans chaque substance de l'universe, qui produit ce
que nous appelons leur communication, et qui fait uniquement l'union de
l'âme et du corps." By its immediate presence, the soul is the substantial
form which unifies the parts of the body.[334]

Leibniz pleads that it is a quite plausible hypothesis. God could give these
substances—metaphysical points—nature or internal forces to produce in
themselves all the appearances they will ever have without interaction with

any other entity or the intervention of any other force. Leibniz stresses that ordinary manners of speaking can be preserved, and that ordinary explanations in physics are still to be made on the principles of mechanics. But, "comme le masse matérielle n'est pas un substance,"[335] it is clear that there is no causal interaction among material things. The primary source of all action, of course, is God; the only secondary sources of action are the metaphysical points or souls which express the universe from different points of view by producing their own perceptions. These substantial forms also unify material bodies.

The "Réponse de M.S.F. à M. de L. B. Z. sur son nouveau sisteme de la communication des substances" appeared in the *Journal des sçavans* of 12 September 1695.[336] Foucher agrees that something like Scholastic forms are necessary for the individuation of unities. He also admits that God could adjust things as Leibniz suggests. Then Foucher says:

> Mais, après tout, à quoi peut servir tout ce grand artifice dans les substances, sinon pour faire croire que les unes agissent sur les autres, quoique cela ne soit pas?

Leibniz's system is, alas, no better than the Cartesians'. Of what good or need is body in such a system? Leibniz, too, has "des corps inutiles que l'esprit ne saurait ni remuer ni connaitre." The Cartesians, at least, are reduced to saying what they do because they develop their system in order to save the principle that there is nothing in common between spiritual and corporeal substances. To Leibniz, Foucher says, "Mais vous, Monsieur, qui pourriez vous en démêler par d'autres voies, je m'étonne de ce que vous vous embarrassez de leurs difficultés." Foucher is not misled by Leibniz's technical adjustments. If occasionalism is to be rejected "parce qu'il suppose inutilement que Dieu considérant les mouvements qu'il produit lui-même dans le corps," then what better is a system where the adjustments are made all at once?[337]

Foucher points out that we still do not know the nature of matter. He feels that Leibniz has missed a sterling opportunity to adjust his system to the facts of experience; we do, after all, experience the interaction of soul and body, whatever either may be essentially. Because Leibniz is not committed to the essential difference of soul and body, Foucher cannot understand why he resorts to occasionalism, pre-established though it be. Hence, Foucher offers a suggestion to repair Leibniz's system.

> Car qui est'ce qui ne conçoit qu'une balance étant en équilibre et sans action, si on ajoute un poids nouveau à l'un de côtés, incontinent on voit du mouvement, et l'un des contrepoids fait monter l'autre, malgré l'effort qu'il fait pour descendre. Vous concevez que les êtres matériels sont capables d'efforts et de mouvement; et il s'ensuit fort naturellement que

le plus grand effort doit surmonter le plus faible. D'autre part, vous reconnaissez aussi que les êtres spirituels peuvent faire des efforts; et comme il n'y a point d'effort qui ne suppose quelque résistance, il est nécessaire ou que cette résistance se trouve plus forte ou plus faible; si plus forte, elle surmonte; si plus faible, elle cède. Or, il n'est pas impossible que l'esprit faisant effort pour mouvoir le corps, le trouve muni d'un effort contraire qui lui résiste tantôt plus, tantôt moins, et cela suffit pour faire qu'il en souffre. C'est ainsi que Saint Augustin explique de dessein formé, dans son livres de la musique, l' action des esprits sur les corps.[338]

Foucher closes his critique by remarking that such questions should not be decided until first principles are established. Such questions are not insoluble, but they depend upon first finding "la marque infaillible de la verite."[339] Once this tie between first principles and the external world is made, then one can proceed to demonstrate truths about the external world from these principles.

Leibniz presents an "Eclaircissement" to answer Foucher in the *Journal des sçavans* for 2 and 9 April 1696.[340] Leibniz insists that his is no arbitrary hypothesis; he is led to it as the only correct one. Hence it is beside the point to ask what its use is, because it is the way things are; one does not ask, for example, what purpose the incommensurability of the side with the diagonal of a triangle serves. However, one is constrained to accept the correspodence theory, because it:

> sert à expliquer la communication des substances, et l'union de l'âme avec le corps par les lois de la nature établies par avance, sans avoir recours ni à une transmission des espèces [Gassendi], qui est inconcevable, ni à un nouveau secours de Dieu [Malebranche], qui paraît peu convenable. Car il faut savoir que, comme il y a des lois de la nature dans la matière, il y en a aussi dans les âmes ou formes; et ces lois portent ce que je viens de dire.

Body is not useless. "Dieu a voulu qu'il y eût plutôt plus que moins de substances, et qu'il a trouvé bon que ces modifications de l'âme répondissent à quelque chose de dehors." It is simply part of God's design. And the soul does know these external bodies, although not through mutual influence. One can still speak of interaction, of course, if one remembers "que l'une est cause des changements dans l'autre en conséquence des lois de l'harmonie."[341] But Leibniz objects to the Cartesian notion of matter as inert extension, which *is* useless.

> Je ne connais point ces masses vaines, inutiles et dans l'inaction, dont on parle. Il y a de l'action partout, et je l'établis plus que la philosophie

reçue; parce que je crois qu'il n'y point de corps sans mouvement, ni de substance sans effort.

However, even with such agreement with Foucher concerning the nature of body as opposed to the Cartesian notion of matter, Leibniz fails to understand Foucher's criticism about saving principles.

Toutes les hypothèses sont faites exprès, et tous les systêmes viennent après coup, pour sauver les phénomènes ou les apparences; mais je ne vois pas quels sont les principes dont on dit que je suis prévenu, et que je veux sauver.

Foucher had said simply that the appearances are that body and soul interact. Leibniz "saves" these appearances, not by blazing a new trail—or reviewing an old one, Augustine's—but by clinging to the Malebranchean principle that there is no interaction between body and soul. Leibniz offers a new way of talking as though there is interaction, which way of talking is inoffensive, if properly understood. But Foucher is not satisfied—as few people ever are initially—with new definitions which preserve the ordinary ways of talking without preserving ordinary beliefs. Foucher sees this in Leibniz as an attempt to make palatable the incredible new metaphysical system of pre-established harmony, despite the obvious fact that interaction takes place between body and soul. Leibniz so far misses the point as to go on to say:

Si cela veut dire que je suis port à mon hypothèse encore par des raisons à priori, ou par certains principes, comme cela est ainsi en effet; c'est plutôt une louange de l'hypothèse qu'une objection.[342]

Leibniz goes on to explain how he has solved the problem of interaction between soul and body which has tumbled so many philosophers. Rather than taking Foucher's suggestion about the influence of forces upon each other on the principle that every effort requires a resistance, Leibniz explains again that for him the efforts are only internally in substances. Effort and resistance seemingly between substances can be explained by pre-established harmony of internal efforts, as is the seeming interaction between material things.[343]

Leibniz closes by saying that he believes that he as much as anyone has followed what is good in Academic method. He thinks everyone should strive to conduct their demonstrations from first principles.[344] However, Leibniz himself does nothing about establishing the principles.

Foucher would certainly have replied had he been capable. He died on 27

April 1696. He surely would have pointed out the Malebranchean principle which determines Leibniz's New System, and would have urged him to cease attempting to save the appearances by building a system around the principle that there is no interaction among substances. Instead, Leibniz should strive to make intelligible what we all experience—the interaction of soul and body—by seeking knowledge of the essences of soul and body which make this interaction possible.

3   LEIBNIZ'S NOTION OF MATTER

Before treating Leibniz's solutions to the epistemological problems raised by Foucher against Malebranche, I must clear up a certain ambiguity concerning matter which has necessarily found its way into these last few pages. Leibniz uses the terms body and matter ambiguously in the writings considered here. The Cartesian notion is that matter is extension, to which Leibniz objects. But when he speaks of the pre-established harmony, Leibniz insists that there are substances—souls or forms—and then matter, which is not a substance, but which operates according to mechanical laws which are in harmony with the internal laws of the substances. He seems to be preserving occasionalism by reducing all the occasions to one. However, Leibniz also remarks that he cannot conceive of this inert extended matter; there is action everywhere, so, presumably, there must be action in matter. Foucher makes the suggestion that the essences of souls and matter may be similar in being centers of force, and thereby can interact. While Leibniz rejects the interaction, there is some suggestion that he believes that matter differs from the metaphysical points only by being extended centers of force.[345] This is unsatisfactory, because Leibniz makes it clear in a paper written in the 1690's that he agrees with Foucher that extension is as phenomenal as color.[346] When Leibniz says in 1693 that all bodies are extended, he goes on to add that one should not confuse extension with the essence of substance.[347]

To determine Leibniz's position on matter at the time of his discussions with Foucher, I consider three papers: "First Truths" of around 1680–1684, "On the Method of Distinguishing Real from Imaginary Phenomens" of the early 1690's, and "On Nature Itself, or On the Inherent Force and Actions of Created Things" published in *Acta eruditorum* of September 1698.[348]

In the first, Leibniz offers as the first truth: "*There is no corporeal substance in which there is nothing but extension, or magnitude, figure, and their variations.*" If this were not true, then there could be two exactly similar corporeal substances, which is absurd. "Hence it follows that there is something in corporeal substances analogous to the soul, which is commonly called form."[349] There are principles of action *in* corporeal substances. However, "Extension, motion, and bodies themselves insofar as they consist in extension and motion alone, are not substances but true phenomena, like rainbows and parhelia."[350] The actual substance of body lacks extension. This option is repeated in the second paper where substances are said to have "metaphysical matter or passive power insofar as they express something confusedly; active insofar as they express it distinctly."[351] In the third paper, Leibniz clearly states that in all things there resides an "active creative force." Cartesian matter would be a mere "flux" and "nothing substantial." This is because the "extension, or the geometric nature of a body, taken alone contains nothing from which action and motion can arise."[352] And whatever does not act has no reason for existence, hence extension does not exist as a substance.[353] These passages support the view that Leibniz believes that material substances are nothing more than centers of power, while all that the Cartesians call matter is merely phenomenal. However, the kinds of power or force must be determined. The natural inertia of bodies indicates that there is a primary matter of mass which is a "passive force of resistance."[354] Activity cannot arise from this passive force, so there must be joined to it "a primitive motive force, which superadded to extension, or what is merely geometrical, and mass, or what is merely material, always acts indeed and yet is modified in various ways by the concourse of bodies, through a conatus or impetus." Leibniz goes on to say:

> It is this substantial principle itself which is called the *soul* in living beings and *substantial form* in other beings, and inasmuch as it truly constitutes one substance with matter, or a unit in itself, it makes up what I call a monad. For if these true and real unities were dispensed with, only beings through aggregation would remain; indeed it would follow that there would be left no true beings within bodies. For even though there are atoms of substance, namely, my monads, which lack parts, there are no atoms of mass or of minimum extension, or any last elements, since a continuum is not composed of points. Furthermore, there is no being that is greatest in mass or infinite in extension, even if there are always things greater than any given things; there is only a being greatest in intension of perfection or infinite in power.[355]

Hence, although Leibniz says that extension as such is not a substance, he retains the elements of Cartesian dualism by making a radical distinction between passive centers of force—matter—which merely resist, and active centers of force which are souls or substantial forms, the unifying principles of material things. The "union" of these two very different forces can be only a manner of speaking derived from the harmony of their actions and passions established by God. Leibniz's reasoning from the passivity of matter to the necessity of an active monad is, then, at least half sophistical, for the monads in no way activate matter; each monad merely reels off its own picture of the world, while matter operates under another set of laws established by God. Monads seem necessary only as unifying principles, and even this implies no real interaction. Foucher might well ask at this point how these monads can be the substantial forms of material things when the union is merely verbal. He would probably go on to point out that the distinction between passive and active centers of force which is analogous to the principle of Cartesian dualism is not really so stringent, for both are centers of force. Where both souls and bodies are composed of centers of force, Foucher would say, there is a possibility of explaining the interaction between them which everyone experiences. Leibniz himself, although he would deny the interaction, can mean the difference only as a matter of degree, for whatever completely lacks active force is not substance.[356]

4   LEIBNIZ'S SOLUTIONS TO CARTESIAN PROBLEMS

Leibniz's New System was developed while he was in active correspondence with Foucher. I now consider the development of Leibniz's specific answers to Foucher's objections to the Cartesian way of ideas.

Leibniz made several notes concerning ideas in the margins of his copy of Foucher's *Réponse* to Desgabets. Concerning page 30 of the *Réponse*, Leibniz comments: "Idea est id quo perceptio sive cogitatio una ab alia differt ratione objeti."[357] The term idea stands either for the quality or form of thought, that is, a modification of the soul, or it stands for the immediate object of perception which is not a modification of the soul. Plato and Malebranche hold the second view, and Leibniz says concerning page 39 of the *Réponse* that in the sense that there is an immediate cause from God of ideas, "il se peut que nous voyions tout en Dieu, et que les idées ou objets immédiés soyent les attributs de Dieu mesme." He says that this is an imprecise way of speaking, however. As for representative ideas, Leibniz comments concerning page 33 of the *Réponse*:

> Les idées, quoy qu'elles ne soyent point étendues, peuvent servir à connoistre l'étendue, et il peut y avoir un rapport entre ce qui est étendue et ce qui ne l'est pas, comme par exemple, entre l'angle et l'arc qui le mesure.[358]

In 1678, Leibniz wrote a short paper entitled "What is an idea?" "First of all," Leibniz says, "by the term *idea* we understand *something which is in our mind*." This eliminates brain traces; thoughts, perceptions, and affections are also eliminated because "*an idea consists, not in some act, but in the faculty of thinking*, and we are said to have an idea of a thing even if we do not think of it, if only, on a given occasion, we can think of it."[359] This does not seem completely satisfactory, for there are methods by which one can reach objects without having ideas of them. So Leibniz says an idea must also express the thing. "That is said to express a thing in which there are relations [*habitudines*] which correspond to the relations of the thing expressed." Such correspondence can be effected by models, the projection of images of solids onto planes, speech, symbols, and equations.

> What is common to all these expressions is that we can pass from a consideration of the relations in the expression to a knowledge of the corresponding properties of the thing expressed. Hence it is clearly not necessary for that which expresses to be similar to the thing expressed, if only a certain analogy is maintained between the relations.[360]

Expressions based in nature do require some similarity, such as between a large and small circle, or some connective relation as between a circle and an ellipse; arbitrary relations, such as between words and ideas, do not require any similarity between the related items. Leibniz says that:

> every entire effect represents the whole cause, for I can always pass from the knowledge of such an effect to the knowledge of its cause. So, too, the deeds of each one represent his mind, and in a way the world itself represents God.[361]

Ideas seem to be natural expressions such as that between a circle and an ellipse.

> That the ideas of things are in us means therefore nothing but that God, the creator alike of the things and of the mind, has impressed a power of thinking upon the mind so that it can by its own operations produce ideas which correspond perfectly to what follows from the nature of things. Although, therefore, the idea of a circle is not similar to the circle, truths can be derived from it which would be confirmed beyond doubt by investigating a real circle.[362]

Note that here, as well as in the example of the arc and angle, Leibniz takes "similar" to mean "exact resemblance." Leibniz is surely aware that the relevant similarity or isomorphism of the relations in that which expresses with those in the thing expressed—even though what represents and what is represented are not in themselves like one another—means that the relation of representation still depends on resemblance, in this case, of the standing relations in that which represents with those in that which is represented. And if the two can exhibit the same pattern of internal relations, they are similar at least to that extent. Thus even an arbitrary sign resembles its object to the extent that each is stable and discretely identifiable. This is to argue as Foucher does that both Cartesian mind and Cartesian matter are alike at least in being substances. It is hard—if not impossible—to think of any situation where something represents something else without there being some ground of supporting resemblance between them, if only that each is in some way an identifiably discrete item.

A short essay by Leibniz, "Meditations on Knowledge, Truth, and Ideas," appears in the *Acta eruditorum* of November 1684.[363] In it, Leibniz distinguishes between obscure concepts such as one has when one remembers seeing a flower in a place but not which flower, and distinct concepts which contain sufficient marks to distinguish an object from all others. Of distinct concepts "we have a *nominal definition*, which is nothing but the enumeration of sufficient marks."[364] Primitive concepts are also distinct, although indefinable, as they are their own marks. "*Real definitions*" are those "through which the possibility of a thing is ascertained," and hence are necessary for perfect knowledge. "An idea is true when the concept is possible; it is false when it implies a contradiction."[365] The goal in knowledge is to reduce all real definitions to indefinable, possible, primitive concepts upon which they depend. Leibniz is doubtful that this can ever be completely accomplished. There is such difficulty in determining which concepts are clear and distinct that it is obvious that the Cartesian principle is defective which states that whatever is clearly and distinctly perceived is true.[366]

Leibniz allows that it can be said that we see all things in God but,

> it must be understood that, even if we saw all things in God, it would still be necessary to have our own ideas also, not in the sense of some kind of little copies, but as affections or modifications of our mind, corresponding to the very object we perceive in God. For, whenever thoughts succeed each other, some change occurs in our mind. There are also ideas in our mind of things of which we are not actually thinking, as the figure of Hercules is in the rough marble.

Hence, even if there are ideas in God, we perceive those ideas by our own ideas, just as we are said to perceive material things by ideas. Whatever is external must be known by way of ideas in our minds or souls.

Leibniz concludes with a remark on the perception of sensible qualities.

> Moreover, when we perceive colors or odors, we are having nothing but a perception of figures and motions, but of figures and motions so complex and minute that our mind in its present state is incapable of observing each distinctly and therefore fails to notice that its perception is compounded of single perceptions of exceedingly small figures and motions. So when we mix yellow and blue powders and perceive a green color, we are in fact sensing nothing but yellow and blue thoroughly mixed; but we do not notice this and so assume some new nature instead.[367]

This passage requires interpretation, for figure and motion are just as "apparent" or sensible for Leibniz as are colors and other sensible qualities. Leibniz seems to be saying that if our senses were fine enough, we would have sensations of nothing but figures and motions. These two qualities are enough for mechanical physics, and no doubt it is because of this that Leibniz makes such a distinction between primary and secondary qualities. In a more complete analysis he would have to go on to say that figure and motion are also secondary, in the sense that they are only effects of substances which are active centers of force.[368]

From this set of papers, then, I conclude that for Leibniz an idea is a modification of the soul which expresses its object. This expression is due to no essential similarity between idea and object, but to a correspondence or analogy of relations which are apparent both in idea and in the object. Whatever we know is known by an idea. An idea is true if it is possible, that is, if it does not contain a contradiction; but to know whether or not an idea really corresponds to its object, one would have to compare idea and object, which is impossible. We are assured of this correspondence, however, by the fact that God made both ideas and objects, and He made ideas to express objects.

Two years after publishing on ideas in the *Acta eruditorum*, Leibniz wrote Foucher a long letter discussing Foucher's *Réponse* to Desgabets. It is in agreeing with Foucher's doubts about the interaction between Cartesian body and soul that Leibniz outlines his New System. Concerning the sixth assumption, that our ideas need not resemble the objects they represent, Leibniz agrees with Malebranche. Leibniz say that:

> il n'est pas necessaire que ce que nous concevons des choses hors de nous, leur soit parfaitement semblable, mais qu'il les exprime, comme un Ellipse exprime un cercle vu de travers, en sort qu'à chaque point du cercle il en reponde un de l'Ellipse et vice versa, suivant une certaine loy de rapport. Car comme j'ay déjà dit, chaque substance individuelle exprime l'univers à sa maniere, à peu pres comme un même ville est exprime diversement selon les differens points de veue.[369]

Leibniz goes on to explain that God has resolved it this way. He says the way to dertermine if extension is a nonessential or accidental phenomenon like color is to find whether there is something more primary which is the essence of material substance. As I have shown, Leibniz discovers substance to be a center of force which, among other things, supports extension. Hence, he offers an argument different from Foucher's for the relegation of extension to the phenomenal realm: Neither extension nor any other sensible quality is the essence of matter. For further discussion, Leibniz refers Foucher to the *Acta eruditorum* article.[370]

On the occasion of receiving Part II of Foucher's *Apologie* in 1687, Leibniz continues to develop his answer to Foucher's problems. He finds that the truth is that "chaque substance (conjointement avec le concours de Dieu) est la cause réelle immediate de ce qui se passe dans elle."[371] In a note written on his copy of the letter but not sent to Foucher, Leibniz says:

> Je prouve mesme que l'estendu, la figure, et le mouvement enferment quelque chose d'imaginaire et d'apparent, et quoyau'on les concoive plus distinctemant que la couleur ou la chaleur, neantmoins, quand on pousse l'analyse aussi loin j'ay fait, on trouve que ces notions ont encor quelque chose de confus, et que, sans supposer quelque substance qui consiste en quelque autre chose, elles seroient aussi imaginaires que les qualités sensibles, ou que les songes bien reglés. Car par le mouvement en luy même, on ne sçauroit determiner à quel sujet il appartient; et je tiens pour demonstrable qu'il n'y a nulle figure exacte dans les corps.[372]

Leibniz has, then, at least three reasons different from Foucher's for saying that primary qualities do not actually belong to material substance as the Cartesians claim: 1) Extension is not the essence of matter, 2) all appearances in the soul are caused by the soul, and 3) the notions of extension, figure, and movement are confused. Even so, it is still permissible and even imperative to do physics according to mechanical principles; as always, it is all right to talk as usual about physical things if one understands the locution. One of the virtues Leibniz finds in his system is that with it one can still talk in ordinary ways.[373]

Leibniz and Foucher thus have many points of agreement. Both disagree with the Cartesians on the essences of substances and mistrust the Cartesian principle of clearness and distinctness as a criterion for true ideas. Foucher believes that Leibniz's system of active forces retains too many of the elements of occasionalism, but sees in it a possible way of making intelligible the interaction between body and soul that we all experience. Leibniz offers the principle of contradiction as the criterion of the truth of ideas, but recognizes with Foucher that this validates only an internal truth and is not a criterion for determining whether or not ideas actually apply to external things. Leibniz agrees that there is a need to search for this ultimate criterion to establish first principles, and Foucher agrees that science can progress by hypothetical systems without it. Leibniz does not insist that the great success of hypothetical science means that it could be absolutely certain (as does Régis[374]), and Foucher does not insist that the uncertainty of first principles means that scientific research should be abandoned (as does La Mothe Le Vayer[375]). But Foucher does believe that the proper work of a philosopher is to search for the criterion. Leibniz, on the other hand, believes that he has reduced all to one principle—the principle of contradiction[376]—and hence is justified in concerning himself with hypothetical science. There remains only the establishment of this one principle to make science certain, and there is need of only a few philosophers—such as Foucher—to work toward this goal.

Had Foucher lived to criticize Leibniz's doctrine of ideas, there would probably have been less agreement. Foucher would have pointed out that an arc and a circle, and a circle and an ellipse, are all extended; thus the analogy of them to idea and material thing cannot hold. He would agree that an idea that is a modification of the soul is necessary to know an external idea in God but, granting the possibility of resemblance between these two spiritual ideas, the problem of resemblance with a material thing would still remain. He would agree that because God is the primary cause of everything, one can, in a manner of speaking,[377] say that we see all things in God. But he would say that Leibniz is, like Malebranche, only making a pious remark which explains nothing when he says that God makes us have ideas which express their objects. Rather, Foucher would undoubtedly say, the fact that all substances are centers of force makes it possible in Leibniz's system for mofidifications of one substance to resemble those of another. Just as he suggests that Leibniz has a notion of substance which would allow him to explain interaction between substances intelligibly (although Leibniz does not do it), so also might Foucher suggest that the New System allows for the possibility that ideas could resemble and hence truly represent their objects. Leibniz solves Foucher's problem by eliminating extension as the essence of matter; Foucher might continue to worry about extension being in the soul.

In concluding this chapter, I must remark that however favorable Foucher was to Leibniz's New System, he would never have accepted it until he found a criterion that assured him that Leibniz's notion of the essence of substance really applies to external substances. Leibniz, if anything, is more doubtful that this ultimate grounding of first principles can ever be accomplished than is Foucher.[378]

Foucher develops his objections to Cartesianism in his criticisms of Malebranche, in his correspondence with Leibniz, and in his dispute with Desgabets. I show how far-reaching these objections are. They extend to any system which retains something of the Cartesian dualism as expressed in the essential difference between mind and matter, and in the causal and epistemological likeness principles. Foucher's criticisms are thus easily applicable to Malebranche's occasionalism and retain their force against Leibniz's New System.

chapter 10

The Downfall of Cartesianism

The downfall of Cartesianism in the late seventeenth century has now been traced to the inability of Cartesians to solve two major problems deriving from conflicts among their metaphysical principles. They could give philosophically satisfactory explanations neither of how minds can know material objects, nor of how mind and matter can causally interact.

The seat of the difficulties is Cartesian ontology, which is dualistic in two respects. First, there is a dualism of created substances, mind and matter, which differ in essence. Second, there is a dualism of types of ontological entities: Whatever exists is either a substance or a modification of substance. The primary Cartesian existents, then, are (besides God) material things modified by size, shape, and motion or rest, and minds modified by sensations and ideas. Problems arose when the Cartesians attempted either to follow or to abandon the principles that essential likeness is necessary between cause and effect, and between idea and object, and that direct acquaintance is necessary for knowledge.

The attack upon Cartesian metaphysics began with consideration of a third aspect which is also dualistic, the epistemological distinction between ideas which represent their objects, and sensations which are non-representative. Because sensations and ideas are all that is directly knowable for Cartesians, they asserted that material things are known mediately by way of representative ideas. The major critic of this view, Foucher, believed that the representative aspect of ideas must be ontologically grounded. He first asserted that because both ideas and sensations are modifications of mind, either both must, or neither can, represent material objects. Foucher then went on to point out that *as* modifications of mind, ideas differ in essence from material objects, and thus are ontologically unlike them. Because the only satisfactory ground he knew of for the representation of an object by an idea is that of essential likeness or resemblance between the two, Foucher concluded that material objects cannot be known by way of Cartesian ideas. Ideas cannot *represent* material objects because ideas do not *resemble* material objects. Foucher also insisted that there can be no causal interaction between unlike substances.

In response to Foucher's criticisms, the orthodox Cartesians claimed that ideas represent material objects without resembling them. Desgabets, La Forge, Rohault, Régis, Le Grand, and Arnauld employed two arguments. They said either that representation by non-resembling ideas is fundamental and thus is not in need of explanation, or that while such representation is inexplicable, it is not impossible. Arnauld in particular defended the claim that it is of the nature of ideas to represent their objects without resembling them. However, even Arnauld's arguments ultimately reduce to the orthodox position that we cannot understand how it is done, but because God creates and knows both mind and matter, He can and certainly does make it so that mind knows matter. The orthodox Cartesians also admitted that causal interaction between unlike substances is inexplicable; they found support for interaction between mind and matter—as for non-resembling representation—only in the unknown ways of God.

Malebranche is one of the first major Cartesians to face these crucial systemic problems. In opposition to the orthodox Cartesians, Malebranche did not reject the causal and the epistemological likeness principles. Admitting that there can be no causal interaction between mind and matter, Malebranche developed occasionalism. And ideas presumably do resemble their objects in some manner, for they are the ideas by which God knows— and thus according to which He created—the world. Ideas are not modifications of mind, Malebranche contended, but are *in* God. Malebranche's doctrine of external ideas is problematic because he retained the traditional principle that whatever exists is either a substance or a modification, while tying to solve some and to avoid other epistemological problems by insisting that ideas are neither. The orthodox Cartesians felt no need to explain how a mind can be directly acquainted with ideas which are modifications of the mind, but they had to call upon God to explain the representation by mental ideas of anything which is unlike ideas. Malebranche could not base direct acquaintance with external ideas upon the relation between a substance and its modifications, nor could he base representation upon the resemblance of such ideas to material objects. If external things must be known mediately, then knowledge of external ideas perhaps also needs mediation. And if external ideas are neither substances nor modifications, they certainly cannot resemble and thus represent material substances and modifications. Foucher, Leibniz, and Arnauld argued that the theory according to which we see all things in God can be viewed charitably only as an expression of piety; Malebranche offers no philosophical clarification or explanation of the issues at hand.

Foucher's criticisms of Cartesian metaphysics were fatal because even the orthodox Cartesians were strongly committed to the causal and epistemological likeness principles. This is most evident in their mechanical explanations of physical events, and their agreement that resemblance between idea and object is the only *understandable* ground for representation of object by idea. The Cartesians admitted that the causal and epistemological issues are crucial. But whether they tried to adhere to the likeness principles (as did

Malebranche) or tried to abandon them (as did the orthodox Cartesians), they still could not explain within the limits of Cartesian ontology how a mind can causally interact with and know material objects.

From shreds and patches of continental metaphysics, Locke cobbled his own version of the way of ideas. Locke said that ideas resemble and thus represent primary qualities of material objects. He provides a possible ontological ground for this resemblance by insisting that extension and thinking are not the essences of matter and mind, but are nothing more than modifications of unknown substances. Mind and matter might, after all, be essentially similar, and then interaction and representation could be explained. Foucher, Leibniz, and even Descartes had explored the possibilities of such a monistic solution; Spinoza, however, was the philosopher who developed—and was vilified for it—that way out. Locke's position, instead, makes clearly evident the inadequacies of the way of representative ideas.

New developments in the way of ideas came by way of Malebranche, and Foucher through Bayle, in the philosophy of ideas of Berkeley. For Berkeley, nothing is like an idea but an idea, thus ideas are all that can be known by way of ideas. Although he eliminated matter (and thus found no problems of causal interaction between unlike substances), Berkeley retained the ontological dualism of *types* of existents, that is, substance and modification. And because he reasoned about ideas always as though they were modifications of the mind, he found the direct acquaintance of a mind with its own ideas unproblematic. But Berkeley decided that ideas which are all passive cannot adequately resemble and thus represent active minds; there can be no ideas of, but only notions of, minds. Cartesian problems derive from unlike substances. The problem of Berkeley's doctrine of notions derived from his recognition of the unlikeness between substance and modification. Berkeley could not explain how we have knowledge of minds.

In the metaphysical systems of substance and modification into which they were introduced, Malebranche's external ideas and Berkeley's notions perform epistemological roles, but they have no ontological place. Malebranche senses that ideas cannot be limited in their representative power by their ontological status if they are to perform in their epistemological role. But neither he nor Berkeley could break away from the use of ontological relations as ground for epistemological relations. Berkeley and the Cartesians were bound, in the last analysis, to the notion that ideas are (and must be) modifications of the mind, because only the relation of a substance to its modifications gives ontological support to the relation of direct acquaintance between a mind and its ideas.

Hume finally abandoned the whole of Cartesian ontology, both the dualism of substances, and the categories of substance and modification. Hume compressed the distinctions between Cartesian sensations and ideas,

Malebranchean sensations and external ideas, and Berkelean ideas and notions. As a *reductio*, Hume argued that if independent existence is the criterion of a substance, then his perceptions are substances. Although perceptions are all ontologically of the same kind and type, and although ideas represent by being like impressions, perceptions are neither substances nor modifications. Hume culminates a tradition of sceptical arguments by abandoning substance philosophy.

In a wider philosophical context, then, Cartesianism inherited the traditional likeness principles and the ontology of substance and modification; its inadequacies are germane to the modern failure of substance philosophy. In the narrower compass of the late seventeenth century, the dependence of Cartesians upon the ontology of substance and modification led to their inability to explain how causal interaction takes place between unlike substances, and how ideas make objects which are unlike them known. This inability deriving from conflicts among basic ontological and epistemological principles in the Cartesian metaphysical system is the major philosophical reason for the downfall of Cartesianism.

Part Three

Cartesian Theology

chapter 11

Transubstantiation among the Cartesians

1 DESCARTES'S THEOLOGICAL AMBITIONS

It is worthwhile to consider a very specific reason (as contrasted to the general epistemological reasons I examine in Part II) for the decline and fall of Cartesianism.[379] Like the problems considered therein, it is a difficulty Cartesians get into because of their adherence to ontological dualism. It also stems from Descartes's desire to be all things to all disciplines. Certainly in the history of modern philosophy few philosophers have been so egotistic and ambitious as René Descartes. During that stretch of time extending between Aristotle and Hegel, few other pilosophers take so personally as their own province the total world-view, sacred and profane. There is, of course, Augustine. Thomas Aquinas and many lesser commentators do work out a Christian-Aristotelian world-view, and philosophers such as Leibniz and Kant do have polymath interests. Both Galileo and Newton understand that they are altering if not overturning a world-view. However, among these giants only Descartes contends that his own, new philosophy should replace that of Aristotle both in science and in religion.

To further his aim, Descartes undertook a major attack on Scholasticism. His scorn for philosophers who ground physics on species, substantial forms, and occult forces is well known, and his role in advancing the mechanistic philosophy of Galileo, Gassendi, and Mersenne is well documented. Here I lay stress on an application of Descartes's philosophy that he had hoped would be as important to religion as are his contributions to the rise of modern science. Despite his occasional protests to the contrary, Descartes had in mind while constructing his philosophical system its implications for the reconstruction of both natural philosophy and Christian theology.

In fact, Descartes was not himself inclined to develop a Cartesian theology. He was occupied with setting out his metaphysical position, with its implications for natural science, in such a way as to avoid sharing Galileo's fate. What he rather hoped was that some theologians, preferably of the dominant Jesuit sect, would base a solid theological structure on Cartesian principles, just as Thomas Aquinas had on Aristotelian principles. Descartes's arrogance was to see himself not as another Thomas Aquinas, but as a modern Aristotle.

Among scholars of Cartesianism, J.-R. Armogathe[380] and Jean Laporte have best documented Descartes's theological ambitions. Laporte cites a letter of 28 January 1641 in which Descartes encourages Mersenne to accommodate theology to Cartesian principles. Descartes says:

> Il n'y aura, ce me semble, aucune difficulté d'accomoder la Theologie à ma façon de philosopher; car ie n'y voy rien à changer que pour la Transubstantiation, qui est extremement claire & aisée par mes principes. Et je seray obligé de expliquer en ma Physique, avec le premier chapitre de la Genese, ce qeu je me propose d'envoyer aussi à la Sorbonne, pour estre examiné avant qu'on l'imprime. Que si vous trouvez qu'il y ait d'autres choses qui meritent qu'on écrive un Cours entier de Theologie, & que vous le vouliez entreprendre, je le tiendray à faveur, & vous y serviray en tout ce que je pourray.[381]

Mersenne had better sense than to try to provide a Cartesian theology. Those who did—Denis Mesland, Emmanuel Maignan, Robert Desgabets, and Pierre Cally—suffered for their pains by having Church sanctions imposed upon them.[382]

Descartes himself made only one detailed attempt to account for Christian dogma with his principles. In his reply to Arnauld's objections to the *Meditations*, Descartes puts forward a Cartesian explanation of transubstantiation. He makes further suggestions in four letters to Mesland. Obviously Descartes believed that he might have in Père Mesland a Jesuit champion. Disabusement was swift. The exchange of letters began in 1644 and was terminated abruptly in 1646 when, as extreme discipline for his commerce with Descartes, Mesland was banished to Canada. He died on the Canadian mission in 1672 without, so far as is known, inquiring further into the subject of transubstantiation.

Why was Mesland dealt with so severely? Undoubtedly it was for the same reasons that led Descartes to drop his guard to make some tentative proposals about Cartesian theology himself. The issue of transubstantiation was crucial for at least three reasons.

First, the doctrine of substantial forms that Descartes held up to ridicule was best known to all Catholic scholars and priests through the role of subsistent accidents in transubstantiation. Second, the sacrament of the Eucharist was the central symbol of the authority and sacredness of the priesthood. Only the ordained could take the sacrament; only they could participate in the miracle.

Third, a major Protestant position was that the Catholic doctrine of transubstantiation leads to idolatry. Among the views of Wycliffe, Hus, Luther, and Calvin that the Catholics deemed most heretical is the opinion that the Eucharist is merely symbolic: Christ is there in spirit, but not in flesh and blood. This was a central point of contention during the Protestant revolution.[383] And as recently as 1965, Paul VI at Italy's National Eucharistic Congress warned against the interpretations of such contemporary Catholic theologians as Piet Schoonenberg, Luchesius Smits, and Edward Schillebeeckx who belittle, ignore, or deny the doctrine of real accidents and actual (as opposed to mystical) transubstantiation.[384] This is still a point on which Protestants are separated from Catholics. The presence of Christ's soul with no actual change of matter is what many Protestants now profess, and this view is close to Descartes's final suggestion about transubstantiation.

If Cartesianism is to provide a metaphysical basis to replace that of Scholasticism, then it is essential that Cartesians give some explanation of transubstantiation other than one dependent on unsupported properties. And given the centrality of the Eucharist, it is surely not surprising that Louis XIV and other guardians of the Church such as Harlay, the bishop of Paris, forbade discussion on a topic so potentially politically disruptive of established hierarchy. Descartes's works were put on the Index *donec corrignatur*, and there is good reason to conjecture that what was to be corrected—or removed—were Descartes's comments on transubstantiation.

In the following, I first outline the several Cartesian explanations of transubstantiation, and some of the objections to them. They are of intrinsic interest for the light they throw on the mechanistic interactions of Cartesian matter, and on the notion of substance that Descartes offers to replace the Thomistic-Aristotelian conception. Then, in evaluating these explanations in contrast to the Scholastic views, I pose some questions about the basic ontological differences between Scholasticism and Cartesianism. It is my contention that the Cartesian explanation of transubstantiation fails, and thus does not support Descartes's attack on substantial forms.

Finally, I argue that the Cartesians' inability to explain transubstantiation satisfactorily on mechanistic grounds is paralleled by an inability to explain the nature of man without resorting to a Scholastic model. In the Cartesian explanation of transubstantiation, the sensible qualities of bread and wine are not unsupported, but are modifications of mind caused by material particles that have no other characteristics than size, shape, and motion. Yet, for Descartes, the mind itself is the form of the composite substance man. At death when the union of body and soul is broken, the liberated soul appears most like a substantial form. The peculiarity of Descartes's attempt to present active thinking itself as a substance stems from his taking the Aristotelian form or essence of man—rationality—to be itself an independent substance.

2   DESCARTES'S EXPLANATIONS OF TRANSUBSTANTIATION

The Cartesian distinction between primary and secondary qualities strikes at the heart of Scholastic physical explanations. When sensible qualities are equated with sensations, the seat of their being is transferred from material objects to the mind. Material objects are thus shorn of a multitude of explanatory principles or species. The only modifications of matter retained are figure, size, and motion with which the causal action and individual identity of material objects are to be explained. The wind of Descartes's change thus blows out of the material world the mist of occult forces, powers, or entities, leaving only a passive mechanical skeleton that has motion imposed upon it and that influences only by impact.

Descartes singles out for special attack the notion of substantial form:

> De plus, c'est une chose entierement impossible & qui ne se peut concevoir sans repugnance & contradiction, qu'il y ait des accidens réels, pource que tout ce qui est réel peut exister separement de tout autre sujet: or ce qui peut ainsi exister separement, est une substance, & non point un accident.[385]

Given the role attributed to real accidents in the miracle of the Eucharist then, it was inevitable that the question of how Descartes explains transubstantiation be raised. Antoine Arnauld sets the problem succinctly in the fourth set of objections to Descartes's *Meditations* in a section entitled "Des Choses Qui Peuvent Arester les Theologiens":

> *Mais ce dont je prevoy que les Theologiens s'offenseront le plus, est que, selon ses principes, il ne semble pas que les choses que l'Eglise nous enseigne touchant le sacré mystere de l'Eucharistie puissent subsister & demeurer en leur entier.*
>
> *Car nous tenons pour article de foy* que la substance du pain estant ostée du pain Eucharistique, les seuls accidens y demeurent. *Or ces accidens sont l'etendue, la figure, la couleur, l'odeur, la saveur, & les autres qualitez sensibles.*
>
> *De qualitez sensibles notre auteur n'en reconnoist point, mais seulement certains differens mouvemens des petits corps qui sont autour de nous, par le moyen desquels nous sentons ces differentes impressions, lesquelles puis après nous apelons du nom de couleur, de saveur, d'odeur &c. Ainsi il reste seulement la figure, l'étenduë & la mobilité. Mais nostre auteur nie que ces facultez puissent estre entenduës sans quelque substance en laquelle elles resident, & partant aussi, qu'elles puissent exister sans elle; ce que mesme il repete dans ses Réponses aux premieres Objections.*
>
> *Il ne reconnoist point aussi entre ces modes ou affections de la substance, & la substance, de distinction autre que la formelle, laquelle ne suffit pas, ce semble, pour que les choses qui sont ainsi distinguées, puissent estre separees l'une de l'autre, mesme par la toute puissance de Dieu.*[386]

In reply, Descartes reiterates that he is "persuade qu'il n'y a rien autre chose par quoy nos sens soyent touchez, que cette seule superficie qui est le terme des dimensions du corps qui est senty ou aperceu par les sens. Car c'est en la superficie seule se fait le contact."[387] This superficies is not just the gross outline of the body, but the superficies of all the tiny particles of which it is composed as well. As these particles are always in motion, the superficies is always changing.

> Enfin, il fait remarquer que, par la superficie du pain ou du vin, ou de quelque autre corps que ce soit, on n'entend pas icy aucune partie de la substance, ny mesme de la quantite de ce mesme corps, ny aussi aucunes parties des autres corps qui l'environnent, mas seulement *ce terme que l'on conçoit estre moyen entre chacune des particules de ce corps & les corps qui les environnent, & qui n'a point d'autre entité que la modale.*[388]

From this it can easily be seen that if the substances of bread and wine are replaced by substances of flesh and blood in such a way that the boundaries are unchanged, "il s'ensuit necessairement que cette nouvelle substance doit mouvoir tous nos sens de la mesme facon que feroient le pain & le vin, si aucune transubstantiation n'avoit este faite." This follows the teaching of the Church "dans le Concile de Trente, section 13, can. 2 & 4, *qu'il se fait une conversion de toute la substance du pain en la substance du Corps de nostre Seigneur Jesus Christ, demeurant seulement l'espece du pain.*"[389]

Because Descartes believes that everyone will agree that all that is meant by species is whatever is required for acting on the sense organs, he sees no reason for preferring the enigmatic intentional species or real accidents to superficies. Descartes sees no reason why the Church should have as a second miracle in the Eucharist real accidents that subsist by themselves. All God need do is "une substance en une autre, & que cette derniere substance demeure precisement souz la mesme superficie sous qui la premier estoit contenuë."[390] Descartes concludes by expressing his hope that this simple, rational explanation will one day be accepted by theologians in place of the incomprehensible explanation based on the doctrine of real accidents.

Descartes probably would have been willing to let the matter rest there had he not been asked further questions by Père Denis Mesland in letters that are not now extant. Mesland was born in Orleans in 1615 and had been a Jesuit since 1630. Descartes hoped that he would champion Cartesian views among the Jesuits.

Mesland's inquires evidently had to do with the role of real accidents and the individuation of Christ's flesh. Whether the presence of real accidents is a second miracle or not, the Scholastic explanation describes a stark situation in which real flesh and blood replace bread and wine. Flesh lies trembling under accidents unnatural to it, the accidents of bread that stand as unsupported shields, concealing the true properties of the underlying substance.

Numerous stories were known of the shield having been dropped, so that the priest saw lying in his hand an actual piece of flesh or, more spectacularly, a tiny, perfectly formed baby.[391] It seems probable that Mesland—sympathetic to Descartes—was worried about the dismissal of these real accidents.

Further, on Cartesian grounds material objects are distinguished by nothing more than size, shape, and motion. If a piece of matter that is Christ's flesh takes on the characteristics of bread, in what way can it possibly remain also Christ's flesh? The Scholastic version is again more satisfying. Christ's flesh on Aristotelian terms is a union of matter and form, which retains its identity as an individuated substance whatever external characteristics it takes on. This is not a matter of unsupported substantial forms, but one of individuating form, which Descartes had banished from his material world along with all other occult entites. To make his explanation as satisfactory as the Scholastic, Descartes obviously had to say more.

Descartes first explains to Mesland that the superficies upon which our sensations depend is nothing but a mode. Like the purported real accidents in the Scholastic explanations, the superficies can remain the same even if the surrounding bodies change, or even if the body in question is replaced with one of exactly similar dimensions. As for the Eucharist:

> Car le corps de I.C. estant mis en la place du pain, & venant d'autre air en la place de celuy qui environnoit le pain, la superficie, qui est entre cet air & le corps de I.C., demeur *eadem numero* qui estoit auparauant entre d'autre air & pain, parce qu'elle ne prend pas son identité numerique de l'identité des corps dans lesquelles elles existe, mais seulement de identité ou resemblance des dimensions.[392]

Thus, like real accidents, the same properties of bread and wine can remain—as superficies—to cover the matter of flesh and blood.

This process of substitution, however, gives rise to another question. How can Christ's body be compressed into the space occupied by a small piece of bread? Descartes puts this question aside because there is difference of opinion in the Church as to whether Christ's whole body or only a piece of his flesh is in the Eucharist. However, he goes on to offer a way of avoiding the question which turns out to be an explanation of transubstantiation completely different from the one he gives to Arnauld. It also provides a way of individuating matter as belonging to Christ.

When we eat bread and drink wine, Descartes now says, the small parts are dissolved and transported throughout our bodies where they become parts of flesh and blood. Were our vision fine enough, we could see "qu'elles sont encore les mesmes *numero*, qui composoient auparavant le pain & le vin."[393] This natural transubstantiation takes place throughout our lives; our bodies change their constituents, grow and diminish in size, yet even when all the parts of a human body change over a long period of years, we call it the same *idem numero*. Such natural transubstantiation took place in Christ's body, too. Hence, "l'unite numerique du corps d'un homme ne depend pas de sa matiere, mais de sa form, qui est l'âme."[394]

In the miraculous transubstantiation of the Eucharist then, there is no necessity for the bread to be replaced with the body or flesh of Christ by the removal of the first and a substitution of the second in a miraculously compressed dimension. All that is required is for Christ's soul to be supernaturally joined to the bread. By such union it is no longer bread, but a part of Christ's flesh, supernaturally transubstantiated by union with his soul. To the observer, the only difference between this flesh and that formed by the natural transubstantiation of bread into flesh is that the bread of the Eucharist is large enough to be seen as bread after it is (miraculously) made a part of Christ's flesh.

This notion of real presence is dangerously close to Lutheran and Calvinist heresies.[395] But beyond that, this explanation suffers from technical difficulties that are examined below. As for the notion of real presence, Descartes himself did not remain long satisfied that it alone is adequate. In a later letter to Clerselier, he combines his first with this second theory. After explaining how the superficies can remain the same when flesh replaces bread, he says that "outre le matière du corps de Iesus Christ, qui est mise sous le dimensions où estoit le pain, l'âme de Iesus Christ, qui informe cette matière, y est aussy."[396] This is Descartes's final word on the matter. Not only is the actual matter of bread replaced by the actual matter of Christ's flesh with the superficies remaining the same, but also the transubstantiated matter is individuated by being united with Christ's soul.

3 DOM ROBERT DESGABETS, CHAMPION OF CARTESIAN TRANSUBSTANTIATION

The Benedictine, Robert Desgabets, was probably the unhappiest of Cartesians. His main published work is a defense of Malebranche, which led that good Oratorian to comment caustically, "*Il me semble que ceux qui se mêlent de deffendre ou de combattre les autres, doivent lire leurs Ouvrages avec quelque soin, afin d'en bien sçavoir les sentimens.*"[397] Desgabets was never banished to Canada, and was even permitted to continue writing. His punishment was that permission was refused for publication of anything after his famous *Critique de la critique de la recherche de la vérité* in 1675.[398]

Desgabet's reputation as a busybody does not stem entirely from his *Critique*. The 1660s and 1670s were years during which Cartesianism was being viewed with more and more official disfavor. Clerselier had hesitated to print Descartes's letters to Mesland on transubstantiation, but had instead circulated copies among the learned and influential, ever hoping to get a sponsor for their publication. Cardinal de Retz explained the disapproving views of the archbishop of Paris and Louis XIV by saying that both Rome and the king knew the danger of novelties. Jacques Rohault had already been forbidden to give public lectures, in part because he defended the viewpoint in the letters,[399] when Desgabets entered the picture.

Desgabet's fifteen-page tract, "Considerations sur l'état présent de la controverse touchant le Très Saint-Sacrement de l'autel, où il est traité en peu de mots de l'opinion qui enseigne que la matière du pain est changée en celle du corps de Jésus-Christ par son union substantielle à son âme et à sa personne divine," published in 1671, was immediately branded as heretical, and Desgabets was forced to disown the opinions expressed in it. Among other things, he says that the authors of the *Art de penser* (Arnauld and Nicole) should agree with his opinions, because they include Descartes's theories in their logic. Arnauld was furious at this, because a modicum of peace had just been attained for the Jansenists. Now Desgabets had given more fuel to Jean Ferrier, Louis XIV's Jesuit confessor and a vicious foe of Jansenism. Desgabets apologized to Arnauld, but the damage had been done. Paul Lemaire says that Desgabet's pamphlet set off the persecutions against the Cartesians in France.[400] Whatever effect it had, it was certainly not Desgabets's first essay on the subject. He left well over three hundred pages of folio manuscript concerning the problem of the Eucharist.[401]

To be fair to Desgabets, one can assume that he realized the importance of the issue of transubstantiation to Cartesianism. If theologians would accept Descartes's explanation, then they no longer would have any strong theoretical objections to the Cartesian metaphysical system. As long as substantial forms, real accidents, and the like were enshrined in one of the greatest mysteries of Christendom, there could be hope that Cartesianism would receive official sanction. Hence Desgabets concentrated his efforts on making the Cartesian explanation of the Eucharist acceptable, to open the way for the Cartesian system of true and certain knowledge.

4   JACQUES ROHAULT'S CLARIFICATION

Jacques Rohault also saw transubstantiation as a central issue in Cartesianism. After Descartes's *Meditations* had been put on the Index, Rohault set about to clarify the explanation of transubstantiation. He says that of course God could cause the miracle of real accidents existing without a subject, but he thinks this is not necessary.[402] Rather, he explains that because sensible qualities are only our own sensations, God could cause us to have sensations of bread and wine although he has actually replaced these substances in our hands with the flesh and blood of Christ.[403] Thus, while a miracle still takes place, it is much easier to explain what happens in the Cartesian way, with sensible qualities as modifications of the soul, than to explain how a real accident, which is only a mode, can subsist without an underlying substance. In the Cartesian case, God merely intervenes in the process of perception upon the occasion of exchanging the substances. In the Scholastic explanation, God would have to separate a mode from its substance, which is contradictory, because it is the nature of a mode to subsist in its substance.

For offering this occasionalist simplification of the Cartesian explanation, Rohault was accused of being a heretic. Paul Mouy, like Lemaire, claims that this debate over transubstantiation touched off the persecution of the Cartesians, but asserts that the principal target was Cartesian physics, not Cartesian theology. Mouy himself, however, carefully documents that the only book put on the Index is the 1650 Amsterdam edition of the *Meditations*, which contains the explanation of the Eucharist in the answers to the "Fourth Set of Objections," and this only *donec corrignatur*. Mouy believes that the major attack is from nonchurchmen, citing Louis XIV's verbal order to the archbishop of Paris, Harlay, to put a stop to the Cartesians' speculations on transubstantiation.[404] However, Louis XIV was concerned to keep order, and it must not be forgotten that his confessor, Jean Ferrier, was a violent anti-Jansenist. An attack on the Cartesians was an attack on Arnauld and Nicole.

5   JEAN-BAPTISTE DE LA GRANGE'S ATTACK

There is further evidence that the explanation of transubstantiation touched off major opposition to the Cartesians. In 1675, Jean-Baptiste de La Grange published *Les principes de la philosophie, contre les nouveaux philosophes Descartes, Rohault, Regius, Gassendi, le P. Maignan, &c.*, which was followed by several more works attacking the new philosophers. It is interesting to note that La Grange, like Malebranche, was a member of the Oratory. Unlike Malebranche, however, La Grange is concerned to present and to protect a philosophy that had been taught for over five hundred years in all the academies of Europe. Most of Scholastic theology is based on its principles, particularly those explanations used to explicate mysteries of Christianity to combat the heretics.[405]

La Grange begins by pointing out that the appeal of Cartesian philosophy rests on its being easier than the Peripatetic. However, there is something very bad in it. Cartesianism ruins a good part of Catholic theology and ordinary philosophy. One need not examine Descartes's works in depth. It is enough to know that he says that Catholic theologians have been deceived for hundreds of years about sensible qualities. So if Descartes's doctrine is not erroneous, it is at least dangerous. All novelties in religion are bad. The major example of Descartes's intent to destroy Catholic theology and ordinary philosophy is in his answer to the "Quatrièmes Objections" to his *Meditations*. There he says that the Scholastic explanation of the Eucharist is incomprehensible! And then he has the audacity to dedicate the *Meditations* to the doctors of the Sorbonne. This is nothing but mockery.[406]

Descartes's explanation of transubstantiation, La Grange contends, is wrong, his principles are wrong, and he is against true philosophy. Without accidental forms, for example, there can be no inherent grace as the Council of Trent defines it. Grace cannot come simply from extension and movement. Descartes says he leaves theology alone, but his explanation of the Eucharist shows that his real intent is to destroy Scholastic theology. Descartes says that the Scholastic theological explanations are false because they are contrary to his philosophy. La Grange says that the proper conclusion from this is just the opposite: Descartes's philosophy is false.[407]

La Grange goes on to attack Emmanuel Maignan, who builds on Descartes's principles. Maignan, like Descartes, mocks accidental forms and thinks that sensible qualities are due to movements of material parts. La Grange points out that there has been no real proof that sensible qualities are not substantial forms. Actually, nothing is as true and useful as substantial forms and sensible qualities in philosophy.[408] La Grange says that he will show this:

> J'examine toutes les qualités spirituelles & sensibles, dont on peut disputer en philosophie, & pretends faire voire que ce sont des Estres entierement distinguée, & differents de la substance dans laquelle ils se trouvent; parce qu'on ne peut pas raisonnablement les explique d'une autre manière.[409]

What the Cartesians do, La Grange says, is take figure and disposition of parts which do distinguish artificial things, and claim that natural things are similarly distinguished. However, all natural things are composed of matter and real substantial forms entirely different from matter that forms give being. Accidental forms such as hardness, heat, and light are also real beings different from body, contrary to Descartes's assertions.[410]

As his major example, La Grange spends three chapters showing how Scholastic principles can be used to explicate transubstantiation, while Cartesian principles cannot. First, quantity is not the same thing as extension or corporeal body.[411] Accidental forms are "Entités, qui ne sont ny corps ny ésprits, dont la nature est de pouvoir perfectionner la substance."[412] The

Cartesian categorization of substance and mode is not complete, hence the Scholastic terms appear to be incredible only by Cartesian definition.[413] A substance is actually something that subsists and can never have a subject, whereas an accident *also* subsists, and can have a subject.[414]

Even peasants believe that sensible qualities are different from spirit and matter. They agree that material substance in itself has no taste, color, and the like, but that these are accidental forms. Hence, La Grange says ironically, even the Cartesians should have no trouble conceiving of these things.[415]

Once all this is understood, it is easy to explain how the body of Christ can be reduced in size and be at many places at once. Contrary to what the Cartesians say, quantity is different from extension, and substantial forms give things the being they have.[416]

Descartes himself is contradictory in his explanations. According to his own principles, if a piece of substance which causes us to have the sensations of bread in the Eucharist is not the same bread as before the miracle, it is another bread. That is, it is a substance with such-and-such a taste, and so on.[417] And if there are superficies that remain after the bread is removed, then they can be nothing but real accidents as the Scholastics define them.[418] As for the question of whether there is deception in the miracle, La Grange says flatly that there is none. After all, Christ tells us that the bread is his body.[419] Ultimately, all the Scholastics need say is that one accident— quantity—is unsupported, and that it supports all the other accidents.[420] Thus, only the simple, general miracle of nonsupport is required. However, the Cartesian (occasionalist) explanation requires a complex, individual miracle for every person experiencing the Eucharist.

La Grange believes that the Cartesians are condemned at the Council of Constance in the form of some propositions of Wycliffe and Hus:

> Tous les Theologiens Catholiques croyent que les Especes du Pain & du Vin, comme le goust, la couleur, la pesanteur & la Dureté, sont des Estres ou des Accidens réels, qui subsistent après la Consecration sans aucur sujet; parce que la substance du Pain, qui estoit leur appuy est totalement convertie au Corps du Fils de Dieu.[421]

Out of forty-five condemned propositions of Wycliffe, the second, that the accidents of bread do not remain without a subject,[422] Descartes says that a cause remains, and so cannot say that the accidents are unsupported.[423]

Finally, Rohault's explanation, that God causes us to have sensations, is even more impossible for,

> il est absurde de dire que les sentimens que nous avons d'un morceau de Pain que nous voyons ou que nous touchons, soient le Accidens du Pain;

ce serout parler autrement que le reste des Hommes. Par le mot d'Accident du Pain, de quelque opinion qui l'on soit, on entend toujours ce qui
est dans le Pain & ce qui est cause des sentimens que nous en avons, &
non pas le sentimens mesmes.[424]

The Cartesians, like the Lutherans, define accident to be a part of
substance when they speak of it as cause. However, it is really different from
substance.[425] And it certainly is different from a sensation that is only an
effect in us caused by the accident.

La Grange goes on to show the necessity of substantial and accidental
forms in physics and philosophy. The Cartesians do not think deeply enough;
they arbitrarily defend substance and mode, denying that there can be any
other sort of being; and they make the ridiculous mistake of confusing
sensations with sensible qualities. This is the result of revolting against
traditional philosophy. La Grange clearly sees the danger of Cartesianism to
Scholasticism. He sincerely believes the Cartesians to be heretical in their
intent to destroy Scholastic physics and philosophy, for this will also destroy
Scholastic theology. And he is led to see the urgency of the need for such a
prolonged defense as he gives by having read the spurious explanations of
transubstantiation given by Descartes, Rohault, Maignan, and others.

6   THE INDIVIDUATION OF THE BODY OF CHRIST

Although a great deal of heat is generated over whether or not real accidents
can be supported without an underlying substance, the crucial issue in the
theological debate between Scholastic and Cartesian philosophers is over the
problem of individuating the matter that makes up Christ's flesh, or body,
and blood. According to the Cartesians, individual pieces of matter are
distinguished only by their modifications and, as the Scholastic critics point
out, these modifications are nothing more than material substance variously
figured. For any given material object, size and shape are the only intrinsic
characteristics it can have, with weight being a function of the extrinsic,
imposed characteristic of motion. The sensible qualities popularly attributed
to bodies are, for the Cartesians, actually properties of the mind caused by
the immediate or mechanically mediated impact of material objects on the
sense organs.

On these grounds, the total replacement of bread by the body of Christ
that takes on or retains the same (or exactly similar) superficies as the bread,
as Descartes first suggests, would result in a total change of all that can be
changed in any piece of matter. What a piece of matter is—whether bread or
flesh—is entirely determined by its distinctive shape or disposition of parts.

If the superficies of a piece of matter is such that it causes us to have sensations as though we were perceiving bread, then we are perceiving bread. If a piece of matter appears to us to be flesh, then it is flesh. There is nothing in Cartesian matter as such to distinguish any part of it from any other part. Therefore, the explanation for transubstantiation that Descartes originally suggests is completely inadequate, because there is no way of identifying the transubstantiated piece of matter—any piece would do—as that of Christ's flesh, or body. Even more damning, Descartes's explanation transforms Christ's body into *real* bread, while the point of the miracle is that Christ's body is supposed to be there in actuality under the accidents of the bread, which is no longer present. Descartes substitutes the real presence of bread for the real presence of Christ's flesh.

These difficulties were probably quite obvious to Descartes, and no doubt they led him to modify his explanation. Thus he goes into great detail to discuss the natural process of digestion and assimilation in which bread and wine are transformed into flesh and blood. However, Descartes's example is flawed. According to his principles, one should *not* be able—contrary to his assertion—even with the most powerful microscope, to discern in flesh or blood the tiny particles of bread or wine that made it up. If one could, the question might arise as to which comes first, bread or flesh. And again, if blood were made up, say, of little particles of wine, then in the gross it would—on Cartesian principles—appear to be wine, not blood, for what makes matter either blood or wine is its shape and disposition, and nothing else. Nor could the tiny particles be shaped as flesh, for example, while the gross shape is that of bread, for Descartes specifically asserts that it is the detailed superficies of all the particles, and not just gross shape, that determines what a chunk of matter is and what sensations it causes. What apparently happens in natural digestion and assimilation then, on Cartesian grounds, is what actually happens. The superficies of the matter we eat are changed into the superficies of the parts of our bodies.

Thus Descartes is led to introduce the notion of the real presence of Christ's soul in the Eucharist. And here he compounds the difficulties of his appeal to natural transubstantiation. He has no ground for saying that any part of Christ's flesh was ever made of actual bread. No part of Christ's body ever had the superficies of bread. Christ's soul was never united with actual bread. Therefore, Descartes's penultimate explanation of the Eucharist by the real presence of Christ's soul in real bread is also unsatisfactory. For this reason he finally argues that the bread and wine are replaced by the matter of Christ's body, which matter remains united to Christ's soul. The miracle then would be that Christ himself—the union of body and soul that is Christ—is transubstantiated into real bread, which is at the same time really Christ. It is essential that this take place if the matter of the bread of the

Eucharist is to be individuated as that of Christ's actual body. And at this point Descartes has diverged sufficiently from his claim to have given an explanation of the miracle of the Eucharist that is more rational and acceptable than the Scholastic explanation, that it is fair to brand his whole attempt a failure.

7 THE DEBACLE OF DESCARTES'S DUALISM

But then, so far as that goes, Descartes's entire metaphysics is a failure. This chapter is part of my eulogy to the greatest and most influential failure in Modern philosophy. Descartes's discussion of transubstantiation so exposed the difficulties of the Scholastic position that orthodoxy was greatly shaken. If Descartes intended to destroy Scholastic theology, he contributed by exposing the doctrine of transubstantiation—however explained—to ridicule. Alan Gabbey[426] and Jacques Roger[427] show how Descartes's philosophy of nature impinges on serious political and religious issues of his day. Richard H. Popkin[428] shows how Cartesian Bible criticism could lead to atheism. I show how Cartesian theology could lead at least to Protestantism.

The battle over transubstantiation raises very serious problems for Cartesian as well as for Scholastic metaphysics, for if the issue of individuating Christ's matter in the Eucharist is crucial in any explanation of transubstantiation, the problem of individuating any human being is crucial to Cartesianism. I contend that Descartes fails to establish a viable dualistic ontology, and that his failure is illuminated by the foregoing discussion.

Cartesian mind is a very peculiar substance. It is *active thinking*, a substantial activity, something very different from passive matter. On any traditional grounds, an activity ought to be grounded in or supported by an actor. Yet there is ample evidence that Descartes truly means to introduce thinking itself as a substance.[429] Of course, Cartesian matter is no less peculiar a substance. Sheer extension, mere empty space, is *what* matter is. As the Scholastics point out, this is to take a property of traditional matter—its quantity or dimensionality—and make this property into a substance. It is not that matter is something that is extended in three dimensions: Cartesian matter just is three-dimensionality.

Quite obviously, Cartesian mind and matter as described in the previous paragraph have many affinities with Scholastic substantial forms. A Scholastic critic might very well say that Descartes takes the (Aristotelian) form and matter of a man, separates them, and then claims (what is impossible) that they can exist separately as independent substances. In fact, man is a union of form and matter. Descartes himself admits this by saying that man is a composite substance, consisting of the union of two substances—mind and matter—in which mind acts as the form of man, and body as man's matter, on the strict Aristotelian model.

That Descartes resorts to this Aristotelian model mitigates somewhat the strength of his attacks on Aristotelianism. Nevertheless, his attempt to present two new substances must stem at least in part from certain difficulties in the Scholastic model of man. Descartes wants mind and matter to be essentially different from and independent of one another so that after death the soul can survive. A Scholastic critic would point out that the matter of man in the Aristotelian union of form (soul) and matter (body) is not *corporeal* matter. However, to the Cartesians, prime matter is as enigmatic as are real accidents, so corporeal matter is the only matter that they find available for union with any form.

After all this is said, the somewhat paradoxical interpretation of Descartes's two substances—mind and matter—as at last derivative from the Aristotelian union of form and matter in the substance, man, remains plausible. In a sense, the two substances of Descartes's dualism are unsupported substantial forms. To say that mind is thinking, and that matter is extension, is to give substantiality to characteristics that on traditional grounds ought themselves to be grounded in an underlying substance.

A conclusion made comprehensible by the foregoing discussion is that Descartes's ontology is—to say the least—most peculiar. Despite this peculiarity, and despite Descartes's own felt need to bring mind and matter back together again when he discusses man, his ontology has of course had a grand career. The ontology of modern science embodies Cartesian matter, and the ontology of phenomenalism enshrines Cartesian mind. It goes without saying that there remain many unsolved problems in the systems based on Cartesian ontology, problems that can be traced to the oddities of these primary ontological entities.

8   THE NATURE OF MAN AMONG THE CARTESIANS

Descartes's final explanation of transubstantiation by the real presence of Christ's soul to individuate the matter transubstantiated is related to another jointly metaphysical and theological problem in Cartesianism, immortality. A man for Descartes is merely an extraordinary and temporary union of a mind and a body. Of the Cartesians, Louis de La Forge is most explicit about what this means for the soul after death.[430] All sensations—sensible qualities—and thus all particular knowledge about existing matter are a result of the union of mind and matter. When this union is broken at death, the mind—now the soul—no longer has any knowledge of the particularities of the material world. All the soul knows are the general truths of intelligible extension, its own self, and God. This is a very hard doctrine—and was despised as much by critics as was the Cartesian view that animals are machines[431]—but the implications would seem to be even harsher than those La Forge delineates.

Individual men are distinguished on Cartesian grounds by their union with this or that body. The particularities of the body's experiences, the sensations and thoughts generated in this union, are what individuate one man from another. After death, without a body, the mind or soul is shorn of all sensory memory and imagination, for these depend on the bodily union. There would thus seem to be nothing remaining to distinguish or to individuate one soul from another. Mankind *extra mundus*, that is, all souls liberated from bodies, would not consist of many separately distinguishable souls, but instead would be merely thinking, the mental substance, just as matter undistinguished into parts or individuated into separate bodies by motion is merely extension. Perhaps mankind in heaven is just the lowest species of angel, of which, as for other angels, there is only one individual to a species because several individuals would be indiscernible and thus identical.

In Descartes's explanation of the Eucharist, he brings in Christ's soul to individuate the transubstantiated matter; in his metaphysical system, it is matter that individuates each man. Christ is unique, of course, and His soul is of a higher order than that of any man. Consequently, to bring in Christ's soul as a universal to explain such things as how the Eucharist can be performed in different places at the same time accords with traditional philosophy. But is there also perhaps only human mind, only one thinking, split into many different souls by union with different individual bodies? Mental substance for Descartes might then parallel material substance, with each individual human soul having existence only as a part of one total thinking, just as each individual material body has existence only as a part of the total extended plenum.

Obviously, their ontology forces Cartesians to hold radical theological views. I have shown that their replacements for Scholastic physics and philosophy necessarily lead to replacements for Scholastic theology. The Cartesian theological views were deemed heretical by the Catholics, and this—like their unpopular notion that animals are machines—led to general disapproval of Cartesianism. Thus the downfall of Cartesianism can be traced not only to general epistemological failures of the way of ideas, but also to religious controversy, in which the debate over transubstantiation is central.

chapter 12

The Cartesianism Theology of Louis de La Forge (1632–1666)

Louis de La Forge, a physiologist, was the most brilliant and consistent of the orthodox Cartesians. Unlike Malebranche, La Forge followed Descartes carefully, and carried his thought to what some contemporaries believed was the bitter end. Much has been made of La Forge's occasionalism.[432] However, his substantive contributions are worth more study than are his few remarks on occasional causes.

In *Traitté de l'esprit de l'homme, de ses facultez et fonctions, et de son union avec le corps, suivant les Principes de René Descartes*,[433] published in 1666, La Forge focuses on matters Descartes treats only briefly. His conclusions startled both Cartesians and non-Cartesians. La Forge found that spirit and matter become human mind and body only in union. All sensible experiences, images, and memories occur only in this union. When a man dies and the immortal spirit is separated from matter, the spirit retains no knowledge of its life united as a mind with a human body. After death, one can have knowledge only of a spirit, God, and intelligible—not sensible—extension.

In developing this conclusion on Cartesian principles, La Forge treats in detail the way in which ideas of particular material objects can be had by man (union of mind and body) but not by spirit (the immortal soul) alone. La Forge's reasonings are detailed, acute, and strictly Cartesian. Rather than trying to argue with La Forge, many simply gave up Cartesianism, rejecting a doctrine that comes to such harsh conclusions about life after death.

Numerous Cartesians expounded Descartes's thought. None carried it so far and so consistently as does La Forge. This makes his *Traitté* the most philosophically important book in the orthodox Cartesian corpus. For this reason, Pierre Clair has recently presented a biographic and bibliographic study of the *Traitté*.[434] This study should be supplemented with the edition of Descartes's *L'Homme* that La Forge produced with Clerselier.[435] However, like Gouhier, Clair stresses only a limited aspect of La Forge, and so also does A. G. A. Balz in his "Louis de la Forge and the Critique of Substantial Forms."[436] Thus I venture here a broader interpretation as a supplement to my *Downfall of Cartesianism, 1673–1712*.[437]

La Forge's *Traitté de l'esprit de l'homme* is a complement to the work of Descartes. Unlike Rohault, Régis, and eminently Antoine Le Grand, La Forge attempts no complete exposition of the Cartesian system. Rather, he focuses his attention on crucial and difficult points, and concentrates his constructive powers on areas of importance that Descartes treats only briefly. Where there is difficulty or obscurity in Descartes's work, La Forge states the problem clearly and does not shrink from giving the orthodox Cartesian solution, even when it may be unsatisfactory to critics. Where expansion of Descartes's system is needed, La Forge proceeds with impeccable logic to a solid Cartesian conclusion. And here again, if the results sometimes disturb even some Cartesians, La Forge does not hesitate. For this careful Cartesian, Descartes's texts set problems, but they also provide the solutions. Thus it is in an exalted sense that La Forge is rightly said to be the most rigid Cartesian. It can be said that he sees only what Descartes does, but yet that he sees more than do most of the Cartesian expositors of his day. His innovation is in explication.

La Forge begins with an examination of the logical structure of substances. He analyzes the notion of essence in such a way that both the essence of a substance and its essential attributes must be distinctly unique to that substance. The attributes that define one substance, for example, are incompatible with the attributes that pertain to another substance. Essential attributes of one substance could not characterize another substance even in succession, assuming what is impossible, that is, that the essential attributes of the second substance could be removed. This points up the fact that the essential attributes of a substance are necessarily related to the substance's essence and, moreover, that they are necessarily interrelated. To apply this abstract discussion about essence, one need only consider that material properties are necessarily subsistent in matter, whose essence is extension. Only extended objects can have size and shape, for example, and whatever has size necessarily has shape, and so on. The thoughts that characterize spiritual substance, and the powers of understanding, willing, remembering, etc., necessarily adhere to the substance whose essence is thinking, and are necessarily interrelated. Matter and spirit then, the only two (created, simple) substances we know, are alike in exhibiting the above mentioned logical characteristics of substance.[438]

Before examining further La Forge's comparison of spirit and matter, I want to remark that his criticism and rejection of Scholastic substantial forms[439] falls out of this analysis of substance with no possible compromise whatever. Essential attributes, modes, accidents, properties, and acts are inconceivable except as belonging to a substance. The term "substantial form" combines two notions in an incoherent compound. It is a contradiction to think of a form—which necessarily must inhere in a substance—as being substantial or as subsisting in itself. Once one understands the logical structure of substance and attribute, one will no longer be bemused by the chimera of substantial form. So although La Forge argues directly against substantial forms, one might expect him to have felt that anyone who follows and accepts the Cartesian analysis of substance will see that such direct argumentation is really superfluous.

But having destroyed a spectre from the past, La Forge had to face a modern union of incompatibles—the ghost and the machine—that is just as difficult to comprehend as are substantial forms. Whatever their utter substantial differences, spirit and matter, which are as essentially unlike one another as any two things can be, are in fact found to be united in the compound substance, man. In man, the thinking spirit becomes a mind that not only can think about spiritual matters, but that also is aware of the human body's actions and of the actions of the external material world upon it. Besides this expanded power of awareness of the body in this union, the spirit gains also the power to control some of the movements of the human body with which it is compounded. Thus the *mind* is much more than a *spirit*; and indeed, the *body* of a man is much more than mere passive *matter*, it is the living instrument of a spirit become mind.[440]

No other Cartesian details this situation with the crispness that La Forge does. And just as he supports the conclusion that no form can be substantial, so also does he support the conclusion that spirit and matter can be united—by further analysis of the notion of substance. We know now that there are only two (created, simple) substances. Let us compare them as substances. First, of course, both spirit and matter are substances with essential attributes. They parallel one another in having properties, and the distinctive properties of matter pertain to it in the same way those of spirit pertain to it. This fashion of being of properties—material and spiritual— just is the substance as determined, the substance in a determinate fashion. Now a substance is conceivable without any properties in particular, but any substance must be particularized to exist. Thus a spirit is individuated by its thoughts, just as a material object is individuated by its shape and place. Furthermore, both spirit and matter exist in time. As a material object is inseparable from its parts which define and limit it, so is a spirit inseparable from its thoughts which define and limit it.[441]

What is the purpose of this extensive paralleling of spirit and matter? For one thing, La Forge apparently thinks that it eases the mystery of how two essentially different substances can be united. But perhaps even more important, there is exposed (and what better phrase can one use for what is obvious once a structure is understood and a problem posed for which it provides an answer?) in this architectonic an answer to the question of how spiritual ideas can represent material objects without resembling them.

Consider: The union of spirit and matter to make man is an observable fact. The united powers of the human mind and the human body are experienced in operation. That spirit and matter are alike as substances makes this union conceivable at least to the extent that there are parallels on which to fasten.

The operant faculty in this union is the will, which affects and is affected by the body.[442] And the spirit can be said to be the "form" of the body if one is careful to remember that this means not that the spirit is the essential attribute of man, but that it is the animating, conscious essence of man.[443] As for the question of how mind and body interact causally, La Forge takes the hard Cartesian line that the animal spirits of the body (somehow) influence the mind and are influenced by the mind in the pineal gland. Little more on the subject can be said than this, by me, or by La Forge. It is here that La Forge says that the mind has ideas on the occasion of material traces on the pineal gland.[444] But this is clearly not occasionalism; it is the employment of a noncommital term when no more operationally descriptive phrase is available. He goes on to say that of course all primary efficient causality comes from God. Secondary causality—among material objects just as much as between mind and body—is really beyond our comprehension. It may be too much to say that it is a total mystery, because at least the mechanical aspects of this secondary causality can be traced out. But we still do not see the causal how. But it is real causality, nonetheless.[445] Thus those commentators who see in La Forge the predecessor of Hume are about as right (or wrong) as those who see in him the predecessor of Malebranche. La Forge marched right up to the problem of causality and stared it in the face; he went just as far as Descartes did, but no farther. Secondary causality is real; we can see its mechanics; God alone knows the inner springs. If this does not satisfy the critics of Cartesianism, it does satisfy the Cartesian conscience.

Now what about that other great problem that results from the Cartesian dualism, the split between our ideas and the material world? How is one to bridge the gap between ideas that are completely spiritual and the material objects the ideas represent? Here again we find that the architectonic provides an answer. For although ideas and material objects are essentially different from one another so that Cartesians must reject the traditional view that ideas represent their objects by resembling them, there is resemblance between spirit and matter as substances.[446] It is this resemblance—as substances—that Descartes harks to in the Third Meditation when he says that the mind could contain the notion of extension eminently even if no material world exists. This is because, as a substance, the mind has as much formal reality as the idea of matter has objective reality. Nevertheless, La Forge does make the usual Cartesian claims, first, that ideas do represent material objects without resembling them; second, that it is the nature of ideas to represent without resembling their objects; and third, that God knows matter by way of nonresembling ideas, so there should be no question about his making it possible for us to know matter by the same way of ideas.[447] But more than this, he goes on to show that—as properties of substances—there can be and often is a one-to-one correspondence between ideas and the material complexes they represent.[448] His word is *conformité*, a conformity between ideas (and sensations) and the material world that is a result of the parallel between spirit and matter as substances, and that is a result of the interaction between the human mind and the human body in the union that is man. A causal theory of nonresembling representative ideas is thus supported by a careful statement of the parallels that exist between spirit and matter despite their essential unlikeness. This is no grand Spinozistic isomorphism between spiritual and material realms. But it is a mode of connection, a way of relation between ideas and material objects, soundly grounded in the Cartesian ontology. (And, one might add, ultimately based on some form of likeness between ideas and material objects, after all.)

This is enough to show La Forge in the role of strict expositor supreme, stretching apart the warp and woof of the Cartesian fabric for all to see. Consider La Forge's theological expansion of Descartes's ideas, a compounding that leads to an unquestionably Cartesian position, but one from which even Cartesians shrink. For believers in an afterlife, often no hope is fonder than that on the other side one will see again one's loved ones, and experience in eternity the delights one once had—or even those one was deprived of—on earth. La Forge shows that a Cartesian can have no such expectations at all. The experience of this material world, one's powers of perception and memory and imagination of material things, or more accurately, of sensible as contrasted to intelligible extension, are all functions of the union of spirit and matter. When a man dies, the compound is broken; the immortal spirit is then freed from mortal coils, but as it flies to heaven, so also flies away all awareness of the material world. Not only is there no more interaction with a human body, there is no memory, no imagination, no thought of sensible things. The spirit goes to spirit's things; the dust to dust.[449]

The conclusion that the disembodied spirit can no longer think of earthly things is an inevitable conclusion of orthodox Cartesianism. As remarked above, certainly spirit can think of matter. A spirit could dream up the notion of extended substance, even if none existed. And of course spirits by themselves can reason about intelligible extension, span the breadths of geometry, and plumb the depths of mathematical physics. What a bodyless spirit cannot do, however, is locate its thoughts on the object of any actual particular material thing, whether the existence of that thing is situated in the past, the present, or the future. The faculty of sensation and the ability to know particular sensible things are properties of the compound substance, man. It is only by being a union of spirit and matter that a man can have those confused ideas—sensations—that alert him to the existence of the sensible world. And it is only with the concurrence of a human body with its material brain that a human mind can imagine the sensible world in his imagination and remember its effects on his body. All this is clearly implied by Descartes; it is exhaustively detailed by La Forge. It was not an enthusiastically greeted conclusion. Along with the Cartesian views that animals are machines and that transubstantiation takes place by nothing more mystical than the rearrangement of minute material particles—views to which it is necessarily related—the view that the Cartesian spiritual heaven is bare of body helped to diminish the popularity of Cartesianism among both devout savants and members of the general public.

A final word can be said about La Forge's position concerning the being of ideas. As modifications of active, thinking substance, ideas are acts. And as spiritual, their termination is within the spirit. In man, their termination is in the mind. They are all alike as modes, but they differ from one another according to their manner of representation, their objects, the faculties they serve, their causes, and their ultimate relations to spirit.[450] In his stress upon the scope of ideas as being acts within the mind, La Forge ranks himself with those such as Antoine Arnauld who believe that individuated acts are enough to account for the knowledge our ideas give us. This is in opposition to those, such as Malebranche, who tend toward the view that individuated ideas are objects of acts of thought, and may, indeed, exist outside individual created spirits, in the mind of God. On the question of the mode of being of ideas, an opponent that La Forge names is Girolamo Fracastoro,[451] an Italian medical doctor born in 1483 in Gerona, who died in 1553. He was an early researcher on syphilis, and wrote an extremely popular clinical and historical poem on the subject in Latin verse, *Syphilis sive De morbo gallica* published in Verona in 1530. This was translated into French, German, and English. (The title of one English translation is *Syphilis or the French Disease*, while the French translations read merely *Syphilis ou le mal vénérien*.) However, La Forge was interested in Fracastoro's dialogue on the soul, *Turrius sive De intellectione*. This work is undated, but it appears in *Hieronymi Fracastorii Veronesis Opera omnia* published in Venice in 1555. According to La Forge, Fracastoro holds an Epicurean position about ideas, with our knowledge of the material world being due to the presentation of material species to the mind by way of the sense organs and the nerves. The forms of the species are then taken and contemplated as *subnotions* by the mind. La Forge stresses that nothing from the outside except motions ever reaches the brain, and that even then the acts of mind that are ideas do not extend outside the mind. Subnotions are rejected as another version of substantial forms. But what does La Forge offer in their place? Once again, we find a Cartesian stopped by the unbridgeable gap between the body and the mind, contending both that the resulting confused ideas really are somehow representative of material bodies on the other side, and that if they do not quite come across, God makes their way even if we do not see how. Thus even Cartesianism compounded fails to explain how we know the material world. But along the way to impasse, La Forge's *Traitté* is a triumph in the detailed working out of what an orthodox Cartesian can know. Unfortunately, it is not enough. Cartesian theories of man, of transubstantiation, and of the afterlife all compound to further the downfall of Cartesianism.

Part IV

The Breakdown of Cartesian Metaphysics

chapter 13

What Moves the Mind? An Excursion in Cartesian Dualism

The commonsense source of Cartesian Dualism is familiar to everyone. Each of us thinks of and experiences himself and others as a combination of a mind that thinks, understands, wills, and has conceptual ideas, sensations, and passions, and of an extended body of a certain size and shape that moves about. It seems clear that bodies interact directly with one another through impact. Thoughts influence each other directly through association. There is also causal interaction between bodies and thoughts; bodies can be moved intentionally, and bodies cause ideas and sensations.

Descartes acknowledges in his ontology the obvious difference between mind and matter. This ontology raises a number of problems that occur to anyone who begins to think about how mind and matter differ, and it provides a way of solving some of them. It is a substance/property ontology; there is one material substance, an extended plenum which, when modified by size, shape, position, and motion, yields a multiplicity of bodies; these modifications define bodies. And there is one kind of mental substance with many instances called minds, each modified by thoughts comprising understandings, willings, conceptual ideas, sensations, and passions; these modifications differentiate minds.

Descartes speaks of material and mental substances as being finite. This means in part that each is limited in its capacity to be modified. That is, matter cannot take on the properties of thought, and mind cannot take on the properties of extension. There is also an infinite substance, God, who is an omnipotent source of being. Finally, there are compound substances, human beings consisting each of a union of a mind with a body.

I know this is familiar. I need to say it as an introduction to my claim that the most important thing to Descartes is the positing and maintenance of his ontological dualism of mind and matter. This is shown by Descartes's refusal to give up the dualism even in the face of two extremely difficult problems he apparently could not solve:

> How can mind and matter interact causally?
> How can mental ideas represent material bodies?[452]

There are two equally primary sources of Descartes's dualism, one in theology and one in physics. Descartes was concerned first of all to uphold

Christian dogma. Anyone reading Descartes's *Replies to the Objections* to his *Meditations* and his *Letters* must conclude that his ontology derives from dogmatic theology. First, God is perfect and unchanging in the sense of not being qualified, and particularly not by extended properties and sensations such as pain. Because God is neither material nor sensible, Descartes must distinguish God sharply from a world of created substances. These substances cannot be attributes or properties of God (Spinoza was vilified for asserting that they are), but must be independent existents, dependent on God only for creation and continuity.

Next, the theological demand that human souls be immortal drives Descartes to his dualism of kinds of substances. It is obvious that bodies are material and disintegrate, so they must be separated from souls which do not.

Finally, the theological demand that each human soul be an independent individual forces Descartes to posit an asymmetrical dualism, for while there need be only one material substance of which bodies are modifications, there must be a plurality of mental substances all of one kind.

In summary, Descartes must posit substances independent of God in being (although created by God) because God cannot be modified; there must be two kinds of substances because human souls must be separate from human bodies; and the dualism must be asymmetric because each human soul must be capable of independent existence. This is how the foundational Cartesian ontological structure derives from dogmatic theological demands.[453]

Now let us derive the same ontology along a line independent of theological dogma. On this view, Descartes is first of all a natural philosopher. His metaphysics derives from physics and physiology, the sciences of matter.[454] The laws of Cartesian physics, based on the single principle of motion, replace the myriad essentialist explanatory principles of Scholastic physics. But the shift is not merely a substitution of one explanatory model— mechanism—for another—essentialism. Matter—or three-dimensional bodies in motion—provides the ontological foundation for Cartesian physics as a substitute for the active forces that provide the ontological foundation for Scholastic physics. The metaphysical core of Cartesianism is a new ontology of passive matter having no internal forces and essential powers. Then Descartes must posit a second substance because human souls obviously do have internal powers, so must be different from matter. No criticism or problem ever shook Descartes's insistence on the dualistic ontology of passive matter and active mind.

From the independent standpoints of theology and physics, then, the ontological dualism of mind and matter is primary. Both theology and physics require that mind and matter be absolutely distinct in essence.

Matter is passive unthinking extension. Mind is active unextended thinking.[455]

Descartes is now faced with three tasks. He must work out the sciences of the two substances, the physics of matter and the psychology of mind. One presumptive advantage of the absolute dualism is that these two sciences can be developed independently. However, once these two sciences are systematized, Descartes must then develop a science of the interaction of mind and matter, and this is his third task. The union of mind and body as a compound substance results in systemic causal interaction which I argue below demands a unification of physics and psychology.

Descartes works out the physics of matter in some detail. He does considerably less on psychology, but enough to imply that the sciences of mind and matter are incompatible because material motion is determined, but some mental action is free. I show to what extent the two sciences derive from the nature of the two substances, and thus provide a more comprehensive picture of why the interaction seems impossible than the usual statement that engagement between the extended and the unextended is inconceivable. I conclude that if the two sciences are incompatible when developed independently by considering mind and matter separately, then when mind and matter are considered in union their causal interaction must be governed either by a third science different from both physics and psychology, or one of these two sciences must be reduced to the other.

There is some evidence that Descartes considers the possibility of a third science in which sensations would be modifications of the compound substance. But Cartesianism cannot tolerate this—mind and matter and their respective modifications must be ontologically distinct—and Descartes does not pursue it. There are strong reasons for reducing one of the sciences to the other. I suggest that Descartes knows this, but does not undertake the reduction because he does not want to give up either of the independent sciences, that is, he does not want to give up the dualism of mind and matter. If physics were reduced to psychology, for example, matter would be reduced to mind. Because Descartes insists on the ontological dualism, he is forced to accept as unsolvable the problem of how mind and matter interact; he is forced to accept the incompatibility of physics and psychology. I argue, however, that Descartes's metaphysics logically leads to the conclusion that psychology must be reduced to physics, a development Descartes did not care to make explicit.

First, let us consider Descartes's physics and his psychology separately. Can we derive Descartes's physics from Cartesian matter? It is not easy. Matter is passive unthinking extension. I show in Chapter 14 and most recent commentators agree that Cartesian matter just *is* extension, sheer three-dimensionality, what we ordinarily call empty space.[456] Some, like Spinoza, believe that in identifying matter with extension, Descartes mistakenly takes the essential attribute of matter to be matter. I argue that this is by no means a mistake on Descartes's part. When Spinoza says that extension is an attribute of God, he is taken to be saying that God is material. Descartes avoids this by taking extension to be an independent substance. This substance is created by God, but because it is not an attribute, Descartes does not make Spinoza's mistake of attributing extension to God. Anyone who tries to avoid Descartes's saying outright that matter *is* extension,[457] thus must contend with this fact: Descartes assures an absolute dualism of mind and matter by holding that the likeness between them deriving from their being equally finite substances is merely in existence and not in essence or substance; as substances they differ totally.[458] To hold this he cannot regard mind as merely a substance with the essential attribute of thinking, nor matter as merely a substance with the essential attribute of extension. Mind must *be* thinking. Thinking *is* the mental substance. Matter must *be* extension. Extension *is* the material substance.

Extension has no limits. It is a plenum. Is it *something*? Matter in any part of the plenum is exactly the same as matter in any other part of the plenum. There is nothing internal or essential to any part of extension that differentiates it from any other part. Thus the plenum is homogeneous, uniform, featureless. Sheer three-dimensional extension is indistinguishable from empty space. But is it *something*? Descartes certainly thinks that matter is something. He speaks of extension as being intelligible in the sense that it can support the shapes of solid Euclidean geometry. Its modes are what we ordinarily call bodies. But how can we comprehend this capacity if we consider extension *only* in itself? Surely the concept of empty space depends on contrast to and relations among bodies conceived in space. But for Descartes, pure matter is homogeneous, featureless extension unmodified by bodies. Considered without bodies, pure extension may be indistinguishable not merely from what we call empty space, but also from what we call nothing. Descartes himself says that if there is nothing between two bodies, then they are adjacent to one another. There are no bodies in pure extension. Is extension then just nothing?

Descartes did not intend this result. But also he did not intend that extension be merely a place in which bodies can be and move about. Bodies are material, they are made out of extension, so extension is meant to be something. I assume, then, that extension *is* something.

Given extension, how are bodies generated? Extension is passive; in itself it is static. The generation and being of bodies in the Cartesian material plenum is not intrinsic to the being of extension. Descartes explicitly designates matter as merely the inert base of bodies, in contrast to Scholastic bodies that become what they are through the occult powers of their bases. The force that generates Cartesian bodies must come from outside the plenum. Descartes thus calls on God to introduce and conserve a certain quantity of motion in the plenum.

How does this outside force generate bodies? If motion were introduced uniformly, the result would be indistinguishable from a static plenum. Thus motion is introduced differently so parts of matter can be distinguished. This causes circular motions in the plenum because the movement of any portion of matter is possible only if a second portion moves out of its way and so on in a circle until an nth portion replaces the first portion. This circular motion creates whorls, and each material body consists of a portion of matter whirling differentially to adjacent portions of matter. The motion of a body determines (and thus is prior to) its size and shape. A body is any portion of matter that maintains its shape in relation to other moving portions of matter. Descartes says the motion of bodies causes eddying—in analogy to whirlpools in rivers—and thus more and more bodies are generated from God's original introduction of motion into the plenum.

Descartes intends to replace Scholastic ontology as an account of the material world. Scholastic physics has a different force—a striving soul—to explain every different effect in the material world. In Descartes's alternative ontology of material things, there are no differences in internal essence, and bodies have no internal powers. The posing of sheer extension as matter reduces every part of the material plenum to essential, powerless similarity. This homogeneity eliminates the entire occult spectrum.

It *does* pose a problem. It eliminates all bodies, too. For the Scholastics, bodies are differentiated by internal essential powers. Descartes must provide a principle of bodily differentiation that is *external* to the essence of inert matter. The brilliance of Descartes's solution is that he shows how all bodies in the material world are generated from one principle of differentiation, and from one initial application of that principle—motion—introduced differentially into the plenum and then conserved.

Bodies are generated because the motion must be circular because extension is a plenum. Descartes assumes that because extension is *something*, moving matter drags other matter into motion—creating the eddies—the eventual result being a world consisting of extremely small bodies moving separately and thus comprising what we would call empty space, somewhat larger bodies comprising light or something like what was once called ether, and even larger bodies such as what we call atoms, molecules, rocks, chairs, human bodies, planets, suns, etc.

Unfortunately, the concept of friction, which is crucial for the proliferation of bodies, is not derivable from the concepts of Cartesian matter and motion. Descartes observes that moving bodies do convey motion to each other in a frictional process. He further observes regular frictional behavior from which he derives laws of motion. These laws of motion could—he points out—have been different from what they are so far as matter and motion are considered in themselves. The laws are God's choice.

Thus, in substitution for Scholastic essentialism, Descartes provides this ontological framework to support a mechanical explanation for material phenomena. He postulates one homogeneous, powerless ontological entity: matter. He has to keep it without internal force to distinguish it from occult substances. But all he has now is extension, and no bodies. He then calls on God to introduce a quantity of motion that differentiates bodies. God must also introduce laws of frictional transference of motion.

This leads to another important result. What God has done cannot be undone except by God, so the quantity of motion is conserved, and bodies are generated and degenerated according to the immutable laws of motion. The world of material bodies in motion, then, is strictly determined. Anyone knowing the original direction and quantity of motion, and the laws of motion, could derive the size, shape, position, and motion of all bodies at all succeeding times. Cartesian physics is deterministic.

I will only mention three discursions on this picture. First, Descartes seems to provide a place and motion, but nothing to move. It is difficult to conceive of sheer extension as moving. Can places themselves move about? They cannot move from place to place, but perhaps they change into different places as they move along. It is hard to conceive of this without a backdrop of space, which Descartes disallows.

Second, perhaps extension does not move, but motion moves through it. The motion of a body would not consist of a moving portion of extension, but of motion causing continuous portions of extension to take on properties of size and shape successively. Thus *places* would not move. But neither would bodies, if bodies are portions of extension. How could sheer *motion* be a body? If a body were a certain quantity of motion of a given size and shape moving through the plenum, then motion begins to look like an occult force that makes a portion of extension take on properties to be the body it is. Or it is just a body moving through empty space. Neither of these is a Cartesian way to go. Yet a body is surely something that moves through space. But for Descartes, neither extension alone nor motion alone nor the two in combination is adequate for showing how a body can move through space.

My final discursive aside is that throughout his discussion of the material plenum, Descartes confuses the relation of part/whole with that of property/substance. When he has portions of the plenum moving around, he treats bodies as parts of a whole. But he says bodies are properties of extension, which is more compatible with the picture of motion causing successive modifications in contiguous portions of static extension, than with the picture of moving portions of extension.

To continue, I have shown how Descartes's physics can be derived from Cartesian matter. Can Descartes's psychology be derived from Cartesian mind?

I now explore mental substance in the depth I have explored material substance. One reason for doing this is that it is necessary for any solution to a basic problem in modern philosophy. In the Cartesian tradition that includes Arnauld, Spinoza, Leibniz, Locke, Berkeley, Hume, Russell, and Wittgenstein of the *Tractatus*, ideas are ontological entities. Here is the problem: What—in an idea—makes that idea to be of its object? Maybe the question is misguided. It certainly is difficult. It is not obviously a stupid question for Descartes, because ontologically Cartesian ideas are modifications or properties of the mind. It is not obviously mistaken to ask: What real characteristic of Cartesian idea makes it be of its object?

However, this question is posterior to another: Given the dualism and the interaction between mind and body that Descartes insists on and that we experience, how does a mind obtain an idea of a particular thing? This is the title question of this chapter: What moves the mind? To answer it, I must examine matter as I do above, and mind as I do below.

We are always being cautioned not to think of the mind the way we think of matter, nor to think of psychology as being a science like physics. I believe, however, that in Descartes's case there are strong parallels between the two substances and the two sciences. I thus elucidate Cartesian mind in terms like those I use in discussing Cartesian matter, and let the results be the argument for the viability of this approach.

First, note that the material parallel to a mind is not the human body with which it is associated, but the entire material plenum. Each mind is an independently existing substance, just as is the material plenum. Bodies are merely modifications of the one material substance, and the mental parallel to these bodies is ideas which are modifications of this or that mental substance.

A mind *is* thinking, an active substance in contrast to matter, a passive substance. Nevertheless, I argue that thinking is a mental plenum, and that—as such—it is in its own way as homogeneous and thus as empty as is the material plenum. For there to be any particular ideas, something must be introduced to a mind the way that motion must be introduced to matter to generate particular bodies. Thus the question: What moves the mind?

A mind—like the material plenum— is intrinsically, essentially empty. I must reconcile this claim with Descartes's statement that each mind contains innate ideas of God or necessary existence, mind or thinking, and matter or extension. There are also innate principles such as that equals added to equals result in equals, that what is contradictory in concept cannot exist, and that where there is a property there must be a substance supporting that property. These innate ideas and principles might be merely capacities or potentialities for having actual ideas. In this sense one might say that a pure mind is empty of actual ideas. This is like saying that pure extension has the capacity to support three-dimensional bodies even when none are actual. It seems to be a fair argument. But it also seems too easy, and perhaps too slick.

I say too slick because Descartes argues that extension really is a three-dimensional something, and not just a capacity to support bodies. He also thinks the innate ideas of mind really are somethings, actual and not just potential. I argue that innate ideas are to the mental plenum as three-dimensionality is to the material plenum, and that the mental plenum is as empty as the material.

Innate ideas are different from particular ideas. Particular ideas are modifications of the mind, just as bodies are modifications of matter. But innate ideas are, I argue, each of them, the mind itself. First, each innate idea is empty, but is something. The ideas of God, mind, and matter are vacant in that they have no content. The essence of God is necessary existence, and whether necessary existence is a property or a substance (if mind *is* thinking, and matter *is* extension, why not say that God *is* necessary existence? Spinoza thought so), this existence is non-describable. One wants to ask *what* exists. Infinite, unitary perfection exists, or an omniscient, omnipotent, etc. God exists, but we cannot comprehend these notions. The idea of God is empty, it is the homogeneous *is* of Parmenides, the night in which all cows are black, the blank page picturing the absolute in the parody issue of *Mind*. Again, it is the emptiness of mind sought by some mystics who would contemplate the infinite. One who has a true idea of necessarily existing perfection has the content-equivalent of an empty mind.

I have already shown that the idea of matter is empty.

The idea of mind is empty because thinking in itself has no content. Descartes does say that thinking is reflexive. When one thinks, one knows that one is thinking. Thinking is self-awareness. What am I? A thinking thing. But I am not an understanding, willing, doubting, or a judging thing unless there is content for thinking to fasten onto. Sheer thinking is content-less. Content must be provided for thinking. My argument is that thinking as such provides no content, just as extension as such provides no bodies. If one looks within—as do philosophers as disparate as Malebranche and Hume—one is bound to find nothing. Unless something external is introduced to the mind—unless something moves the mind to make particular ideas with particular contents—the mind will be as empty as the featureless, unmoved material plenum. The content-equivalent of a mind thinking only of itself is the void.

One might protest that Descartes claims that if one thinks of God, one knows that God exists, and that if one thinks of thinking, one knows that oneself exists. I argue that there is no content to these claims. What is one thinking about when one knows that God exists but does not know what God is? Nothing. What is one thinking about when one is thinking of bare thinking? Nothing. One might say that at least we know the difference between the ideas of God, mind, and matter. But then we would have to know how they differ, which we do not, for Descartes says, "Substance cannot be first discovered merely from the fact that it is a thing that exists, for that fact alone is not observed by us."[459] Even if one knows that an innate idea exists, one does not know its content. After finding that he exists, Descartes asks, "What am I?" And if one knows only that three innate ideas exist, one cannot distinguish them.

Finally, one might argue that this nothing of which one is thinking is something because it exists as an object of thought. My point is that it is nothing in the sense of having no content. However, each of these innate ideas is something in the sense of being an existent. Each, I argue, is equivalent to the existing mind itself. As such, they are indistinguishable.

I am not the only one to interpret Descartes this way. Louis de La Forge reasoned that at death after separation from the body, the soul has no memory of particular bodies and events, and can think only of God, matter, and mind in general.[460] The soft-headed interpretation of this is that one could at least spin out the general truths of divinity, mathematics, and the laws of thought while whiling away eternity. The hard-headed view is that with nothing to move the mind, one's thoughts would be of nothing.

I conclude that the self-reflexive innate idea of the mind is the mind. It is a contentless nothing, and as such is equivalent to the contentless innate ideas of God and matter. And what are they? They are not modifications of the mind, they are not particularized. All three innate ideas must be nothing but the mind itself. But what of the innate principles? These, too, are empty because they are general statements that reduce to $A = A$. What you know if you know only that A exists, but not what A is, is nothing. And what you know if you know only in general that $A = A$ is also nothing.

So even if there are an infinite number of innate principles in the mind, they are empty tautologies. They offer no particular, determinate content. What else could these principles *be*, if not the empty mind itself? Innate ideas and principles are empty thinking itself, the pure mental substance.

God introduced motion into the featureless plenum of the homogeneous material deep, thereby creating particular bodies. I ask: What moves the mind? What introduces particular ideas into the mind? What differentiates the featureless homogeneous mental plenum into particular ideas of particular things?

Descartes says that the interation of a particular body with a mind causes that mind to have a particular idea of that body. My question, again, is this: What moves the mind in the sense of producing particular ideas of particular bodies? The initial answer is, obviously: Particular bodies move the mind. Now here is the conclusion we are led to: To say that bodies move the mind is to say that moving bodies move the mind, and this is to say that the motion that differentiates bodies is what moves the mind, and this is to say that what moves the mind is the motion God introduces into the material plenum. There is an order of logical priority here. There would be no particular ideas of particular bodies unless there were particular bodies. The motion *of* bodies produces the ideas. Thus the motion that produces bodies produces particular ideas. The homogeneous mental plenum is differentiated into particular ideas by the motion that differentiates the material plenum into particular bodies. God moves the mind with the motion he introduces into matter.

Thus *all* particular ideas are produced by bodies.

There are extremely serious consequences for Cartesianism in this outcome. I think Descartes is aware of them, but does not work them out because he wants to—and does—claim that human minds have free will. Thus, Cartesian psychology cannot be a strictly deterministic science like physics. Free will is extraneously introduced to the mental plenum just as friction is to the material, and the laws of psychology are no more intrinsic or essential to mere thinking than are the laws of physics to mere extension. Given free will, the laws of thinking must accommodate undetermined inputs. Setting this up systematically would be quite difficult, which is perhaps why Descartes never does it. It may in fact be incoherent.

I conclude by arguing that Descartes's insistence on the interaction of mind and matter forces him to reconcile the two sciences, physics and psychology. Either both are deterministic, or both are not. The evidence is strongest for the view that both are deterministic. This would mean that there are no undetermined thoughts, no free will, a conclusion Descartes does not want to draw.

Descartes talks about reasoning, but he does not go into detail about the dynamics of the mind. We can freely associate ideas in imagination. The most striking manifestation of free will, however, is our apparent ability to move our own body and with it other bodies intentionally, by willing it. The mind evidently has the power to move bodies (reciprocating bodily movements that cause ideas). Descartes says practically nothing about the will's power to move bodies. And most commentators conclude that because mind and body are substantially different, there is no way of explicating *how* they interact.[461] But there is a more crucial reason than this why mind and matter cannot interact: On Descartes's account, the laws of material motion are deterministic; the laws of will are not. Because the movements of bodies are determined, even if the mind could get in there and push, so to speak, it could not penetrate matter unless something gave. Because the quantity of motion is constant, the mind cannot introduce or withdraw motion. Thus some Cartesians suggest that the mind can change the *direction* of motion. But this is impossible, for the production of bodies in the plenum depends on an initial differential introduction of motion in given directions. Not only is quantity of motion determined, but also direction. If a mind changed the determined direction of motion of any body, it would alter the whole material system. There just is no way undetermined will could change the determined motions of bodies in the material system. So we can go beyond the elementary objection that mind and body cannot engage. Even if they could, the material system would repel the advances of mind.

But if anything, Descartes is an Empiricist. Obviously mind and matter interact. Descartes is not going to be satisfied with the impotent occasionalism of Malebranche who shows only how it *appears* that mind and body interact. Descartes insists on robust interaction.

And he can have it if he is willing to pay the price. I argue that Descartes has the integration set up, he just does not want to go the distance. Descartes is first of all a physicist. He is most concerned to detail the science of matter. He posits matter to get rid of the little souls of Scholasticism. He does retain one, the human soul, which unfortunately interferes with the deterministic science of matter.

We have to assume that the two realms, mind and matter, are integrated. The two dynamic systems have to be unified into one system. Either the caprice of free will infects the compound system, or the whole system is deterministic. Now we get down to the ground in answering the question: What moves the mind? The motion that differentiates particular bodies causes particular ideas in the mind. Otherwise the mind would have no content. There would be no differentiation in the mind at all unless bodies acted on it. The ideas the mind has are determined by the determined motion of bodies. These particularly introduced ideas are the primary ontological elements in the system of the mind from which all other ideas—those of memory and imagination—are spun off. Is this spinning off merely capricious? No. We do know some of the laws of the association of ideas. Descartes should face the task of delineating a totally deterministic science of psychology. The particular ideas introduced by the motion of bodies would in turn determine all the flights and fancies of the mind. In a reflex arc the particular ideas introduced would initiate mental responses, such as willings. As there are whorls in matter so bodies can move, there must be circlings of ideas in the mind, so the desiring and willing that flow back to the pivot point of mind/body interaction determine the movements of bodies in lawfully integrated ways. The compound system I am describing is fully deterministic. Psychology is integrated with physics. The motion of bodies initiates an integrated deterministic motion of mind. Cartesian science is unified.

Why not the other way around? In essence, both mind and matter are empty. Deterministic friction is introduced from outside to matter just as free will is introduced from outside to mind. Unification could go either way. Why not make free will dominant and introduce caprice into physics? Descartes does not go that direction. Neither did God, originally. Did He not set the heavens in motion before He introduced human thinking on the scene? In any event, Descartes comes down heaviest on the material side. He has God introduce motion to the material plenum, differentiating bodies. The motion of bodies differentiates the particular ideas of the mind. I argue that this means the circling of ideas in the mental plenum is just as deterministic as the circling of bodies in the material plenum. I do not think Descartes wants to draw this conclusion. But if Cartesian physics is deterministic, and mind and matter interact, that is the way it has to be.

chapter 14

Descartes Knows Nothing

The defense of reason is crucial in maintaining the viability of Cartesian metaphysics because philosophers who take seriously Descartes's admonition "to meditate seriously with me" often find it impossible to reach that "certain and evident knowledge of the truth" that is Descartes's stated goal.[462] There are doubts that Descartes can know anything at all. I contend with these critical philosophers that the First Meditation embeds Descartes so deeply in agnosticism that he can know neither that anything exists, nor, supposing he could know that something exists, what any existing thing is. Descartes is bereft of knowledge both of the existence and of the essence of anything. I conclude that Descartes knows nothing.

I mean three things by "nothing." First, "nothing" means empty of cognitive content. Thus, in "What Moves the Mind? An Excursion in Cartesian Dualism,"[463] I argue that Descartes's innate ideas of mind, matter, and God are vacuous. Descartes's major innate ideas—of thinking, of extension, and of necessary existence—are empty of content, and in this sense Descartes knows nothing of these universal essences.

Second, my arguments may suggest that Descartes opens the door on being as nothingness. Perhaps Descartes knows nothing in this existential sense, but I do not develop that possibility here.

Finally, the primary sense in which Descartes knows nothing is that he knows no thing, neither in essence nor in existence. It is in this failure to know particular things in the world that Cartesian metaphysics breaks down.

The question of existence is metaphysically less crucial than the question of essence. The denial that Descartes can know even that he himself exists, however, appears to be counter-intuitive, so I begin by examining Cartesian reasons for doubting whether anything exists. Then on the assumption that external objects do or can exist, I argue that Descartes cannot know what they are.

That is, I take the metaphysically significant sense of "Descartes knows nothing" to be the claim that even if he knows that something exists, he cannot know what that thing is. So we could give Descartes knowledge of the existence of things. And the point of doing so would be just to show the cognitive vacuity of mere knowledge of existence. A thing of which one knows no characteristics, but only that it exists, is known no better than if it were uncharacterized. What is uncharacterized is nothing, so to know nothing of a thing's characteristics is little better than, if not the same as, to know nothing.

The slippage of language in this last sentence leads to a crucial question, as old as Plato: Can one know that something exists without knowing what it is? Descartes obviously claims that knowledge of the existence of something can be independent of knowledge of its essence. Given this separation, Descartes attempts to make two moves generally thought to be impossible or illegitimate in philosophy: from existence to essence, and from essence to existence.

Using the *cogito*, as foundation, Descartes claims to go from knowledge only of the existence of something to knowledge of what that thing—a thinking mind—is. And in the ontological proof, Descartes tries to go from knowledge only of the essence of something to knowledge that that thing—God—exists. I argue that Descartes fails in these attempts. But more than that, even if he could go from one to the other, after the First Meditation, Descartes can have knowledge of neither essence nor existence of anything.

I

In the First Meditation, Descartes proceeds through several stages of doubt that can be ordered as follows:

1. External things exist with characteristics such as color and shape, and in relations such as cause and effect, but because of the possibility that my senses and reason might provide incorrect reports about these things' sensory and conceptual modes, I cannot know for certain that the external things I am now perceiving and conceiving are as I perceive and conceive them to be.

2. External things exist with sensory and conceptual modes, but because of the possibility that these modes are different from the sensory and conceptual modes through which I perceive and conceive these things, I cannot know for certain that the external things I am now perceiving and conceiving are like my perceptions and conceptions of them.

3. External things exist with characteristics such as color and shape, and in relations such as cause and effect, but because of the possibility that I may be hallucinating or dreaming, I cannot know for certain that the perceptions and conceptions I am now having are of external things that exist.

4. External things might or might not exist with sensory and conceptual modes, but because of the possibility that God, a demon, or I myself might be the cause of the perceptions and conceptions I am now having even if no things exist, I cannot know for certain that any external things exist at all.

In summary, if I assume that I have knowledge that an external thing exists, and of the properties of external things in general, then I can doubt (1) that I have correct knowledge of its properties, (2) that I have any knowledge of its properties, and (3) that I am perceiving and conceiving it or any existing thing. Then if I doubt both that external things exist and that I know their properties in general, I can doubt (4) that I am perceiving and conceiving any existing thing at all. Descartes takes these arguments to be conclusive concerning the dubitabity of knowledge of both the existence and essence of external things.

In the First Meditation, Descartes also casts doubt on reason. In parallel with the above stages, even if I assume that my reasoning processes are generally reliable or consistent, I can still doubt rational inferences because (1) sometimes I make mistakes and have lapses of memory, (2) the relations among existing things may differ from representations of them by reason, and (3) reasoning while hallucinating and dreaming may be of nonexistent things. Finally, (4) because of the possibility of the demon, I can doubt that I am reasoning about any existing things at all. Descartes later substantiates this fourth possibility by insisting on a voluntaristic God Who can create things whose descriptions are contradictory to our reason, or that we cannot conceive of without contradiction.[464]

II

What happens if these reasons for doubt are taken seriously? First, consider the fallibility of memory. In his *Censura philosophiae Cartesianae*, Pierre Daniel Huet attacks Descartes by insisting on the activity or discursiveness of all thinking, even of those thoughts expressing simple relations.[465] Huet suggests that as an argument, the *cogito* cannot be expressed as "I think, therefore I am," but rather in some such form as, "I think, therefore I was," or "I think, therefore I will be," or "I thought, therefore I was," or "I thought, therefore I am," or "I thought, therefore I will be," but never "I think" and "I am" in the same moment. The two members of all of the above expressions are different thoughts separated in time. The conclusion of any argument is always dubitable because, as Descartes himself admits, discursive reasoning is dependent on memory which is not trustworthy from moment to moment.

Descartes very soon denies that the *cogito* is an argument.[466] The *cogito* may be expressed in the form of an argument, but when pressed Descartes claims that he knows his own existence by intuition. Every momentary act of thinking that I exist—even that of doubting it—involves the apodictic certainty that I do exist.[467] Descartes thus tries to save knowledge of his own existence by eliminating a dubitable discursive argument and basing certainty on instantaneous intuition.

Elsewhere, however, Descartes claims that we can grasp arguments atemporally and thus avoid the doubts attendant on discursive reasoning. He urges us to practice intuiting even extensive arguments all at once, in a single intuition.[468] Thus even if the *cogito* were an argument, we could intuit the truth of "Everything that thinks exists; I think; therefore, I exist." Fallible memory is foiled.

Alas, a problem remains. Suppose the *cogito* is not an argument. Eliminate "therefore." We still have a complex proposition, "I think, I am." In the instantaneous intuition of this proposition we still must grasp the relation between "I think" or a thing that is thinking, and "I am" or a thing's existence. Descartes himself admits that reason can be deceived in its comprehension of the relations of compatibility or logical connection even of two simple ideas intuited at the same moment. So whether the *cogito* is either an argument or merely two related concepts, grasping it intuitively does not guarantee its truth.

Thus, when thinking and thinker are put in relation—discursively or logically—this attribution of relation can then be doubted either by challenging memory required in following an argument, or by challenging reason required in recognizing logical connection. That is, even if memory were trustworthy, I can doubt that a thinker exists because I could be wrong about the relation between thinking and thinkers. And this on two levels: Acts may generally imply actors, but I could be mistaken in this specific case. On a deeper level—think of the Eucharist[469]—God may have created this act without an actor, this property without a supporting substance, this thinking without a thinker.

Moreover, even supposing there is a thinker, how do I know that this thinker is I? Again I could be mistaken, or God could have done what is contradictory to our reason but is not impossible for God, acquaint me with some thinking that appears to be mine but really belongs to another, or even to no one at all.

Because the thinker is separate or distinguishable from the thinking, one can know neither that something is thinking nor who is thinking. Hume was by far not the first to look within and not find himself. Descartes cannot know that the thing whose existence and essence he thinks he knows is himself.

Following the arguments above, I conclude that by the time Descartes asks "qu'est-ce donc que je suis?" and discovers that he is "Une chose qui pense,"[470] he has gone far beyond the limits that serious consideration of his reasons for doubting experience and reason demand. Even supposing that Descartes knows that something exists, to assert what this something is, that it is a mind or soul or self or thinking thing, is to claim to know how it is characterized, and Descartes himself has forever put a gulf between our representative perceptions and conceptions on the one side, and the true nature of the things that may or may not exist on the other side. Two philosophers who take him seriously on this are Locke and Kant. They see that even if the *ego* is an internal thing, it is still external to the perceptions and conceptions representative of it. Another who sees this is Descartes's deviant disciple, Malebranche, who deduces as a major implication of the First Meditation that the essence of mind—like the essence of body—is unknown unless and until revealed by God.[471]

Descartes cannot know that he exists because this knowledge depends on either experience, memory, or reason, all dubitable according to (1), (2), (3), and (4) above; nor can he know what he is, for ultimately this depends on trust in the verisimilitude of an idea of mind, which is most thoroughly ruled out by argument (4). The crux of Huet's objection is that the setting of two notions in relation is both discursive and complex, and if discursive then memory can fail, and if complex then reason can fail. "I think" and "I am" are distinct notions; the *cogito* is thus a dubitable proposition; thus I can doubt my own existence.

III

Is there a way out? It certainly is not through what must be one of the most difficult discursive arguments in the literature, Descartes's attempted demonstration that clarity and distinctness are the criteria of certainty.[472] This argument is valid, but as also in the case of Arnauld's circle,[473] it is clearly ingenuous if not illegitimate to use reason to establish criteria to be used in turn to certify reason when reason itself is in doubt. Does Descartes forget his reasons for doubting reason? No. I think Descartes expects to be saved by intuition.

Consider: If the existence of God is assured by discursive argument, then it can be challenged on grounds of possible memory failure. But suppose we know God's existence by intuitive grasp of an argument or logical relation all at once. Then it can be doubted on the possibility that reason is relating two items—God and existence—incorrectly. This possible error can be avoided, however, if, as in the ontological proof, God's existence and his essence are identical.[474] Descartes would have to argue that here one does not see that two items are related, but rather that one intuits a single, simple idea. God's essence is existence. In connotation, to know the idea of God is equivalent to knowing the idea of necessary existence. In denotation, the idea of God refers to a necessarily existent thing. If I have an idea of God, then I know that He exists. But what is He? He is existence, necessary existence. And if the equation of identity holds, one cannot in this instance argue that it is impossible or illegitimate to go from knowledge of essence to knowledge of existence or vice versa. They are the same.

But Descartes fails even here. The idea we have of God could be without referent, deceptively emplaced by the demon or by God Himself. We could intuit God's existence and simply be deceived, even if our reason informs us that it is a contradiction to conceive of a nonexisting God. Again, to intuit God's necessary existence, Descartes must equate His perfection with His existence. Then if the idea of His perfection includes any content other than that He exists—for example, that He is not a deceiver—the idea of God would be complex and thus dubitable because of possible confusions of reason.

Finally, suppose that we accept the proof of God's existence. If the idea of God is merely the idea of existence, even necessary existence, is it not vacuous? Sheer existence is without character, and thus is unknowable as a thing. Existence is not a thing. As remarked above, I argue for the emptiness of content of Descartes's idea of existence in "What Moves the Mind?" And it seems to me that it is fair to say that to know the mere existence of God is to know nothing.

This is to present the ontological proof as Descartes's supreme attempt to make it impossible in this case to drive a wedge between knowing that something exists and knowing what it is, for God is His existence. The idea of God is simple in the sense of noncomplex. But since propositions such as the *cogito* are complex, Descartes says that only what is comprehensible—or clear and distinct—in nondiscursive intuition is certain. The noncomplex thus merges with anything complex that can be comprehended in intuition as though it were simple.

To complete this picture, I suggest that Descartes further claims that the ideas of God, mind, and matter are innate in order to avoid at least those sceptical problems that would arise if they were said to be caused by perceptual and abstractive processes.

If one could trust innate ideas, then, in the order of knowledge God would be best known, for the idea of God is a simple identity of essence and existence that is open to immediate intuition. Next, mind is better known than body, because—Descartes claims—we can intuit both the existence and the essence of mind. But Descartes believes that he has an intuitive grasp only of the essence and not of the existence of matter.

Descartes's interpretation of the *cogito* as intuited is thus seen as an attempt to gain knowledge that something exists, a gambit at least as old as Augustine. The gambit does not work, but even if did, one could not proceed metaphysically because of inability to know what the essence is of this thing that exists. The offering of innate ideas of mind, matter, and God is inadequate because their source and application are dubitable. A stronger move is to provide in one intuition knowledge both of essence and of existence, and this is done in the ontological proof of God. And here to escape problems of discursiveness and of complexity, the intuition is of a single notion, necessary existence, which is both God's essence and His existence.

I argue above that Descartes fails to grasp either his own existence or essence intuitively. And I stress that innate ideas are not as such guarantors of certain knowledge, for either the demon or God could have made them appear to refer to existents when they do not. Given these difficulties, Descartes's attempted way out of scepticism is by way of intuitive knowledge of the innate simple idea of God that presumably is not susceptible to mistake, misinterpretation, memory failure, or deception. But even were this true, the idea of sheer existence is contentless, so in the end Descartes knows nothing.

IV

Suppose one could intuit that something exists. I present Descartes here as making the claim for this intuition in two instances, in the *cogito* for his own existence, and in the ontological proof for God's existence. Descartes himself makes the case that these two existents can be reached in the same intuition, that in intuiting his own existence he also intuits God's existence.[475] Can two separate entities be known to exist in a single intuition? Given that we are not certain that we know the true essence of mind, but we do know in the *cogito* that something exists, and given that God's essence just is His existence which we know intuitively also in the *cogito*, then perhaps the "I" being intuited is not an individual mind or soul, but—as Spinoza posits—merely a mode of an attribute of God. Not "I think" but "It thinks." But this—on Descartes's sceptical grounds—would be much less than Spinoza himself provides, for all that is known is that something exists, not what it is, not that its essence is thinking or extension or anything other than existence itself.

What I contend above is that because Descartes cannot argue to the conclusion that he exists, he claims that he intuits that he exists. And because he cannot argue to the conclusion that his essence is thinking, he provides the innate idea of mind. Also, Descartes cannot argue to the conclusion that God exists, so he says that he intuits that God exists. And he cannot argue to the conclusion that God's essence is existence, so he identifies the innate idea of God with the idea of necessary existence, which means that in intuiting God's existence he intuits God's essence at the same time. Finally, if intuiting that I exist is a part or the whole of intuiting that God necessarily exists, then it may be that there is only one primary intuition. I might be mistaken in thinking that I exist. Perhaps in the *cogito* I discover only that God exists.

The conclusion I take to be devastating to Cartesian metaphysics is that even if Descartes knows that he exists and/or that God exists, he can know nothing about what either of these existing things is. He cannot know his own essence, and the essence of God is mere existence. God is not characterized substantively. And thus we come again to the crux: Descartes wants to claim that knowledge that something exists is certain and metaphysically foundational. It might be allowed to be certain, but how can it be foundational? Descartes tries to provide a foundation by contending that God's essence is His existence, so that here knowledge of existence is knowledge of essence. But knowledge of mere existence is knowledge of nothing rather than knowledge of something. Descartes has no knowledge of anything of which he knows what it is. He cannot know even that what exists is a thing.

V

Supposing that Descartes has knowledge of finite existents, what he then needs is intuitive certainty about the essences of existing mind and matter. But Descartes shows how to doubt that any thing has the essence of matter, and Malebranche goes on to doubt that we know the essence of mind.

I show above that Descartes's argument that in knowing God's essence we know that He exists because His essence = existence provides no substantive knowledge of God, because existence is not a *what*. Existence is neither characterized nor does it characterize anything. Gassendi and Kant firmly separate the what of a thing from its existence, so that we can discuss modes, attributes, properties, natures, and essences without knowing whether anything so characterized exists. The ontological proof does suggest, however, that in knowing that a thing exists, we might have a way of knowing what it is. Knowledge of an existent thing could give knowledge of essence if the existent thing is a substance and substance = essence.

Thus in an heroic attempt to avoid doubt about finite essences, Descartes equates the essences of mind and matter not with the existence *per se* of these things, but with their substances. He says that thinking just *is* the substance mind, and extension just *is* the substance matter.[476] This equation of essence and substance—like the equation of God's essence and existence—can be seen as an attempt to avoid sceptical attack as follows.

If the essence and substance of the mind are the same, then Descartes encounters his mind's substance in intuiting that he exists, and in grasping this existent substance he also grasps its essence. And so in the single intuition of the *cogito*, Descartes knows not only that he exists, but also what he is, a thinking thing.

Consider that if essences of things were separable or distinguishable from substances of things, then it would be possible to be mistaken about an existing thing's essence. One might be misled into speculating, for example, that matter can think. And one might possibly apprehend an essence when there is no substance there at all. Descartes would certainly want to avoid such a separation because it makes knowledge of the mind's essence dubitable to (1), (2), (3), and (4) listed above. (Descartes finds such a separation in the Scholastics' use of unsupported substantial accidents to explain transubstantiation to be absurd.[477]) If one does not separate substance and essence—as Descartes does not—and if in intuiting the existence of a substance one also intuits its essence (if its essence is, so to speak, its existent substance), then one gets *what* with *that*, knowledge of essence at the same time as knowledge of existence. This is one explanation of why Descartes wants to say that mind just *is* thinking, and matter just *is* extension. Then if one does intuit the existence of a substance, one necessarily also at the same time intuits its essence, and then one does know something more than mere existence.

But attempts based on essence being identical to substance fail. The case of matter shows the primary reason why. Suppose there were no existing matter. Could we still intuit the essence of matter? Yes, because there is an innate idea of matter. Thus we can have knowledge of intelligible extension even if no sensible extension or material world exists. In this case we cannot go from the essence to the existence of finite substance. The ability to think about the essences of possibly nonexistent substances makes it possible always to ask how one knows that the essence that is being intuited at the same time one intuits that something exists is the essence of just that existent thing. Descartes accepts this impasse for matter.

But Descartes claims that we can go from the intuition of the existence of finite substance to intuition of or knowledge of the essence of finite substance in the case of mind. (Presumably we could also go from the intuition of the existence of matter to knowledge of the essence of matter if we could intuit the existence of matter, which we cannot.) Descartes insists that he or "I" cannot intuit the essence of mind without a mind's existing, for intuiting is thinking which is identical with an existing mind. So in knowing the essence of mind, do I know that a mind exists? No. Because essence and existence are not identical for mind, intuiting essence is not the same as intuiting existence in the case of mind (nor is it in the case of matter).

More than that, one cannot go even from *intuiting* the essence or existence of mind (or of anything) to knowing that a mind exists. I may appear to exist when thinking or intuiting is going on, but no mind is necessary: God could make a thought of a mind even though no mind exists. Descartes never succeeds in equating—or in making intelligible his attempted equation of—essence and substance in the cases of mind and matter, no more than he does in his attempt to equate essence and existence in the case of God.

VI

Knowledge of existence and essence are separate, not merely because given an essence, the existence of something with that essence is merely possible, but also because given an existent, Descartes's totally free voluntarist God is not committed to the existent's being of this or that essence: It could be of any essence, or of none at all. So the arguments that Descartes cannot reason or intuit that if he is thinking, then he is a thinking thing, do not get to the depth of Cartesian nescience. It is not just that you might be wrong, but more that God is not committed to giving the essence of a thinking thing to the existing thing that thinks. And given that the essence of God Himself is only existence, He is not committed to giving any existent any essence at all beyond its sheer existence. If the way to know what something is, is to know its essence, and not merely that it exists, then we cannot ever know for sure what anything is.

Descartes reaches this impasse in some part by insisting on God's infinite power to do anything. This voluntarism is the ground from which the demon rises. Thus in rejecting the possibility that independent of God there are eternal essences (for example, noncontradictory eternal truths), Descartes goes to the other extreme of positing an existing God that is independent of—even void of—all essence. Descartes's God of sheer unrestricted existence must be void of characterizing essence, otherwise He cannot be free to do or be as He wills. And of course this is a way of giving ontological underpinning to the doctrine of negative theology. God is totally unlike any attribution of essence that we could make of him, not merely because the essences we know are finite or otherwise different from God's essence, but because God has no characterizing essence at all.

Descartes thus can know nothing of God, nor of mind, nor of matter. Neither essence nor existence of any thing can be known. This is the final breakdown of Cartesian metaphysics. It is impossible for a Cartesian even to begin.

VII

It is hard to avoid some such conclusions as these. And yet, nothing so indicates the pervasive intent of philosophers to get on with the tasks of system, truth, and knowledge, as does the denial of the strength and import of Descartes's scepticism. Having read a great quantity (but far from all) of the secondary literature on Descartes, I am impressed with how protective it is of the great man, how the commentators shield him from his own method of doubt.[478] Descartes is, of course, a genius, and we all know that Western philosophy is in many ways ineradicably Cartesian. Nevertheless, Descartes literally knows nothing. Reason fails him, and he never attains certainty *about* *anything*. He knows it. His contemporaries know it. And his commentators know it. I show it.

In the end, why do so many of Descartes's commentators come to the defense of reason? Why, for that matter, does Descartes take scepticism so seriously? As Desmond M. Clarke shows so competently, Descartes is quite happy with probabilistic "moral" certainty in empirical science.[479] What could be so important that Descartes would be concerned also to find "absolute" certainty? A clear answer is provided by Richard H. Popkin, who shows the religious origin of Descartes's *Meditations*.[480] Descartes is concerned about salvation.

Probabilism is all very well in natural science. But in saving one's soul, it is important to know which is the true religion. This is an answer to the question that puzzles many twentieth-century philosophers as to why anyone would bother to search for certainty or take scepticism seriously. The theological implications of Cartesian dualism—and scepticism—are profound. Descartes's was the first modern attempt to provide a metaphysical foundation for religion. Descartes delved deeper than most philosophers have since, and thus his empty results are the more resounding. Nobody needs certainty for science. But as both Pascal and Kierkegaard betray, only certainty is satisfactory for religion. Descartes's goal is certainty but his lot is doubt. This is the final breakdown of Cartesian metaphysics.

Notes

Chapter 1

Full data on works cited throughout this book are given in the Bibliography.

1. Norman Kemp Smith, *Studies in the Cartesian Philosophy*.
2. Richard A. Popkin, *The History of Scepticism from Erasmus to Descartes*; *The History of Scepticism from Erasmus to Spinoza*.
3. Wilfrid Sellers, *Philosophical Perspectives*.
4. Jaakko Hintikka, "*Cogito, Ergo, Sum*: Inference or Performance?."
5. Gustav Bergmann, "Some Remarks on the Philosophy of Malebranche."
6. *Ibid.*
7. Bertrand Russell, *A Critical Exposition of the Philosophy of Leibniz*.
8. Robert G. Turnbull, in classes I took from him at the University of Iowa in the 1950s. I learned about structural history from Bergmann, and while writing my M.A. thesis with Turnbull.
9. Two excellent, recent examples of this approach by young scholars are: Brian E. O'Neil, *Epistemological Direct Realism in Descartes' Philosophy* and Daisie Radner, *Malebranche: A Study of a Cartesian System*.
10. Richard A. Watson, *The Downfall of Cartesianism, 1673–1712: A Study of Epistemological Issues in Late Seventeenth-Century Cartesianism*. Revised as Part Two, herein.
11. Gregor Sebba, "What is 'History of Philosophy'?."
12. *Ibid.*, p. 252.
13. *Ibid.*
14. Jack W. Meiland, *Scepticism and Historical Knowledge*.
15. But they can be extensive. See: Hugh Trevor-Roper, *Hermit of Peking: The Hidden Life of Sir Edmund Backhouse*.
16. Sara K. Shute made detailed criticisms of several versions of this chapter and has serious reservations about my claim that formal analyses depend on historical contexts. I also appreciate commentary on earlier versions by Edwin B. Allaire, Harry M. Bracken, James E. Force, Jack W. Meiland, David Fate Norton, Jerome P. Schiller, and Margaret D. Wilson.

Chapter 2

17. Smith, *Studies in the Cartesian Philosophy*.
18. As scientists, Cartesians are satisfied with probabilism. See chap. 6 herein and *Descartes's Philosophy of Science* by Desmond M. Clarke.
19. For a more expanded account see, *e.g*, chaps. 9 and 10 of S. J. Curtis's *Short History of Western Philosophy in the Middle Ages*.
20. Translated from *Il Saggiatore* by Edwin Arthur Burtt in *The Metaphysical Foundations of Modern Physical Science*, p. 75.
21. *Ibid.* p. 78.
22. See Burtt, *Metaphysical Foundations*; Crombie, "Galileo Galilei; A Philosophical Symbol"; and Koyré, "Galileo and Plato."
23. Brett, *Philosophy of Gassendi*, pp. 63 ff.; Thomas, *Philosophie de Gassendi*, pp. 80 ff.
24. Gassendi, *Dissertations*, p. 474.
25. Thomas, *Philosophie de Gassendi*, pp. 83 ff., 122, 137.
26. Brett, *Philosophy of Gassendi*, pp. 72 ff.
27. Mandon, *Étude sur le syntagma philosophicum de Gassendi*, p. 76.

Chapter 3

28. Previous studies of Foucher are: Rabbe, *Étude philosophique*; Gouhier, "La première polémique de Malebranche"; Popkin, "L'abbé Foucher et le problème de qualités premières"; and in Popkin, "The Sceptical Crisis and the Rise of Modern Philosophy, III." The biographical information that follows is taken primarily from these studies as well as from Bouillier, *Histoire de la philosophie cartésienne*.
29. Baillet, *La vie de monsieur Descartes*, pt. 2, p. 439.
30. Rabbe, *Étude philosophique*, p. 5.
31. Gouhier, "La première polémique de Malebranche," pp. 31 ff.
32. Foucher, *Sur la mort de la reine* and *De la sagesse des anciens*. The drama is entitled *L'Empereur Leonce*.
33. Huet to Nicaise, 25 juillet 1687, in Cousin, *Fragments philosophiques*, vol. 3, pp. 153–154; quoted in Rabbe, *Étude philosophique*, p. x.
34. Menage, *Menagiana*, pp. 358 ff. Menage says Foucher "sçat parfaitement l'histoire des Philosophes" and ranks him side by side with Huet as historian.
35. Barber, *Leibniz in France from Arnauld to Voltaire*, pp. 4 ff.
36. Leibniz, "Extrait d'une lettre . . . sur quelques axiomes de philosophie"; Foucher, "Extrait d'une lettre . . . sur quelques axiomes de philosophie"; Leibniz, "Réponse"; Leibniz, "Sistême nouveau"; Foucher, "Réponse"; Leibniz, "Eclaircissement."
37. Foucher *Sur la mort de la reine*.
38. *Ibid.* p. 3.
39. Foucher, *Traité des hygrometres*.
40. Foucher au Leibniz [1685?], in Gerhardt, *Philosophischen Schriften*, vol. 1, pp. 379–380.
41. Foucher au Leibniz, 8 decembre 1684, in Gerhardt, *Philosophischen Schriften*, vol. 1, pp. 376–378.
42. Ouvrard au Nicaise, 24 septembre 1675, in Cousin, *Fragments philosophiques*, vol. 3, pp. 154–155; quoted in Rabbe, *Étude philosophique*, pp. 7–8.
43. Foucher, *De la sagesse es anciens* and *Lettre sur la morale des Confucius*.
44. Leibniz au Nicaise, 1697; quoted in Rabbe, *Étude philosophique*, p. VIII.
45. Foucher au Leibniz, 5 mai 1687, in Gerhardt, *Philosophischen Schriften*, vol. 1, pp. 388–389.
46. Foucher, *Histoire*, p. 10.
47. Foucher, *Apologie*, pp. 31–32.
48. *Ibid.* p. 83.
49. *Ibid.* p. 25.
50. Foucher, *Histoire*, p. 67.
51. Foucher, *Apologie*, pp. 31, 38.
52. *Ibid.* p. 31.
53. *Ibid.* pp. viii–ix.
54. Foucher, *Histoire*, p. 80.
55. Foucher, *Apologie*, p. 56.
56. *Ibid.* pp. 5–8, 44–45.
57. *Ibid.* pp. 88, 102, 107; Foucher au Leibniz, aoust 1692, in Gerhardt, *Philosophischen Schriften*, vol. 1, pp. 406–409.
58. Foucher, *Apologie*, p. 47; *Histoire*, p. 217.
59. Foucher, *Apologie*, p. 12.
60. *Ibid.* p. 102–103.
61. *Ibid.* p. 108. Menage, *Menagiana*, pp. 360–361, reports similar comments by Foucher on the subject of two logics. Academic logic "enseigne à découvrir la verité & . . à bien penétrer les principes." Such a logic is possible, Foucher says, "par après tout, les idées component les paroles & le language de l'esprit." Thus, "il est nécessaire de travailler à une *Grammaire des Idées*."
62. Foucher, *Apologie*, pp. 36, 46.
63. Foucher, *Histoire*, pp. 140.
64. Foucher, *Apologie*, p. 72.

65. *Ibid.* p. 129.
66. Foucher, *Histoire*, pp. 132–133.
67. *Ibid.* p. 120.
68. Foucher, *Apologie*, p. 75.
69. Foucher, *Histoire*, pp. 140, 199.
70. Foucher, *Apologie*, pp. 91–93.
71. Foucher, *Histoire*, p. 141.
72. *Ibid.* pp. 196–198.
73. Foucher, *Apologie*, p. 154.
74. *Ibid.* p. 86.
75. *Ibid.* pp. 86–87.
76. *Ibid.* p. 88.
77. *Ibid.* pp. 90–91.
78. *Ibid.* p. 95.
79. *Ibid.* p. 100.
80. *Ibid.* p. 87.
81. *Ibid.* pp. 152, 156.
82. *Ibid.* pp. 148–149.
83. *Ibid.* pp. 145–146.
84. *Ibid.* pp. 12–13.
85. *Ibid.* pp. 121–130.
86. Foucher, *Histoire*, pp. 187–188.
87. Foucher, *Apologie*, pp. 131–132, 135, 137, 140–141, 147.
88. Foucher, *Histoire*, p. 187.
89. Foucher, *Apologie*, pp. 111–112.
90. Foucher, *Histoire*, p. 76.
91. Foucher, *Apologie*, p. 113.
92. Foucher, *Histoire*, p. 92.
93. Foucher, *Apologie*, p. 85.
94. Foucher, *Histoire*, pp. 187–188.

Chapter 4

95. Le Grand, *An Entire Body of Philosophy*; Malebranche, *De la recherche de la vérité*; Desgabets, *Critique de la critique de la recherche*; Desgabets, *Supplément*; La Forge, *Traitté de l'âme humaine*; Rohault, *Traité de physique*; Régis, *Systême de philosophie*; Arnauld, *Des vrayes et des fausses idées.*
96. On Foucher see Chapter 3.
97. Lamaire, *Le cartésianisme chez les Bénédictins*, pp. 39–42.
98. *Ibid.* p. 149.
99. La Forge, *Traitté de l'âme humaine*, in *Oeuvres philosophiques*, p. 209.
100. Foucher, *Critique de la recherche*, pp. 44 ff.
101. Du Hamel, *Réflexions critique*; Bayle, "Pyrrhon," remark B, and "Zeno d'Elee," remarks G and H, in *Dictionnare*; Huet, *Censura Philosophia Cartesianae.*
102. Foucher, *Histoire*, pp. 187–188.

Chapter 5

103. The first volume of the first edition of 1674 is available in vol. 1 of *Oeuvres complètes de Malebranche*, ed. André Robinet. All references hereafter to the *Recherche* are to this edition.
104. Hereafter cited as *Critique.*
105. Malebranche, "Preface," p. 496.

106. Malebranche, *Recherche*, p. 43.
107. *Ibid.*
108. *Ibid.* p. 42.
109. *Ibid.* p. 67.
110. *Ibid.* pp. 78–79.
111. *Ibid.* p. 79.
112. *Ibid.* p. 84.
113. *Ibid.* p. 92.
114. *Ibid.* p. 122.
115. *Ibid.* p. 66.
116. *Ibid.*
117. *Ibid.* p. 381.
118. *Ibid.* p. 415.
119. *Ibid.* pp. 413–414.
120. *Ibid.* pp. 425–426.
121. *Ibid.* p. 431.
122. *Ibid.* p. 433.
123. *Ibid.* p. 408.
124. *Ibid.* p. 437.
125. *Ibid.* p. 445.
126. *Ibid.* p. 450.
127. *Ibid.* pp. 442–443.
128. Foucher, *Apologie*, pp. 5–8, 44–45.
129. Foucher, *Critique* p. 4.
130. *Ibid.* p. 13.
131. *Ibid.* pp. 21, 25, 32, 36, 44, 50, 62.
132. *Ibid.* pp. 44–45.
133. *Ibid.* p. 47.
134. *Ibid.* pp. 48–49.
135. *Ibid.* pp. 32–33.
136. *Ibid.* pp. 50–52.
137. *Ibid.* p. 52.
138. *Ibid.* pp. 53–56.
139. *Ibid.* pp. 56–60.
140. *Ibid.* pp. 61–64.
141. *Ibid.* pp. 64–66, 77–78. (The pagination jumps from 66 to 77 although the text is continuous.)
142. *Ibid.* pp. 79–80.
143. Malebranche, "Preface," pp. 495–496.
144. *Ibid.* p. 498.
145. *Ibid.* p. 496.
146. Malebranche, *Recherche*, pp. 162–164.
147. *Ibid.* p. 445.
148. Foucher, *Critique*, pp. 116–119.
149. *Ibid.* pp. 119–120.
150. *Ibid.* p. 122.
151. Malebranche, "Preface," pp. 496–497.
152. Gouhier, "La première polémique de Malebranche," p. 35.
153. Malebranche, "Preface," p. 497.
154. Ouvrard au Nicaise, 24 septembre 1675, in Cousin, *Fragments philosophiques*, vol. 3, pp. 154–155.
155. Malebranche, *Recherche*, p. xxvii.
156. *Réponse pour la critique à la preface*, pp. xiv, xx, 4, 6.
157. *Ibid.* pp. 17–20, 26, 29, 42.
158. *Ibid.* pp. 103–108. For further examination of this point, see Chapter 8.
159. *Réponse pour la critique à la preface*, pp. 112–113.

160. *Ibid.* p. 107.
161. *Ibid.* pp. 40–43.
162. Foucher au Leibniz, [1685?], in Gerhardt, *Philosophischen Schriften*, vol. 1, p. 379.
163. Foucher au Leibniz, 28 avril 1695, in Gerhardt, *Philosophischen Schriften*, vol. 1, p. 422. Foucher altered the terminology of Sextus Empiricus. According to Sextus, Pyrrhonists doubt that they know anything, while Academic sceptics dogmatically assert that nothing can be known. Foucher called dogmatic sceptics Pyrrhonists and referred to his own mitigated scepticism as Academic philosophy.
164. Foucher au Leibniz, decembre 1684, in Gerhardt, *Philosophischen Schriften*, vol. 1, pp. 377–378.
165. Foucher au Leibniz, 12 aoust 1678, in Gerhardt, *Philosophischen Schriften*, vol. 1, p. 375.
166. Foucher au Leibniz, 26 avril 1679, in Gerhardt, *Philosophischen Schriften*, vol. 1, p. 376.
167. *Ibid.*
168. Foucher, *Critique*, pp. 20–23; *Réponse pour la critique à la preface*, pp. 13–14, 80–82.
169. Foucher, *Critique*, pp. 21, 44–50; Foucher au Leibniz, 30 mai 1691, in Gerhardt, *Philosophischen Schriften*, vol. 1, pp. 397–399.
170. Foucher, *Apologie*, p. 156.

Chapter 6

171. Desgabets, *Critique de la critique de la recherche*.
172. A study of Desgabets and many writings not published during his lifetime are found in Lemaire, *Le cartésianism chez le Bénédictins*. See also Armogathe, *Theologia Cartesiana*, and Bouillier, *Histoire de la philosophie cartésienne*. Quotations that follow from Desgabets's *Supplement* are taken from the many selections in Lemaire.
173. Desgabets, *Supplement*, p. 150.
174. *Ibid.* pp. 197–198.
175. *Ibid.* pp. 149, 178–179.
176. Desgabets, *Critique de la critique de la recherche*, pp. 6, 16, 27.
177. *Ibid.* p. 55.
178. *Ibid.* p. 96.
179. *Ibid.* p. 103.
180. *Ibid.* pp. 115–117.
181. *Ibid.* pp. 119–120.
182. *Ibid.* p. 121.
183. *Ibid.* p. 107.
184. *Ibid.* p. 12.
185. *Ibid.* p. 165.
186. *Ibid.* pp. 202–203.
187. *Ibid.* pp. 200-201.
188. Foucher, *Réponse à la critique de la critique de la recherche*, pp. 30–31.
189. *Ibid.* p. 53.
190. *Ibid.* pp. 71–88.
191. *Ibid.* pp. 42–46.
192. *Ibid.* p. 59.
193. *Ibid.* pp. 34–35.
194. *Ibid.* p. 35.
195. Desgabets, *Supplement*, p. 179.
196. Desgabets, *Supplement*, p. 179.
197. On La Forge, see Balz, "Louis de La Forge and the Critique of Substantial Forms"; Bouillier, *Histoire de la philosophie cartésienne*; Clair (ed.), *Oeuvres philosophiques: Louis de la Forge*; Damiron, *Essai sur l'histoire de la philosophie*.
198. La Forge, *Traitté de l'âme humaine*, in *Oeuvres philosophiques*, ed., Pierre Clair, pp. 165–167.

199. *Ibid.* pp. 112, 173.
200. *Ibid.* pp. 157 ff.
201. *Ibid.* p. 175.
202. *Ibid.* p. 173.
203. *Ibid.* p. 175.
204. *Ibid.* pp. 173 ff.
205. Bouillier, *Histoire de la philosophie cartésienne*, vol. 1, p. 503.
206. Damiron, *Essai sur l'histoire de la philosophie*, vol. 2, p. 458.
207. On Rohault see Balz, "Clerselier, 1614–1685, and Rohault, 1620–1675"; Bouillier, *Histoire de la philosophie cartésienne*; Damiron, *Essai sur l'histoire de la philosophie*; Mouy, *Le dévelopment de la physique cartésienne.*
208. Rohault, *System of Natural Philosophy*, trans. John Clarke. (I use the English translation because the copy of the French original in the Bibliothèque Nationale was either lost or misplaced at the time I did my research there, and I have not been able to locate another copy.)
209. *Ibid.* pp. 23–24.
210. *Ibid.* pp. 115, 118, 248.
211. *Ibid.* p. 119.
212. *Ibid.* pp. 236–237.
213. *Ibid.* pp. 245–246, 248.
214. Foucher, *Critique de la recherche*, pp. 64–66, 77–80. (Because of a pagination mistake there are no pages numbered 67–76.)
215. Rohault, *System of Natural Philosophy*, p. 11.
216. On Régis see Bouillier, *Histoire de la philosophie cartésienne*; Damiron, *Essai sur l'histoire de la philosophie*; Mouy, *Le développement de la physique cartésienne*; Fontenelle, "Éloge de Régis."
217. Régis believes that his *Système de philosophie, contenant la logique, la metaphysique, la physique, et la morale* is one of the first and most complete of its kind. "*Nous entendons par SYSTEME,*" he says, "non une seule hypothese, mais'un amas de plusieurs hypotheses dependantes les unes des autres, & tellement liées avec les premieres vérités qu'elles en soient comme des suites & des dependances nécessaires" (*Système*, vol. 1, pp. 275–276). Régis provides an entire interrelated system of philosophy. He begins with logic which treats of self-evident principles. His metaphysics is derived from these logical principles. Then the physics is grounded in the truths of metaphysics, and finally his moral philosophy is derived from the truths of physics: "Ainsi la Morale suppose la Physique; la Physique suppose la Métaphysique; & la Métaphysique la Logique: & par ce moyen toutes les parties de la Philosophie ont un tel rapport, & une telle liaison ensemble, que j'ay crû que le tout que resulte de leur assemblage, pouvoit justement estre appellé *le Système générale de la Philosophie.* C'est par ce Système qu'on pourra réduire les vérités les plus élognees aux premieres principes" (*Système*, vol. 1, p. x). Régis thus sees all knowledge as comprehended in one complete system. One can have certain knowledge, and contrary to Mouy's interpretation in his *Le développement de la physique cartésienne* (p. 166), Régis's physics is not probabilistic, but only problematic. Régis is a true rationalistic physicist. See my article "A Note on the Probabilistic Physics of Régis."
218. Régis, *Système de philosophie*, vol. 1, pp. 73–74.
219. *Ibid.* p. 77.
220. Mouy thinks it does (*Le développement de la physique cartésienne*, pp. 148–149).

In explaining how complex ideas are composed of simple ideas, Régis points out that one must be careful to determine whether or not complex "idées sont véritablement claires toutes les fois qu'elles paroissent l'estre . . . car une idée peut estre composée d'un si grand nombre d'autres idées que l'esprit n'aura pas assez d'étenduë pour les embrasser toutes à la fois; c'est ce que l'experience fait voir en une figure de mille côtez, l'idée de laquelle ne nous représente pas plus clairement cette figure qu'un autre figure d'un nombre de côtez different." (*Système*, vol. 1, p. 49). Mouy takes this passage to mean that Régis does not distinguish ideas from pictorial images. But this is clearly not Régis's meaning. For Régis, the division between simple and complex ideas is made on what the soul can understand in a single action. Ideas of simple geometric figures can be, but ideas of complex geometric figures composed of simple ones cannot be understood in a single action, but must be pondered over. Another example Régis might accept is that of the simple idea of a wheel compared to the complex idea of a clock.

221. Régis, *Système de philosophie*, vol. 1, pp. 180–181.
222. *Ibid.* pp. 112–133. Régis, *L'Usage de la raison et de la foy*, pp. 1–10.
223. Régis, *L'Usage de la raison et de la foy*, pp. vi–vii, 90–95.
224. Régis, *Système de philosophie*. vol. 1, pp. 162–163.
225. Du Hamel, *Réflexions critiques*, pp. 33–35.
226. *Ibid.* pp. 27–28.
227. *Ibid.* pp. 30–41.
228. Régis, *Réponse aux réflexions critiques*, pp. 8–11.
229. Du Hamel, *Lettre*, p. 16.
230. On Le Grand see Bouillier, *Histoire de la philosophie cartésienne*; Sidney Lee, *Dictionary of National Biography; Nouvelle biographie générale.*
231. Le Grand, *An Entire Body of Philosophy*, bk 1, pp. 1–2.
232. *Ibid.* pp. 9–10.
233. *Ibid.* p. 1.
234. *Ibid.* p. 22.
235. *Ibid.* p. 9.
236. *Ibid.* p. 17.
237. *Ibid.* p. 50.
238. *Ibid.* p. 326.
239. *Ibid.* p. 15.
240. *Ibid.* pp. 18–19.
241. *Ibid.* p. 284.
242. *Ibid.* p. 140.
243. *Ibid.* p. 284.
244. On Arnauld, with respect to the issues concerning ideas, see Church, *A Study in the Philosophy of Malebranche*; Damiron, *Essai sur l'histoire de la philosophie*; Delbos, "La controverse d'Arnauld et de Malebranche sur la nature et l'origine des idees"; García-Gómez, *The Problem of Objective Knowledge in Descartes, Malebranche, and Arnauld*; Kremer, *Malebranche and Arnauld: The Controversy Over the Nature of Ideas*; Lovejoy, " 'Representative Ideas' in Malebranche and Arnauld"; Malebranche, *Recueil de toutes les réponses . . . à M. Arnauld.*
245. In his *Malebranche and Arnauld*, Kremer treats the controversy between Malebranche and Arnauld in detail, concentrating on the problem of the way in which ideas are caused to be of their objects.
246. Arnauld, *Des vraies et des fausses idées*, in *Oeuvres* (1780), vol. 38, p. 198. References hereafter are to this edition.
247. *Ibid.* pp. 198–199, 228, 335, 342; *Defense, Oeuvres* (1780), vol. 38, p. 383.
248. Arnauld, *Des vraies et des fausses idées*, p. 198.
249. *Ibid.* p. 193.
250. *Ibid.* p. 194.
251. Foucher also, I argue in Chapter 5, finds that Malebranche begins in the *Recherche* with a Cartesian notion of idea and then later shifts the meaning of the term without warning. Damiron (*Essai sur l'histoire de la philosophie*, p. 482), after outlining Arnauld's objections to Malebranche, says that if he were to give Foucher's objections he would just be repeating those of Arnauld. This is not entirely true. Although Arnauld believes that both sensations and ideas are mental modifications, he retains their essential difference, which Foucher denies. Foucher's major criticism concerning the unexplained notion of nonresembling representative ideas holds against Arnauld as much as against any other Cartesian.
252. Arnauld, *Des vraies et des fausses idées*, p. 199.
253. *Ibid.* p. 181.
254. *Ibid.* p. 198.
255. *Ibid.* p. 187, 309–313.
256. *Ibid.* p. 199.

Chapter 7

257. I take the orthodox Cartesians to be equating essence with substance. Thinking, as the essence of mind, is the substance of mind, and not the essential attribute of mind; extension, as the essence of matter, is the substance of matter, and not the essential attribute of matter. One could know essential attributes, as Locke says, without knowing the thing in itself; the Cartesians claim to know the thing in itself, i.e., its substance, not just its essential attribute. See also Chapter 14.
258. Sextus Empiricus, *Against the Logicians*, pp. 311 ff.
259. Smith, *Studies in the Cartesian Philosophy*, pp. 229 ff.
260. Le Grand, *An Entire Body of Philosophy*, bk. 1, p. 50.
261. *Ibid.* pp. 199–202; I use this example because it is so ingenious, but I must point out that according to it similar poles should attract and opposite poles should repel. This is because when two poles with the same direction of twist are pointed at one another, outstreaming particles would intertwine, as Le Grand envisions is the case when the opposite poles face one another. And the outstreaming particles from poles of opposite twist are the ones that would hit head on, and thus would repel. So far as I know, no one else has pointed out this defect in the theory.
262. To any objection that no true cause can produce effects that do not resemble it, Régis, for example, replies in his *Système de philosophie* (vol. 1, p. 124) that then "Dieu même ne seroit pas une véritable cause, parce que tous les effects qu'il produit, sont d'une nature différente de la sienne."
263. Actually, the causal likeness principle is not preserved in the sense required. What Malebranche shows is that any sense of effective causal interaction between two unlike substances is meaningless. God *creates* mind and matter rather than causally interacting with them. Hence, in substituting this creative "interaction" for causal interaction, Malebranche does not, after all, preserve the *causal* likeness principle.
264. Malebranche, *De la recherche de la vérité*, p. 413.

Chapter 8

265. Lough, "Locke's Reading During His Stay in France." Among the books Lough lists as owned by Locke are two copies of Malebranche's *Recherche de la vérité* (247, 254), three copies of Desgabets's *Critique de la critique de la recherche* (248, 253, 256), two copies of Foucher's *Critique de la recherche* (246, 257) and one copy of Foucher's *Réponse pour la critique à la preface* (257).
266. Locke, *An Essay Concerning Human Understanding*, 1, 1, 8. (Because there is no standard edition of the *Essay*, references are made only to book, chapter, and paragraph.)
267. *Ibid.* 2, 8, 9–10.
268. *Ibid.* 2, 23, 11.
269. *Ibid.* 4, 1, 1.
270. *Ibid.* 4, 4, 3.
271. *Ibid.* 2, 13, 19.
272. *Ibid.* 2, 23, 15.
273. *Ibid.* 2, 30, 2.
274. *Ibid.* 2, 8, 23–24.
275. Yolton, *John Locke and the Way of Ideas*.
276. Locke, *Essay*, 4, 4, 6.
277. *Ibid.* 4, 4, 4.
278. Le Grand's *An Entire Body of Philosophy* was published in 1694. Malebranche's last *Éclaircissement* to the *Recherche* was published in 1712. For the influence of Bayle and Malebranche on Berkeley, see Luce's *Berkeley and Malebranche*.
279. On Berkeley's relation to scepticism see Popkin's "Berkeley and Pyrrhonism."

280. Luce, *Berkeley and Malebranche*; Watson, "Berkeley in a Cartesian Context"; Bracken, *Berkeley*.

281. Berkeley, *Three Dialogues between Hylas and Philonous*, pp. 171 ff.; *A Treatise Concerning the Principles of Human Knowledge*, principles 8–15, pp. 44–77.

282. Berkeley, *Three Dialogues*, p. 236.

283. *Ibid.* pp. 242–243, 257–258, 216.

284. *Ibid.* p. 206; *Principles*, principle 8, p. 44.

285. This dependence need not necessarily mean that the dependent item is a property or modification. Spinoza seems to believe it does. Certainly one of the problems in insisting upon a substance's dependence upon God is that this might mean that the substance is a modification of God. Substances can be said to be causally dependent upon God, but even here there is a tradition of supposing that God's causal activity is merely the flowering of his potentialities. Leibniz, for example, conceives a monad as having the power to cause and support as effects its own modifications. In this sense, the distinction between causal dependence and dependence in the sense of being a modification is but nominal. For a Spinozistic treatment of Descartes see Vernon, *The Metaphysical Role of Ideas in the Philosophy of Descartes*.

286. For example, in Luce, *Berkeley and Malebranche*, and in Popkin, "The New Realism of Bishop Berkeley."

287. See also Fritz, "Berkeley's Self—Its Origin in Malebranche"; Bracken, "Berkeley and Mental Acts"; Bracken, "Berkeley and Malebranche on Ideas"; Bracken, *Berkeley*; Gueroult, *Berkeley*.

288. Berkeley, *Principles*, pp. 61–62.

289. Berkeley, *Three Dialogues*, pp. 240–241.

290. "Lettre de monsieur Descartes à monsieur C.L.R. servat de réponse à un recueil de principales instances faites par monsieur Gassendi contre les precedentes réponses," in Adam and Tannery, vol. 9–1, p. 213; English translation, "Letter from M. Descartes to M. Clerselier to Serve as a Reply to a Selection of the Principle Objections taken by M. Gassendi to the Preceding Replies," in Haldane and Ross, vol. 2, p. 132.

291. Berkeley, *Three Dialogues*, pp. 231 ff.

292. Could an active mind have a passive modification? It must be argued here that a passive idea is not inert in the sense that Cartesian matter is. As a modification of an active substance, an idea would have to be active as opposed to inert, but it could be passive in the sense that the shape of a moving ship is in motion but does not activate the motion. The passiveness of an idea would be that its being—or activity—is provided by the mind.

293. Berkeley, *Three Dialogues*, p. 232.

294. Note that this is the source of a great difficulty about telepathy. If I were directly acquainted with your thoughts, would not those thoughts be my thoughts—modifications of my mind? And then how could they be your thoughts, modifications of your mind? The empirical facts are that we never have anyone else's thoughts. A good explanation for this is that thoughts are modifications of a mind; a particular thought cannot modify two minds at once (although of course two people can think of the same thing at the same time). I am directly acquainted only with my own thoughts because the relation I bear to them—like the relation of a substance to its modification—is such as to make them unsharably mine alone.

295. Hume, *A Treatise of Human Nature*, pp. 232 ff.

296. On Hume's relation to scepticism, see four articles by Richard H. Popkin: "David Hume: His Pyrrhonism and his Critique of Pyrrhonism," "David Hume and the Pyrrhonian Controversy," "The Sceptical Crisis and the Rise of Modern Philosophy, III," and "The Sceptical Precursors of David Hume." For a different viewpoint and the best overall commentary on Hume's philosophy, see Norman Kemp Smith, *The Philosophy of David Hume*.

297. Hume, *Treatise*. pp. 232 ff. Hume is not entirely original on the issues with which I am concerned here, sometimes following Bayle, as Kemp Smith delicately remarks, "with almost verbal consistency." For an introduction to Bayle's influence on Hume, see Smith, *The Philosophy of David Hume*, pp. 325–338.

298. Hume, *Treatise*, pp. 1–7.
299. *Ibid.* p. 233.
300. *Ibid.* p. 252.
301. *Ibid.* pp. 128–131, 189, 191, 228. Hume also has problems concerning the comparison of an idea with the impression of which it is a copy. If they are had at the same time, the greater vivacity of the impression may make it impossible to distinguish the weaker idea. If they occur at separate times, then they cannot be directly compared.
302. *Ibid.* p. 3.
303. *Ibid.* p. 15.
304. *Ibid.* p. 241.
305. *Ibid.* pp. 241, 16, 66–68.
306. Although Hume might be happy with the destructive role I attribute to him, he is not satisfied with his own explanations of mind and the relations between ideas and impressions. See *Treatise*, pp. 633–636.

Chapter 9

307. "Briefwechsel zwischen Leibniz und Foucher," ed. by Gerhardt, pp. 363–427.
308. See Chapter 3.
309. Leibniz, *Nouveaux essais sur l'entendement*, ed. by Gerhardt, p. 355.
310. Leibniz, "Leibniz au Foucher, [1676]," p. 369.
311. *Ibid.* p. 370.
312. *Ibid.* pp. 372–373.
313. *Ibid.* pp. 373–374.
314. Leibniz, "De Modo Distinguendi Phaenomena Realia ab Imaginariis." Quotations are from the English translation, "On the Method of Distinguishing Real from Imaginary Phenomena," p. 604.
315. "Foucher au Leibniz, [1685?]," p. 379.
316. "Leibniz au Foucher, 1686," p. 381.
317. *Ibid.* p. 382.
318. *Ibid.* p. 383.
319. Leibniz, "Eclaircissement de nouveau systême de la communication des substances," p. 255.
320. "Leibniz au Foucher [1687?]," p. 390.
321. "Foucher au Leibniz, Paris, 30 mai 1691," p. 399.
322. "Foucher au Leibniz, Paris, 31 decembre 1691," p. 401.
323. "Leibniz au Foucher, janvier 1692," p. 402.
324. *Ibid.* p. 406.
325. "Foucher au Leibniz, Paris, aoust 1692," pp. 407–408.
326. "Leibniz au Foucher, 17/27 octobre 1692," p. 410.
327. "Foucher au Leibniz, Paris, mars 1693," pp. 412–413.
328. "Foucher au Leibniz, [1685?]," p. 380.
329. "Leibniz au Foucher, 1686," pp. 382–383.
330. *Ibid.* p. 383.
331. Leibniz, "Sistême nouveau de la nature & de la communication des substances, aussi bien que de l'union qu'il y a entre l'âme & le corps." The page references which follow are to the reprint of this article in Janet, *Oeuvres philosophiques de Leibniz*.
332. *Ibid.* pp. 636–637.
333. *Ibid.* p. 640.
334. *Ibid.* pp. 641–642.
335. *Ibid.* pp. 642–644.
336. Foucher, "Réponse de M. S. F. à M. de L. B. Z. sur son nouveau sistême de la communication des substances." The page references which follow are to the reprint in Janet, *Oeuvres philosophiques de Leibniz*.

337. *Ibid.* p. 647.
338. *Ibid.* pp. 647–648.
339. *Ibid.* p. 648.
340. Leibniz, "Eclaircissement du nouveau sistême de la communication des substances." The page references which follow are the reprint in Janet, *Oeuvres philosophiques de Leibniz.*
341. *Ibid.* pp. 650–651.
342. *Ibid.* p. 651.
343. *Ibid.* pp. 652–653.
344. *Ibid.* p. 652.
345. Leibniz, "On Nature Itself, or on the Inherent Force and Actions of Created Things," pp. 809 ff.
346. Leibniz, "On the Method of Distinguishing Real from Imaginary Phenomena," p. 606.
347. Leibniz, "Lettre sur la question si l'essence du corps consiste dans l'étendu," p. 631. The page reference is to the reprint in Janet, *Oeuvres philosophiques de Leibniz.*
348. Leibniz, "Primae Veritates"; quotations are from the English translation, "First Truths." Leibniz, "De Modo Distinguendi Phaenomena Realia ab Imaginariis"; quotations are from the English translation, "On the Method of Distinguishing Real from Imaginary Phenomena." Leibniz, "De Ipsi a Natura, sive de Vi Insita, Actionibusque Creaturarum; pro Dynamicus suis confirmandis illustrandisque"; quotations are from the English translation, "On the Nature Itself, or on the Inherent Force and Actions of Created Things to Serve to Confirm and Illustrate the Author's Dynamics."
349. Leibniz, "First Truths," p. 416.
350. *Ibid.* p. 417.
351. Leibniz, "On the Method," p. 607.
352. Leibniz, "On Nature Itself," pp. 809–817.
353. *Ibid.* p. 824.
354. The universe is a *plenum.* Leibniz, "First Truths," p. 415.
355. Leibniz, "On Nature Itself," pp. 818–819.
356. *Ibid.* p. 824.
357. Leibniz, "Excerpta ex notis meis inauguralibus ad Fucherii responsionem in Malebranchium critica," in Rabbe, *Étude philosophique,* p. XLI. Some of these notes are translated as "Notes on the Reply of Foucher to the Criticism of his Criticism of the *Recherche de la verité*" by Loemker in *Philosophical Papers.* Loemker's translation of the quoted passage is: "An idea is that by which one perception of thought differs from another with respect to its object" (p. 241).
358. Leibniz, "Excerpta ex notis meis," p. XLI.
359. Leibniz, "Quid sit Idea." ["What Is an Idea?"] p. 317. Quotations are from the English translation.
360. *Ibid.* p. 318.
361. *Ibid.* pp. 318–319.
362. *Ibid.* p. 319.
363. Leibniz, "Meditationes de Cognitione, Veritate et Ideis." Quotations are from the English translation, "Meditations on Knowledge, Truth, and Ideas."
364. *Ibid.* p. 449.
365. *Ibid.* p. 452.
366. *Ibid.* pp. 452–453.
367. *Ibid.* p. 454.
368. Leibniz, "On the Method," pp. 606–607.
369. "Leibniz au Foucher, 1686," p. 383.
370. *Ibid.* p. 384.
371. "Leibniz au Foucher [1687?]," p. 391.
372. *Ibid.* p. 392.
373. Leibniz, "On Nature Itself," p. 817; Leibniz, "Sistême nouveau," p. 643, page reference to the reprint in Janet, *Oeuvres philosophiques de Leibniz.*
374. See Chapter 6.
375. Popkin, *The History of Scepticism,* pp. 93–94.

376. "Leibniz au Foucher [1687?]," p. 393.
377. "Foucher au Leibniz, Paris, 28 avril 1650," p. 423.
378. "Leibniz au Foucher [1676]," p. 373.

Chapter 11

379. Leonora Cohen Rosenfield examines another such specific reason for general disabusement with Cartesianism in her excellent book, *From Beast-Machine to Man-Machine: Animal Soul in French Letters from Descartes to La Mettrie*. On the other hand, contrary to what one might think, Descartes's mistaken physics was not held against the Cartesians, in part because several of them were good physicists, and in part because—like Malebranche—they admitted their errors and adopted Newtonian principles. As I remark in Chapter 7, Samuel Clarke thought it perfectly appropriate to present Rohault's *Traité de physique* in Latin and English translations with a few corrections as a Newtonian text.
380. J.-R. Armogathe. *Theologia Cartesiana: L'explication physique de l'Eucharistie chez Descartes et Dom Desgabets.*
381. Jean Laporte, *La Rationalisme de Descartes*, p. 339; "Descartes au Mersenne, 28 janvier 1641," in *Oeuvres de Descartes*, Adam & Tannery, vol. 3, pp. 295–296.
382. Laporte, *La Rationalisme de Descartes*, p. 317.
383. James Thomson Shotwell, *A Study in the History of the Eucharist*, p. 1.
384. Anonymous, "Beyond Transubstantiation: New Theory of Real Presence"; R. P. Desharnais, "Letter on Transubstantiation"; Frank Kinkaid, "Letter on Transubstantiation."
385. Descartes, "Sixièmes Réponses," AT, vol. 9(1), pp. 234–235; Latin: vol. 7, p. 434; English: HR, vol. 2, p. 250.
386. Arnauld, "Quatrièmes Objections," AT, vol. 9(1), p. 169; Latin: AT, vol. 7, pp. 217–218; English: HR, vol. 2, p. 95.
387. Descartes, "Quatrièmes Réponses," AT, vol. 9(1), p. 192; Latin: AT, vol. 7, p. 249; English: HR, vol. 2, p. 117.
388. *Ibid.* p. 193; Latin, p. 250–251; English, pp. 118.
389. *Ibid.* p. 194; Latin, p. 251; English, p. 118.
390. *Ibid.* p. 196; Latin, p. 255; English, p. 121.
391. See Ronald Layman, "Transubstantiation: A Test Case for Descartes's Theory of Space," who perpetuates this naive "sandwich" interpretation of Christ's flesh under a layer of bread.
392. "Descartes au Mesland, 9 fevrier 1645?," AT, vol. 4, pp. 164–165.
393. *Ibid.* p. 168.
394. "Descartes au Mesland, mai 1645?," AT, vol. 4, p. 346.
395. Laporte, *La rationalisme de Descartes*, p. 416. Descartes's contributions to Protestant arguments are discussed by Walter Rex in his *Essays on Pierre Bayle and Religious Controversy*, pp. 121 ff.
396. "Descartes au Mesland, 2 mars 1646," AT, vol. 4, p. 373.
397. Nicolas Malebranche, "Avertissement contre Desgabets et Foucher," placed at the head of vol. 2 of *De la recherche de la vérité*; reprinted in *Oeuvres complètes de Malebranche*, ed. André Robinet, vol. 2 (ed. Geneviève Rodis-Lewis), p. 500. This is, of course, just a version of Malebranche's *bon mot* against Foucher (see Chapter 6). It was as dangerous to defend Malebranche as to attack him.
398. Lemaire, *Le cartésienisme chez de Bénédictins*, p. 54.
399. Jacques Rohault, *Entretiens sur la philosophie*, reprinted in Pierre Clair, *Jacques Rohault (1618–1672) bio-bibliographie avec l'édition critique des Entretiens sur la philosophie*. See also Henri Gouhier, "Jacques Rohault et l'histoire de la polémique sur l'eucharistique" in *Cartésianisme et augustinisme au XVIIème siécle*, pp. 71–80.
400. Lemaire, *Le cartésienisme chez les Bénédictins*, pp. 123–133. See also Armogathe, *Theologia Cartesiana.*
401. Lemaire, *Le cartésienisme chez les Bénédictins*, p. 11.

402. Jacques Rohault, *Traité de physique*, pp. 41–42. See also Rohault, *Entretiens sur la philosophie.*
403. Rohault, *Traité de physique*, p. 57.
404. Paul Mouy, *Le développement de la physique cartésienne, 1646–1712*, pp. 169–170.
405. Jean-Baptiste de La Grange, *Les principes de la philosophie, contre les nouveaux philosophes Descartes, Rohault, Regius, Gassendi, le P. Maignon, & c.*, vol. 1, pp. vi–ix.
406. *Ibid.* pp. 1–2.
407. *Ibid.* pp. 3–4.
408. *Ibid.* pp. 39–42.
409. *Ibid.* p. 43.
410. *Ibid.* pp. 52–53.
411. *Ibid.* p. 101.
412. *Ibid.* p. 102.
413. *Ibid.* p. 128.
414. *Ibid.* p. 133.
415. *Ibid.* p. 127.
416. *Ibid.* p. 106.
417. *Ibid.* pp. 120–121.
418. *Ibid.* p. 123.
419. *Ibid.* p. 125.
420. *Ibid.* p. 135.
421. *Ibid.* p. 110.
422. *Ibid.* p. 111.
423. *Ibid.* p. 117.
424. *Ibid.* p. 118.
425. *Ibid.* p. 132.
426. Alan Gabbey, "Philosophia Cartesiana Triumphata: Henry More, 1646–1671."
427. Jacques Roger, "The Cartesian Model and Its Role in Eighteenth-Century 'Theory of the Earth.'"
428. See Chapter 14 herein.
429. Richard H. Popkin, "Cartesianism and Biblical Criticism."
430. Louis de La Forge, *Traitté de l'âme humaine*, pp. 135, 151–152; see also Chapter 12 herein.
431. Rosenfield, *From Beast-Machine to Man-Machine.*

Chapter 12

432. See the recent excellent studies by Pierre Clair, "Louis de la Forge et les origines de l'occasionalisme," and Henri Gouhier, "Louis de la Forge," in his *Cartésianisme et augustinisme au XVIIème siècle.*
433. La Forge, *Traitté de l'esprit de l'homme.*
434. *Louis de La Forge: Oeuvres philosophiques.* Édition annotée avec une étude bio-bibliographique présentée par Pierre Clair.
435. *L'Homme de René Descartes et un traitté de la formation du foetus du mesme auteur, avec les remarques de Louys de la Forge, docteur en medecine, demeurant a La Fleche, sur le traitté de l'homme de René Descartes, et sur les figures par luy inventees.*
436. Balz, *Cartesian Studies*, pp. 80–105.
437. See Part II herein.
438. La Forge, *Traitté de l'esprit de l'homme*, page references to Clair's edition, pp. 111 ff.
439. *Ibid.* p. 77.
440. *Ibid.* pp. 204 ff.
441. *Ibid.* pp. 105 ff.
442. *Ibid.* pp. 176 ff., 204 ff.
443. *Ibid.* p. 247.
444. *Ibid.* pp. 244, 178.
445. *Ibid.* pp. 235 ff.

446. *Ibid.* pp. 174 ff.
447. *Ibid.* pp. 175 ff.
448. *Ibid.* pp. 224 ff.
449. *Ibid.* pp. 279 ff., especially p. 291.
450. *Ibid.* pp. 157 ff.
451. *Ibid.* pp. 170 ff.

Chapter 13

452. I consider these issues in Part II.
453. I show one way it is not adequate in Chapter 11.
454. For a defense of this view see Hiram Caton, *The Origin of Subjectivity: An Essay on Descartes.*
455. I outline this position in "Cartesianism," *The Encyclopaedia Britannica*, vol. 3, pp. 968–970.
456. S. V. Keeling, *Descartes*, pp. 125–126, 144–147, 280–287. Bernard Williams, *Descartes: The Project of Pure Enquiry*, pp. 227–230. Margaret Dauler Wilson, *Descartes*, says that "Descartes does maintain that matter in general or as a whole is 'just extension'" but she continues "or more exactly, a subject with extension as its only essential attribute" (pp. 85–86). I deny that extension is ontologically an attribute of substance; extension is a substance, cf. Alexandre Koyré, "Introduction" in Elizabeth Anscombe and Peter Thomas Geach (trs. and eds.) *Descartes: Philosophical Writings*; Koyré says that for Descartes "Body is neither less nor more than extension" (p. xliii).
457. In *Meditation II*, Descartes concludes that the concept of matter discovered from examining a piece of wax contains "rien que quelque chose d'estendu" (AT, vol. 9[1], p. 24; English: HR, vol. 1, p. 154). Descartes repeats this view in *Sixièmes réponses* where he says body is only "une substance étenduë en longueur, largeur & profondeur" (AT, vol. 9[1], p. 239; Latin: vol. 7, p. 440; HR, vol. 2, p. 254), and in *Principles of Philosophy*, Principle 11, titled *"En quel sens on peut dire du'il [l'espace] n'est point different du corps qu'il contient"* where he concludes: "Apres avoir ainsi examiné cette pierre, nous trouverons que la veritable idée que nous en avons consiste en cela seul *que nous appercevons distinctement* qu'elle est *une substance* étendue en longueur, largeur & profondeur; or cela mesme est compris en l'idée que nous avons de l'espace, non seulement de celuy qu'on appelle vuide." (AT, Latin: vol. 9[2], pp. 68–69; AT, vol. 8[1], p. 46; English: HR, vol. 1, p. 259).
458. *Principles of Philosophy*, Part 1, Principles 52 and 53, AT, vol. 9(2) pp. 47–48; Latin: vol. 8(1), pp. 105–107; English: HR, vol. 1, p. 240. The title of Principle 53 is *"Que chaque substance a un attribut principal, & que celuy de l'âme est la pensée, comme l'extension est celuy du corps."* Commentators who take extension to *be* the material substance must contend that Descartes does not mean that an attribute is an ontological category different from that of substance.
459. Descartes, *Principles*, Part 1, Principle 52.
460. Louis de La Forge, *Traitté de l'esprit de l'homme*, page references to Pierre Clair, *Louis de La Forge: Oeuvres philosophique*, pp. 279 ff., especially p. 291. I treat this issue in Chapter 12.
461. See Part II.

Chapter 14

462. Descartes, "Preface to the Reader," in *Meditations on First Philosophy*. HR, vol. 1, p. 139; Latin: AT, vol. 7, p. 9.
463. See Chapter 13 herein.
464. "Mais, tout au contraire, parce qu'il s'est déteriminé à faire les choses qui sont au monde, pour cette raison, comme il est dit en Genese, *elles sont tres-bonnes*, c'est à dire que la raison de

leur bonté depend de ce qu'il les a ainsi voulu faire. . . . Il est aussi inutile de demander comment Dieu eust peu fare de tout eternité que deux fois 4 n'eussent pas este 8, &c., car j'avoue bien que nous ne pouvons pas comprehendre cela. . . . Ainsi donc il ne faut pas penser quey *les veritez eternelles dépendent de l'entendement humain, ou de l'existence des choses,* mais seulement de la volunté de Dieu, qui, comme un souverain legislateur, les a ordonnees & establies de toute eternite." Descartes, "Sixièmes réponses," AT, vol. 9(1), pp. 236–237; Latin: AT, vol. 7, pp. 435–436; English: HR, vol. 2, pp. 250–251. The concept of a square circle is contradictory to our reason; I cannot conceive of my own nonexistence without contradiction.

465. Huet, *Censura philosophiae Cartesianae.*

466. "Mais quand nous apercevons que nous sommes des choses qui pensent, c'est une premiere notion qui n'est tirée d'aucun syllogism; & lorsque quelqu'un dit: *Je pense, donc je suis, ou j'existe,* il ne conclut pas son existence de sa pensée comme par la force de quelque syllogisme, mais comme une chose connuë de foy; il la void par une simple inspection de l'esprit." Descartes, "Secondes réponses," AT, vol. 9(1), p. 110; Latin: AT, vol. 7, p. 140; English: HR, vol. 2, p. 38. Objections II." Haldane and Ross, vol. 2, p. 38.

467. "*Je suis, je existe,* est necessairement vraye, toutes les fois que je la prononce, ou que je la concoy en mon esprit. . . . *Je suis, j'existe*: cela est certain; mais combien de temps? A sçavoir, autant de temps que je pense." Descartes, "Seconde meditation," AT, vol. 9(1), pp. 19–21; Latin: AT, vol. 7, pp. 25–27; English: HR, vol. 1, pp. 150–151.

468. "Rule XI. *If, after we have recognized intuitively a number of simple truths, we wish to draw any inference from them, it is useful to run them over in a continuous and uninterrupted act of thought, to reflect upon their relations to one another, and to grasp together distinctly a number of these propositions so far as is possible at the same time. For this is a way of making our knowledge much more certain, and of greatly increasing the power of the mind.*" Descartes, *Rules for the Direction of the Mind,* HR, vol. 1, p. 33; Latin: AT, vol. 10, p. 407.

469. See Chapter 11 herein.

470. "Mais je ne connois pas encore assez clairement ce que je suis, moy qui suis certain que je suis. . . . Un autre [attribut de l'âme] est de penser; & je trouve icy que la pensée est un attribut qui m'appartient; elle seule ne peut estre détachée de moy. . . . Je n'admets maintenant rien qui ne soit necessairement vray: je ne suis donc, precisement parlant, qu'une chose qui pense, c'est à dire un esprit, un entendement ou une reason, qui sont des termes dont la signification m'estoit auparavant inconuë. Or je suis une chose vraye, & vrayment existante; mais quelle chose? Je l'ay dit: une chose qui pense. . . . Mais qu'est-ce donc que je suis? Une chose qui pense." Descartes, "Seconde meditation," AT, vol. 9(1), pp. 19–22; Latin: AT, vol. 7, pp. 25–28; English: HR, vol. 1, pp. 150–153.

471. Malebranche, "XI. Éclaircissement. Sur le chapitre septième de la seconde partie du troisième libre. Ou je prouve: Que nous n'avons point d'idée claire de la nature ni des modifications de notre âme." Geneviève Rodis-Lewis, ed., *Oeuvres de Malebranche,* vol. 3, p. 163.

472. "Je suis certain que je suis une chose qui pense; mais ne sçay-je donc pas aussi ce qui est requis pour me rendre certain de quelque chose? Dans cette premiere connoissance, il ne se recontre rien qu'une claire & distinct perception de ce que je connois; laquelle de vray ne seroit pas suffisante pour m'assurer qu'elle est vraye, s'il pouvoit jamais arriver qu'une chose que je concevrois ainsi clairement & distinctement se trouvast fausse. Et partant il me semble que des-ja je puis establer pour regle generale, que toutes les choses que nous concevons fort clairement & fort distinctement, sont toutes vrayes." Descartes, "Troisième meditation," AT, vol. 9(1), p. 27; Latin: vol. 7, p. 35; English: HR, vol. 1, p. 158.

473. "*Il ne me reste, plus qu'un scruple, que est de sçavoir comment il se peut deffendre de ne pas commettre un circle, lorsqu'il dit que* nous ne sommes assurez que les choses que nous concevons clairement & distinctement sont vrayes, qu'à cause que Dieu est ou existe.

"*Car nous ne pouvons estre assurez que Dieu est, sinon parce que nous concevons cela tres-clairement & tres-distinctement; doncques, auparavant que d'estre assurez de l'existence de Dieu, nous devons estre assurez que toutes les choses que nous concevons clairement & distinctement sont toutes vrayes.*" Arnauld, "Quatrièmes objections," AT, vol. 9(1), p. 166; Latin: AT, vol. 7, p. 214; English: HR, vol. 2, p. 92.

474. "Je trouve manifestement que l'existence ne peut non plus este separée de l'essence de Dieu, que de l'essence d'un triangle rectiligne la grandeur de ses trois angles égaux à deux droits . . . l'existence est unseparable de luy [Dieu]. . . . Car y a-t-il rien de soy plus clair & plus manifest, que de penser qu'il a un Dieu, c'est à dire un estre souverain & parfait, en l'idée duquel seul l'existence necessaire ou eternelle est comprise, & par consequent qui existe?" Descartes, "Cinquième meditation," AT, vol. 9(1), pp. 52–55; Latin: AT, vol. 7, pp. 66–69; English: HR, vol. 1, pp. 181–183. Descartes does not here say explicitly that God's essence is identical with his existence, but when Arnauld says of God that *"parce qu'il est un estre infini, duquel l'existence est son essence"* ("Quatrièmes objections," AT, vol. 9[1], p. 166; Latin: AT, vol. 7, p. 213; English: HR, vol. 2, p. 92), Descartes agrees that "en Dieu l'existence n'est point distinguée de l'essence" ("Quatrièmes réponses," AT, vol. 9[1], p. 188; Latin: AT, vol. 7, p. 243; English: HR, vol. 2, p. 113). Also, in reply to Gassendi's objection that existence is not a property or perfection ("Objections Quintae," AT, vol. 7, pp. 260–263; English: HR, vol. 2, pp. 185–187), Descartes says *"God is His existence"* ("The Author's Reply to the Fifth Set of Objections," HR, vol. 2, p. 228; Latin: AT, vol. 7, p. 383).

475. "Il faut necessairement conclure que, de cela seul que j'existe, & que l'idée d'un estre souverainement parfait (c'est à dire de Dieu) est en moy, l'existence de Dieu est tres-evidemment demonstrée. . . . Mais de cela seul que Dieu m'a crée, il est fort croyable qu'il m'a en quelque facon produit a son image & semblance, & que je conçoy cette ressemblance (dans laquelle l'idée de Dieu se trouve contenuë) par la mesme faculté par la quelle je me conçoy moy-mesme; c'est à dire que, lorsque je fais reflexion sur moy, non seulement je connois que je suis un chose imparfaite, incomplete, & dependante d'autruy, qui tend & qui aspire sans cesse à quelque chose de meilleur & de plus grand que je ne suis, mais je connois aussi, en mesme temps, que celuy duquel je dépens, possede en soy toutes ces grandes choses ausquelles j'aspire, & dont je trouve en moy les idées, non pas indefiniment & seulement en puissance, mais qu'il en joüit en effect, actuellement & infinment, & ainsi qu'il est Dieu." Descartes, "Troisième meditation," AT, vol. 9(1), pp. 40–41; Latin: AT, vol. 7, p. 51; English: HR, vol. 1, p. 170.

476. "*Principle 53. Que chaque substance a un attribut principal, & que celuy de l'âme est la pensée, comme l'extension est celuy du corps.*

Mais, encore que chaque attribut soit suffisant pour fare connoistre la substance, il y en a toutesfois un. . . . en chacune, qui constitue sa nature & son essence, & de qui tous les autres dependent. A sçavoir l'estendue en longueur, largeur & profondeur, constitue la nature de la substance corporelle; & la pensée constitue la nature de la substance qui pense. . . . *Principle 63. Comment on peut avoir des notions distinctes de l'extension & de la pensée, en tant que l'une constitue la nature du corps, & l'autre celle de l'âme.*

Nous pouvons aussi considerer la pensée & l'estendue comme *les choses principales* qui constituent la nature de la substance intelligente & corporelle; & alors nous ne devons point les concevoir autrement que comme la substance mesme qui pense & qui est estenduë, c'est à dire comme l'âme & le corps . . . pource qu'il y a quelque difficulté à separer la notion que nous avons de la substance de celles que nous avons de la pensee & de l'estenduë." Descartes, *Principes*, Part I, AT, Vol. 9(2), pp. 48, 53–54; Latin: AT, vol. 8(1), pp. 25, 30–31; English: HR, vol. 1, pp. 240, 245–246.

477. See Chapter 11 herein.

478. Among recent commentators who ignore Descartes's scepticism, say he was not serious about it, offer easy and inadequate ways out of it, and/or defend reason for Descartes in various ways are the following:

Caton, Hiram, *The Origin of Subjectivity, An Essay on Descartes.* New Haven: Yale University Press, 1973.

Curley, E. M. *Descartes Against the Skeptics.* Cambridge: Harvard University Press, 1978.

Frankfurt, Harry G. *Demons, Dreamers, and Madmen: The Defence of Reason in Descartes's Meditations.* Indianapolis: Bobbs-Merrill, 1970.

Gäbe, Lüder. *Descartes's Selbstkritik, Untersuchungen zur Philosophie des Jungen Descartes.* Hamburg: Felix Meiner, 1972.

O'Neil, Brian E. *Epistemological Direct Realism in Descartes's Philosophy*. Albuquerque: University of New Mexico Press, 1974.

Ree, Jonathan. *Descartes*. New York: Pica Press, 1975.

Rodis-Lewis, Genevieve. *L'Oeuvre de Descartes* (2 volumes). Paris: J. Vrin, 1971.

Williams, Bernard. *Descartes, The Project of Pure Enquiry*. London: Harvester Press. 1978.

Wilson, Margaret Dauler. *Descartes*. London: Routledge & Kegan Paul, 1978.

479. Clarke, Desmond M. *Descartes's Philosophy of Science*. University Park: Pennsylvania State University Press, 1982.

480. Popkin, Richard H. *History of Scepticism from Erasmus to Spinoza*. Berkeley: University of California Press, 1979.

Bibliography

Adam, Charles, and Paul Tannery, eds. *See* Descartes, *Oeuvres.*

Allaire, Edwin B. "The Attack on Substance: Descartes to Hume," in *Dialogue* 3 (1964): 284–287.

— "Berkeley's Idealism," in *Theoria* 29 (1963): 231–244.

— "Existence, Independence, and Universals," in *The Philosophical Review* 69 (1960): 485–496.

Alquie, Ferdinand. *La découverte metaphysique de l'homme chez Descartes.* Paris: Presses Universitaires de France, 1950.

— "Descartes et l'ontologie négative," in *Revue internationale de philosophie* 12 (1950): 153–160.

Anonymous. "Beyond Transubstantiation: New Theory of Real Presence," in *Time,* July 2 (1965): 52–53.

Armogathe, J.-R. *Theologia Cartesiana: L'explication physique de l'eucharistie chez Descartes et Dom Desgabets.* International Archives of the History of Ideas 84. The Hague: Martinus Nijhoff, 1977.

Arnauld, Antoine. *Défense de M. Arnauld, docteur de Sorbonne, contre la réponse au livre des vraies & des fausses idées.* Cologne: Nicolas Schouten, 1684. Also in *Oeuvres* 38 (1780).

— *La logique, ou l'art de penser.* Paris: C. Saureux, 1662. "Objectiones Quartae," in Adam and Tannery, eds., *Oeuvres de Descartes* 7 (1964): 196–218; "Quatrièmes objections," in Adam and Tannery, eds., *Oeuvres de Descartes* 9–1 (1964): 153–170; "Fourth Set of Objections," in Haldane and Ross, eds., *The Philosophical Works of Descartes* 2 (1934): 89–95.

— *Oeuvres de messire Antoine Arnauld, docteur de la maison et societé de Sorbonne.* Paris: Sigismond d'Arnay, 1780.

— *Des vrayes et des fausses idées, contre ce qu'enseigne l'auteur de la recherche de la vérité.* Cologne: Nicolas Schouten, 1683. Also in *Oeuvres* 38 (1780).

Aschenbrenner, Karl. "Bishop Berkeley on Existence in the Mind," in *George Berkeley,* University of California Publications in Philosophy 29, pp. 37–64. Berkeley: University of California Press, 1957.

Baillet, Adrien. *La vie de Monsieur Descartes.* Paris: Daniel Horthemels, 1691.

Balz, Albert G. A. *Cartesian Studies.* New York: Columbia University Press, 1951.

— "Clerselier, 1614–1684 and Rohault, 1620–1675," in *Cartesian Studies,* pp. 28–41.

— "Louis de la Forge and the Critique of Substantial Forms," in *Cartesian Studies,* pp. 80–104.

Barber, W. H. *Leibniz in France from Arnauld to Voltaire: A Study in French Reactions to Leibnizianism, 1670–1760.* Oxford: Clarendon Press, 1955.

Bayle, Pierre. *Dictionnaire historique et critique.* 5th ed. revue, corrigée, et augmentée. Amsterdam: Compagnie des Libraries, 1784.

— "Pyrrhon, Remark B," in *Dictionnaire* 4: 668–671.

— "Zeno d'Elee, Remarks G & H," in *Dictionnaire* 5: 598–603.

Beer, Henry. *Du scepticisme de Gassendi.* Traduction de Bernard Rochot. Paris: Albin Michel, 1960.

Belaval, Yvon. *Leibniz critique de Descartes.* Paris: Gallimard, 1960.

Bergmann, Gustav. "Russell's Examination of Leibniz Examined," in *Philosophy of Science* 23 (1956): 175–203.

— "Some Remarks on the Philosophy of Malebranche," in *The Review of Metaphysics* 10 (1956): 207–225.

Berkeley, George. *Three Dialogues between Hylas and Philonous*. In Luce and Jessop, eds., *The Works of George Berkeley* 2 (1949).

— *A Treatise Concerning the Principles of Human Knowledge*. In Luce and Jessop, eds., *The Works of George Berkeley* 2 (1949).

— *The Works of George Berkeley, Bishop of Cloyne*. Edited by A. A. Luce and T. E. Jessop. London: Thomas Nelson and Sons, 1949.

Boas, George. *Dominant Themes of Modern Philosophy, A History*. New York: Ronald Press, 1957.

Boas, Marie. "Establishment of the Mechanical Philosophy," in *Osiris* 10 (1952): 412–541.

Bonno, Gabriel. *Les relations intellectuelles de Locke avec la France (d'après des documents inédits)*. University of California Publications in Modern Philology 38–2, pp. 37–264. Berkeley: University of California Press, 1955.

Bouillier, Francisque. *Histoire de la philosophie cartesienne*. Paris: Durand, 1854.

Bouwsma, O. K. "Descartes' Evil Genius," in Bouwsma, *Philosophical Essays* (1965): 85–97.

— *Philosophical Essays*. Lincoln: University of Nebraska Press, 1965.

Bracken, Harry M. *Berkeley*. London: Macmillan, 1974.

— "Berkeley and Malebranche on Ideas," in *The Modern 'Schoolman* 41 (1963): 1–15.

— "Berkeley and Mental Acts," in *Theoria* 26 (1960): 140–146.

— "Berkeley's Realisms," in *Philosophical Quarterly* 8 (1958): 1–15.

— *The Early Reception of Berkeley's Immaterialism: 1710–1733*. Rev. ed. The Hague: Martinus Nijhoff, 1965.

Brett, G. S. *The Philosophy of Gassendi*. London: Macmillan, 1908.

Brodbeck, May. "Descartes and the Notion of a Criterion of External Reality," in Royal Institute of Philosophy, *Reason and Reality*, London: Macmillan, 1972: 1–14.

Broughton, Janet and Ruth Mattern. "Reinterpreting Descartes on the Notion of the Union of Mind and Body," *Journal of the History of Philosophy* 16 (1978): 23–32.

Buchenau, Arthur. "Idee und Perzeption. Ein Beitrag zur Ideenlehre Malebrances," in *Philosophische Abhandlungen, Herman Cohen zum 70. Geburtstag Dargebracht*, Berlin: Cassirer, 1912: 135–151.

— "Über Malebranches Lehre von der Warheit und ihre Bedeutung für die Methodik der Wissenschaften," in *Archiv für die Geschichte der Philosophie* 16 (1910): 145–184.

Burtt, Edwin Arthur. *The Metaphysical Foundations of Modern Physical Science*. Rev. ed. New York: Harcourt, Brace and Co., 1932.

Cartesio nel Terzo Centenario nel "Discorso del Metodo." Supplemento Speciale al volume XIX, *Rivista di Filosofia Neo-Scolastica*, Milano: Società Editrice "Vita e Pensiero," 1937.

Cassirer, Ernst. *Das Erkenntnisproblem in der Philosophie und Wissenschaft der Neueren Zeit*. Berlin: E. Cassirer, 1906, 1911.

— "Descartes et l'idée de l'unité de la science," in *Revue de synthese* 7 (1937): 7–28.

Caton, Hiram. *The Origin of Subjectivity: An Essay on Descartes*. New Haven: Yale University Press, 1973.

Church, Ralph Withington. *A Study in the Philosophy of Malebranche*. London: George Allen & Unwin, 1931.

Clair, Pierre, ed. *See* La Forge, *Oeuvres philosophiques*.

— *Jacques Rohault (1618–1672) bio-bibliographie avec l'édition critique des entretiens sur la philosophie*. Centre d'Histoire des Sciences et des Doctrines, Recherches sur le XVIIème siècle 3. Paris: Centre Nationale de Recherche Scientifique, 1978.

— "Louis de la Forge et les origines de occasionalism," in *Recherches sur le XVIIème siècle*. Paris: Centre Nationale de Recherche Scientifique, 1976: 63–72.

Clarke, Desmond M. *Descartes' Philosophy of Science*. University Park: Pennsylvania State University Press, 1982.

Clatterbaugh, Kenneth C. "Descartes's Causal Likeness Principle," in *Philosophical Review* 89 (1980): 379–402.

Collins, James. *Interpreting Modern Philosophy*. Princeton: Princeton University Press, 1972.

Cousin, Victor, ed. *Fragments philosophiques pour faire suite aux cours de l'histoire de la philosophie*. 4th ed. Paris: Ladrange et Didier, 1847.

Couteret, Louis, ed. *See* Leibniz, *Opuscules et fragments*.

Crombie, A. C. "Galileo Galilei: A Philosophical Symbol," in *Actes du VIIIe Congrès International d'Histoire des Sciences*, Florence, 3–9 September 1956: 1089–1095.

Cummins, Phillip D. "Berkeley's Likeness Principle," in *Journal of the History of Philosophy* 4 (1966): 63–69.

— "Perceptual Relativity and Ideas in the Mind," in *Philosophy and Phenomenological Research* 24 (1963): 202–214.

Curley, E. M. *Descartes Against the Sceptics*. Cambridge: Harvard University Press, 1978.

Curtis, S. J. *A Short History of Western Philosophy in the Middle Ages*. London: MacDonald & Co., 1950.

Damiron, M. Ph. *Essai sur l'histoire de la philosophie en France, au XVIIe siecle*. Paris: L. Hachette, 1846.

Delbos, Victor. *Étude de la philosophie de Malebranche*. Paris: Bloud & Gay, 1924.

Descartes, René. "Descartes à Clerselier. Egmond, 2 mars 1646," in Adam and Tannery, eds., *Oeuvres de Descartes* 4: 373.

— "Descartes à Mersenne [Leyde, 28 janvier 1614]," in Adam and Tannery, eds., *Oeuvres de Descartes* 3: 292–300.

— "Descartes à P. Mesland. [Egmond, 9 fevrier 1645?]," in Adam and Tannery, eds., *Oeuvres de Descartes* 4: 161–172.

— "Descartes à P. Mesland. [Egmond, mai 1645?]," in Adam and Tannery, eds., *Oeuvres de Descartes* 4: 215–217.

— *L'homme de René Descartes et un traitté de la formation du foetus du mesme auteur, avec les remarques de Louys de la Forge, docteur en medecine, demeurant à La Fleche, sur le traité de l'homme de René Descartes, et sur les figures par luy inventees*. Paris: Charles Angot, 1664.

— "Lettre de monsieur Descartes à monsieur C.L.R. servant de réponse à un recueil des principales instances faites par monsieur Gassendi contre les precedents réponses," in Adam and Tannery, eds., *Oeuvres de Descartes* 9–1: 202–217; "Letter from M. Descartes to M. Clerselier to Serve as a Reply to a Selection of the Principal Objections taken by M. Gassendi to the Preceding Replies," in Haldane and Ross, eds., *The Philosophical Works of Descartes* 2: 125–134.

— *Oeuvres de Descartes*. Edited by Charles Adam and Paul Tannery. Paris: J. Vrin, 1964.

— *Philosophical Letters*. Anthony Kenny, tr. and ed. Oxford: Clarendon Press, 1970.

— *The Philosophical Works of Descartes*. Edited and translated by Elizabeth S. Haldane, and G. R. T. Ross. New York: Dover, 1934.

— "Reponsio ad Quartas Objectiones," in Adam and Tannery, eds., *Oeuvres de Descartes* 7: 218–256; "Réponses de l'auteur aux quatrièmes objections," in Adam and Tannery, eds., *Oeuvres de Descartes* 9–1: 170–197; "Reply to the Fouth Set of Objections," in Haldane and Ross, eds., *The Philosophical Works of Descartes* 2: 98–122.

— "Reponsio ad Sextas Objectiones," in Adam and Tannery, eds., *Oeuvres de Descartes* 7: 422–447; "Réponses de l'auteur aux sixièmes objections," in Adam and Tannery, *Oeuvres de Descartes* 9–1: 225–244; "Reply to the Sixth Set of Objections," in Haldane and Ross, eds., *The Philosophical Works of Descartes* 2: 241–258.

Desgabets, Robert. *Critique de la critique de la recherche de la vérité, où l'on découvre le chemin qui conduit aux connoissances solides. Pour servir de réponse à la lettre d'un academicien.* Paris: Jean Du Puis, 1675.

— "Supplément à la philosophie de M. Descartes." Manuscript, date unknown. Extracts in Lemaire, *Le cartésienisme chez les Bénédictins*.

Desharnais, R. P. "Letter on Transubstantiation." *Time*, July 16 (1965): 6.

Du Hamel, Jean. *Lettre de monsieur Du Hamel, ancien professeur de philosophie de l'universite de Paris, pour servir de replique à Monsieur Régis.* Paris: publisher unknown, 8 mars 1699.

— *Réflexions critiques sur le systême cartésienne de la philosophie de Mr. Régis.* Paris: E. Couterot, 1692.

Fitzgerald, Desmond J. "Descartes: Defender of the Faith," in *Thought: Fordham University Quarterly* 34 (1959): 383–404.

— *The Unity of Man in Descartes: A Study of Descartes' Treatment of a Medieval and Renaissance Problem.* Ph.D. dissertation. University of California, 1950.

Fontenelle, Bernard le Bovier de. "Éloge de Régis," in *Éloges de Fontenelle*, edited by Francisque Bouillier, Paris: Garnier Freres, n.d.: 14–21.

Foucher, Simon. *Critique de la recherche de la verité, où l'on examine en même-tems une partie des principes de Mr Descartes. Lettre, par un academicien*, Paris: Martin Coustelier, 1675; facsimile reprint, New York: Johnson Reprint Corporation, 1969.

— *Dissertation sur la recherche de la verité, contenant l'apologie des academiciens, où l'on fait voir que leur maniere de philosopher est la plus utile pour la religion, & la plus conforme au bon sens, pour servir de réponse a la critique de la critique, &c. avec plusieurs remarques sur les erreurs des sens & sur l'origine de la philosophie de Monsieur Descartes.* Paris: Estienne Michallet, 1687.

— *Dissertations sur la recherche de la verité, contenant l'histoire et les principes de la philosophie des academiciens. Avec plusieurs réflexions sur les sentimens de M. Descartes.* Paris: Jean Anisson, 1693.

— *Dissertations sur las recherche de la verité, ou sur la logique des academiciens.* Dijon: publisher unknown, 1673.

— "L'empereur Léonce." Manuscript, date unknown.

— "Extrait d'une lettre de M. Foucher chanoine de Dijon, pour répondre à M. de Leibniz sur quelques axiomes de philosophie," in *Journal des sçavans* (Amsterdam) 21 (16 mars 1693): 182–186.

— "Foucher au Leibniz, Paris, 12 aoust 1678," in Gerhardt, ed., *Philosophischen Schriften* 1: 374–375.

— "Foucher au Leibniz, Paris, 26 avril 1679," in Gerhardt, *Philosophischen Schriften* 1: 376–377.

— "Foucher au Leibniz, Paris, 8 decembre 1684," in Gerhardt, *Philosophischen Schriften* 1: 377–379.

— "Foucher au Leibniz [1685?]," in Gerhardt, *Philosophischen Schriften* 1: 379–380.

— "Foucher au Leibniz [1686]," in Gerhardt, *Philosophischen Schriften* 1: 380–385.

— "Foucher au Leibniz, Paris, 5 mai 1687," in Gerhardt, *Philosophischen Schriften* 1: 388–394.

— "Foucher au Leibniz, Paris, 30 mai 1691," in Gerhardt, *Philosophischen Schriften* 1: 397–399.

__ "Foucher au Leibniz, Paris, 31 decembre 1691," in Gerhardt, *Philosophischen Schriften* 1: 400–402.

__ "Foucher au Leibniz, Paris, aoust 1692," in Gerhardt, *Philosophischen Schriften* 1: 406–409.

__ "Foucher au Leibniz, Paris, mars 1693," in Gerhardt, *Philosophischen Schriften* 1: 410–414.

__ "Foucher au Leibniz, Paris, 28 avril 1695," in Gerhardt, *Philosophischen Schriften* 1: 421–423.

__ *Lettre sur la morale de Confucius, philosophe de la Chine.* Paris: Daniel Horthemels, 1668.

__ *Sur la mort de la reine.* Paris: publisher unknown, 1666.

__ *Nouvelle dissertation sur la recherche de la verité, contenant la réponse à la critique de la critique de la recherche de la verité, où l'on découvre les erreurs des dogmatistes, tant anciens que nouveaux, avec une discution particuliere du grand principe des cartesiens.* Paris: Robert de la Caille, 1679.

__ *Nouvelle façon d'hygrometres.* Place and publisher unknown, 1672.

__ *Réponse à la critique de la critique de la recherche de la verité sur la philosophie des académiciens.* Paris: Robert de la Caille, 1676.

__ "Réponse de M.S.F. à M. de L.B.Z. sur son nouveau sistême de la communication des substances, proposé dans les journaux du 27 juin & du 4 juillet 1695," in *Journal des sçavans* (Amsterdam) 23 (12 septembre 1695): 639–646; reprinted in Janet, ed., *Oeuvres philosophiques* 1: 645–648.

__ *Réponse pour la critique à la préface du second volume de la recherche de la verité, où l'on examine le sentiment de M. Descartes touchant les idées, avec plusieurs remarques pour les sciences.* Paris: Charles Angot, 1676.

__ *De la sagesse des anciens, où l'on fait voir que les principales maximes de leur morale ne sont pas contraires au christianisme.* Paris: Dezailliers, 1682.

__ *Traité des hygrometres ou machines pour mesurer la secheresse et l'humidité de l'air.* Paris: Estienne Michallet, 1686.

Frankfurt, Harry G. *Demons, Dreamers, and Madmen: The Defense of Reason in Descartes' Meditations.* Indianapolis: Bobbs-Merrill, 1970.

Frits, Anita D. "Berkeley's Self – Its Origin in Malebranche," in *Journal of the History of Ideas* 15 (1954): 554–572.

__ "Malebranche and Immaterialism of Berkeley," in *The Review of Metaphysics* 3 (1949–50): 59–80.

Gabbey, Alan. "Philosophia Cartesiana Triumphanta: Henry More, 1646–1671," in Lennon, *Problems of Cartesianism*; 171–250.

Gäbe, Lüder. *Descartes' Selbstkritik.* Hamburg: Felix Meiner, 1981.

Galileo Galilei. *Dialogues Concerning Two New Sciences.* Translated by Henry Crew and Alfonso de Salvio. New York: Macmillan, 1914.

__ *Il saggiatore nel quale con bilancia escuista e giusta si ponderano le cose contenute nella libra astronomica e fillosofica.* Rome: Giacomo Mascardi, 1923.

Garciá-Gómez, Sara Fernández. *The Problem of Objective Knowledge in Descartes, Malebranche, and Arnauld.* Ph.D. dissertation. New York: New School of Social Research, 1979.

Gassendi, Pierre. *Dissertations en forme de paradoxes contre les aristotéliciens (Exercitationes Paradoxicae Adversus Aristoteleos) Livres I et II.* Texte latin établi, traduit, et annoté par Bernard Rochot. Paris: J. Vrin, 1959.

Gerhardt, C.J., ed. "Briefwechsel zwischen Leibniz und Foucher." In *Philosophischen Schriften* 1: 363–427.

__ ed. *See* Leibniz, *Philosophischen Schriften.*

Gilson, Etienne. *Etudes sur le rôle de la pensée médiévale dans la formation du système cartésien.* Paris: J. Vrin, 1951.

__ *God and Philosophy.* New Haven: Yale University Press, 1941.

__ *Index Scolastico-Cartésien.* Paris: Felix Alcan, 1913.

—, *La liberte chez Descartes et la théologie.* Paris: Felix Alcan, 1913.

Gouhier, Henri. *Cartésianisme et augustinisme au XVIIème siècle.* Paris: J. Vrin, 1978.

— "La crise de la théologie au temps de Descartes," in *Revue de théologie et de philosophie* (Lausanne) 4 (1954): 19–54.

— "Descartes et la religion," in *Cartesio* (1937): 417–424.

— *Essais sur Descartes.* Paris: J. Vrin, 1949.

— "Les exigences de l'existence dans la metaphysique de Descartes," in *Revue internationale de philosophie* 12 (1950): 123–152.

— "Jacques Rohault et l'histoire de la polémique sur l'Eucharistique," in Gouhier, *Cartésianisme et augustinism* (1978): 71–90.

— "Louis de la Forge," in Gouhier, *Cartésianisme et augustinism* (1978): 58–67.

— "Le malin genie dans l'itinéraire cartésien," in *Revue de philosophie* 6 (1937): 1–21.

— *La pensée métaphysique de Descartes.* Paris: J. Vrin, 1962.

— *La pensée religieuse de Descartes.* Paris: J. Vrin, 1924.

— *La philosophie de Malebranche et son expérience religieuse.* Paris: J. Vrin, 1948.

— "La première polémique de Malebranche," in *Revue d'histoire de la philosophie* 1 (1927): 25–48, 168–191.

— *Les premières pensées de Descartes: Contribution a l'histoire de l'anti-renaissance.* Paris: J. Vrin, 1958.

— "La preuveon ontologique de Descartes," in *Revue internationale de philosophie* 8 (1954): 295–303.

— *La vocation de Malebranche.* Paris: J. Vrin, 1926.

Grabmann, Martin. "Die Philosophie des Cartesius und die Eucharistialehre des Emmanuel Maignan O. Minim," in *Cartesio* (1937): 425–436.

Grossman, Reinhardt. "Digby and Berkeley on Notions," in *Theoria* 26 (1960): 17–30.

Gueroult, Martial. *Berkeley.* Paris: Aubier, 1956.

— *Descartes selon l'ordre des raisons.* Paris: Aubier, 1953.

— *Malebranche.* Paris: Aubier, 1955–1959.

— *Nouvelle réflexions sur la preuve ontologiques des Descartes.* Paris: J. Vrin, 1935.

Haldane, Elizabeth S., and Ross, G.R.T., eds. See Descartes, *The Philosophical Works of Descartes.*

Hintikka, Jaakko. "*Cogito, Ergo, Sum*: Inference or Performance?" in *The Philosophical Review* 71 (1962): 3–32.

Huet, Pierre-Daniel. *Censura Philosophiae Cartesianae.* Paris: Horthemels, 1689.

— "Huet au Nicaise (25 juillet 1697)," in Cousin, *Fragments philosophiques* 3: 151–152.

Hume, David, *Enquiries Concerning the Human Understanding and Concerning the Principles of Morals.* Edited by L.A. Selby-Bigge. 2nd ed. Oxford: Clarendon Press, 1902.

— *A Treatise of Human Nature.* Edited by L.A. Selby-Bigge. Oxford: Clarendon Press, 1888.

Janet, Paul, ed. See Leibniz, *Oeuvres philosophiques.*

Keeling, S.V. *Descartes.* 2nd ed. London: Oxford University Press, 1968.

Kemp Smith, Norman. *New Studies in the Philosophy of Descartes: Descartes as Pioneer.* London: Macmillan, 1952.

— *The Philosophy of David Hume: A Critical Study of Its Origins and Central Doctrines.* London: Macmillan, 1941.

— *Studies in the Cartesian Philosophy.* London: Macmillan, 1902.

Kenny, Anthony. *Descartes: A Study of His Philosophy*. New York: Random House, 1968.
— See Descartes, *Philosophical Letters*.
Kinkaid, Frank. "Letter on Transubstantiation," in *Time*, July 16 (1965): 6.
Koyré, Alexandre. *Essai sur l'idee de dieu et less preuves de son existence chez Descartes*. Paris: Ernest Leroux, 1922.
— *Études galiléennes: I. A l'aube de la science classique*. Paris: Hermann & Cie, 1939.
— "Galileo and Plato," in *Journal of the History of Ideas* 4 (1943): 400–428.
— "Galileo and the Scientific Revolution of the XVII Century," in *The Philosophical Review* 52 (1943): 333–348.
— "Introduction," in Anscombe, Elizabeth and Peter Geach, trs. and eds., *Descartes: Philosophical Writings*, Edinburgh: Nelson, 1954: vii–xliv.
— "Galileo and Plato," in *Journal of the History of Ideas* 4 (1943): 400–428.
— "Galileo and the Scientific Revolution of the XVII Century," in *The Philosophical Review* 52 (1943): 333–348.
Kremer, Elmar J. *Malebranche and Arnauld: The Controversy over the Nature of Ideas*. Ph.D. dissertation. Yale University, 1961.
La Forge, Louis de. *Louis de La Forge: Oeuvres philosophiques, avec une étude bio-bibliographique*. Édition annotée par Pierre Clair. Paris: Presses Universitaires de France, 1974.
— *Remarques. . .sur le traité de l'homme de Rene Descartes. . .*See Descartes, *L'Homme*, 1664.
— *Traitté de l'âme humaine, de ses facultés et fonctions et de son union avec le corps, d'après les principes de Descartes*. Paris: Theodore Girard, 1666. Also in Clair, ed., *Oeuvres*.
La Grange, Jean-Baptiste de. *Les principes de la philosophie, contre les nouveaux philosophes Descartes, Rohault, Regius, Gassendi, le P. Maignon, &c.*. Paris: G. Josse, 1675.
— *Traité des éléments et des météores, contre les nouveaux philosophes Descartes, Rohault, Gassendi, le P. Maignon, & c.*. Paris: Vve Josse, 1679.
Landormy, P. "La mémoire corporelle et la mémorie intellectuelle dans la philosophie de Descartes," in *Histoire de la Philosophie*. Paris: Armand Colin, 1902: 259–298.
Laporte, Jean. "La connaissance de l'étendue chez Descartes," in *Études d'histoire de la philosophie française au XVIIe siècle*, Paris: J. Vrin, 1951: 153–193.
— "L'étendue intelligible selon Malebranche," in *Études d'histoire de la philosophie française an XVIIe siècle*, Paris: J. Vrin, 1951: 153–193.
— *Le rationalisme de Descartes*. Paris: Presses Universitaires de France, 1950.
Layman, Ronald. "Transubstantiation: A Test Case for Descartes's Theory of Space," in Lennon, *Problems of Cartesianism* (1982): 149–170.
Le Grand, Antoine. *An Entire Body of Philosophy, According to the Principles of the Famous Renate des Cartes, in three Books: I. The Institution. . .II. The History of Nature. . .III. A Dissertation of the Want of Sense and Knowledge in Brute Animals. . .*, London: Samuel Roycraft, 1694; facsimile reprint, New York: Johnson Reprint Corporation, 1972.
Lefevre, Roger. *La bataille du "cogito."* Paris: Presses Universitaires de France, 1960.
— *Le criticisme de Descartes*. Paris: Presses Universitaires de France, 1958.
— *L'humanisme de Descartes*. Paris: Presses Universitaires de France, 1957.
— *La vocation de Descartes*. Paris: Presses Universitaires de France, 1956.
Leibniz, Gottfried Wilhelm. *Discours de métaphysics et correspondance avec Arnauld*. Introduction, texte et commentaire par Georges Le Roy. Paris: J. Vrin, 1957.
— "Eclaircissement du nouveau sistême de la communication des substances, pour servir de reponse à ce qui en a été dit dans le journal du 12 sept. 1695," in *Journal des sçavans* (Amsterdam) 24 (2 et 9 avril 1696): 255–258; 259–263; reprinted in Janet, ed., *Oeuvres philosophiques de Leibniz* 1: 649–653.
— "Excerpta ex notis meis inauguralibus ad Fucherii responsionem in Malebran-

cium critica," in Rabbe, *Étude philosophique*: XL–XLII; "Notes on the Reply of Foucher to the Criticism of his Criticism of the *Recherche de la verité*," in Loemker, ed., *Philosophical Papers and Letters*: 241–242.

— "Extrait d'une lettre de Monsr. de Leibniz a Mr. Foucher chanoine de Dijon, sur quelques axiomes de philsophie," in *Journal des sçavans* (Amsterdam) 20 (2 juin 1692): 365–369.

— "De Ipsi Nature sive de Vi Insita, Actionibusque Creaturarum; pro Dynamicus suis confirmandis Illustrandisque," *Acta Eruditorum Lipsiensum*, septembre 1698: 427–440; "On Nature Itself, or on the Inherent Force and Actions of Created Things to Serve to Confirm and Illustrate the Author's Dynamics," in Loemker, ed., *Philosophical Papers and Letters*: 808–824.

— "Leibniz au Foucher [1676]," in Gerhardt, ed., *Philosophischen Schriften* 1: 369–374.

— "Leibniz au Foucher, 1686," in Gerhardt, *Philosophischen Schriften* 1: 380–385.

— "Leibniz au Foucher [1687?]," in Gerhardt, *Philosophischen Schriften* 1: 390–394.

— "Leibniz au Foucher, javier 1692," in Gerhardt, *Philosophischen Schriften* 1: 402–406.

— "Leibniz au Foucher, 17/27 octobre 1692," in Gerhardt, *Philosophischen Schriften* 1: 409–410.

— "Leibniz au Nicaise, 1697," in Rabbe, *Étude philosophique*: VIII.

— "Lettre sur la question si l'essence du corps consiste dans l'étendu," *Journal des savants*, 18 juin 1691: 259–261; reprinted in Janet, ed., *Oeuvres philosophiques de Leibniz* 1: 627–629.

— "Meditatones de Cognitione, Veritate et Ideis," *Acta Eruditorum Lipsiensum*, novembre 1684: 537–542; reprinted in Gerhardt, ed., *Philosophischen Schriften* 4: 422–426; "Meditations on Knowledge, Truth, and Ideas," in Loemker, ed., *Philosophical Papers and Letters*: 448–481.

— "De Modo Distinguendi Phaenomena Realia ab Imaginariis," (date unknown), in Gerhardt, ed., *Philosophischen Schriften* 7: 319–322; "On the method of Distinguishing Real from Imaginary Phenomena," in Loemker, ed., *Philosphical Papers and Letters*: 602–607.

— "Nouveaux essais sur l'entendement par l'auteur du systeme de l'harmonie prééstablie," in Gerhardt, *Philosophischen Schriften* 5.

— *Oeuvres philosophiques de Leibniz*. Edited by Paul Janet. Paris: Felix Alcan, 1900.

— *Opuscules et fragments inédits de Leibniz, extraits des manuscripts de la Bibliothèque Royale de Hanovre*. Edited by Louis Couteret. Paris: Felix Alcan, 1903.

— *Philosophical Papers and Letters*. Edited and translated by Leroy E. Loemker. Chicago: University of Chicago Press, 1890.

— *The Philosophical Works of Leibniz*. New Haven: Tuttle, Morehouse & Taylor, 1890.

— *Die Philosophischen Schriften von Gottfried Wilhelm Leibniz*. Edited by C. J. Gerhardt. Berlin: Weidmannsche, 1875–1890.

— "Primae Veritates, (ca. 1680–84)," in Couteret, ed., *Opuscules et fragments*: 518–523; "First Truths," in Loemker, ed., *Philosophical Papers and Letters*: 411–417.

— "Quid sit Idea, (1678)," in Gerhardt, ed., *Philosophischen Schriften* 7: 263–264; "What Is an Idea?" in Loemker, ed., *Philosophical Papers and Letters*: 317–319.

— "Réponse de Mr. de Leibniz à l'extrait de la lettre de Mr. Foucher chanoine de Dijon, insérée dans le Journal du 16 mars 1693," in *Journal des sçavans* (Amsterdam) 21 (3 aoust 1693): 527–529.

— "Sistême nouveau de la nature & de la communication des substances, aussi bien que de l'union qu'il y a entre l'âme & le corps. Par M.D.L.," in *Journal des sçavans*

(Amsterdam) 23 (27 juin & 4 juilliet 1695): 444–454; 455–462; reprinted in Janet, ed., *Oeuvre philosophiques* 1: 635–644.

Lemaire, Paul. *Le cartésienisme chez les Bénédictins. Dom Robert Desgabets son systême, son influence et son école, d'après plusieurs manuscrits et des documents rares ou inédits*. Paris: Felix Alcan, 1901.

Lennon, Thomas M. "Philosophical Commentary," in Nicolas Malebranche, *The Search After Truth* and *Elucidations of the Search After Truth*. Translated by Thomas M. Lennon and Paul J. Olscamp. Columbus: Ohio State University Press, 1980: 755–848.

—, John M. Nichols, and John W. Davis, eds., *Problems of Cartesianism*. Montreal: McGill/Queens University Press, 1982.

Lenoble, Robert. *Mersenne ou la naissance du mécanisme*. Paris: J. Vrin, 1943.

— "Origines de la pensée scientifique moderne," in *Encyclopédie de la Pléide: histoire de la science* 5: 369–534. Paris: Gallimard, 1957.

— "La psychologie cartésienne," in *Revue internationale de philosophie* 12 (1950): 160–189.

Lewis, Geneviève. "L'âme et la durée d'après une controverse cartesienne." *Revue internationale de philosophie* 12 (1950): 190–209.

— *L'individualité selon Descartes*. Paris: J. Vrin, 1950.

— *Le probleme de l'inconscient et le cartesianisme*. Paris: Presses Universitaires de France, 1950.

Lewis, George F. "Letter on Transubstantiation," in *Time*, 16 July 1965: 6.

Locke, John. *An Early Draft of Locke's Essay Together with Excerpts from his Journals*. Edited by R. I. Aaron and Jocelyn Gibb. Oxford: Clarendon Press, 1936.

— *An Essay Concerning Human Understanding*. Edited by A. C. Fraser. Oxford: Clarendon Press, 1894.

Loeb, Louis E. *From Descartes to Hume: Continental Metaphysics and the Development of Modern Philosophy*. Ithica and London: Cornell University Press, 1981.

— "Is There a Problem of Cartesian Interaction?" *Journal of the History of Philosophy* 23 (1985): 227–231.

Loemker, Leroy E., ed. *See* Leibniz, *Philosophical Papers and Letters*.

Lough, John. "Locke's Reading During His Stay in France," in *The Library, A Quarterly Review of Bibliography*. Transactions of the Bibliographical Society, 3rd ser., no. 8 (1953): 229–258.

— *Locke's Travels in France 1675–1679 as Related in his Journals, Correspondence and other Papers*. Cambridge: Cambridge University Press, 1953.

Lovejoy, Arthur O. "'Representative Ideas' in Malebranche and Arnauld," in *Mind* 32 (1923): 449–464.

— *The Revolt Against Dualism: An Inquiry Concerning the Existence of Ideas*. New York: W. W. Norton, 1930.

Luce, A. A. *Berkeley and Malebranche, A Study in the Origins of Berkeley's Thought*. London: Oxford University Press, 1934.

— *Berkeley's Immaterialism*. London: Thomas Nelson and Sons, 1945.

— and T. E. Jessop, eds. *See* Berkeley, *Works*.

Malebranche, Nicolas. "Avertissement contre Desgabets et Foucher," in Robinet, ed., *Oeuvres complètes de Malebranche* 2: 500–503.

— *Oeuvres complètes de Malebranche*. Edited by André Robinet. Paris: J. Vrin, 1962.

— "Preface contre le livre de Foucher," in Robinet, ed. *Oeuvres complètes de Malebranche* 2: 480–499.

— *De la recherche de la vérité où l'on traite de la nature de l'esprit de l'homme, et de l'usage qu'il en doit faire pour éviter l'erreur des sciences.* Paris: André Prelard, 1674–1675. Reprinted as follows: Edited by Geneviève Lewis, Paris: J. Vrin, 1945. Edited by Désiré Roustan and Paul Schrecker, in *Oeuvres completes de Malebranche* 1, Paris: Boiven, 1938. Edited by Geneviève Rodis-Lewis, in Robinet, ed., *Oeuvres complètes de Malebranche* 1, 2, 3. Paris: J. Vrin, 1962–1964.

— *Recueil de toutes les réponses du père Malebranche, prestre de l'Oratoire, à monsieur Arnauld, docteur de Sorbonne.* Rotterdam: R. Leers, 1694.

Mandon, L. *Étude sur le syntagma philosophicum de Gassendi.* Montpellier: Pierre Grollier, 1858.

Maritain, Jacques. *The Dream of Descartes, Together with Some Other Essays.* New York: Philosophical Library, 1944.

Meiland, Jack W. *Scepticism and Historical Knowledge.* New York: Random House, 1965.

Menage, Gilles. *Menagiana, ou les bons mots et remarques critiquese, historiques, morales & d'érudition, de Monsieur Menage, recueillies par ses amis.* Paris: Veuve Delaulne, 1729.

Mouy, Paul. *Le développement de la physique cartésienne, 1646–1712.* Paris: J. Vrin, 1934.

O'Neil, Brian E. *Epistemological Direct Realism in Descartes' Philosophy.* Albuquerque: University of New Mexico Press, 1974.

Ouvrard, René. "Ouvrard au Nicaise, 24 septembre 1675," in Cousin, ed., *Fragments philosophiques* 3: 154–155.

Peters, Klaus. "Die Dialektik von Existenz und Extension: Eine Untersuchung zum 'cogito, ergo, sum,' " in Klaus Peters, Wolfgang Schmidt, and Hans Heinz Holz, *Erkenntnigeswisssheit und Deduktion: Zum Aufbau der philosophischen Systeme bei Descartes, Spinoza, Leibniz.* Darmstadt und Neuwied: Hermann Luchterhand, 1975: 7–55.

Pintard, René. *Le libertinage érudit dans le premère moitie du XVIIe siècle.* Paris: Bowin, 1947.

Popkin, Richard H. "L'abbé Foucher et le problème des qualités premières," in *Bulletin de la société d' étude du XVIIe siècle,* no. 33 (1957): 633–647.

— "Berkeley and Pyrrhonism," in *The Review of Metaphysics* 5 (1951–1952): 223–246; reprinted in *Highroad to Pyrrhonism,* pp. 297–318.

— "Cartesianism and Bible Criticism," in Lennon, *Problems of Cartesianism*: 61–81.

— "David Hume and the Pyrrhonian Controversy," in *The Review of Metaphysics* 6 (1952–1953): 65–81.

— "David Hume: His Pyrrhonism and His Critique of Pyrrhonism," in *Philosophical Quarterly* 1 (1950–1951): 385–407; reprinted in *Highroad to Pyrrhonism*: 103–132.

— "Did Hume Ever Read Berkeley?" in *The Journal of Philosophy* 56 (1959): 535–545; reprinted in *Highroad to Pyrrhonism,* pp. 277–288.

— "The High Road to Pyrrhonism," in *American Philosophical Quarterly* 2 (1965): 18–32.

— *The High Road to Pyrrhonism.* Studies in Hume and Scottish Philosophy 2. Edited by Richard A. Watson and James E. Force. San Diego: Austin Hill Press, 1980.

— *The History of Scepticism from Erasmus to Descartes.* Assen: Van Gorcum, 1960.

— *The History of Scepticism from Erasmus to Spinoza.* 4th ed. Berkeley: University of California Press, 1979.

— "The New Realism of Bishop Berkeley," in *George Berkeley,* University of California Publications in Philosophy 29, Berkeley: University of California Press, 1957: 1–19; reprinted in *Highroad to Pyrrhonism*: 319–338.

— "The Sceptical Crisis and the Rise of Modern Philosophy, III," in *The Review of Metaphysics* 7 (1953–1954): 499–510.

— "The Sceptical Precursors of David Hume," in *Philosophy and Phenomenological Research* 16 (1955): 61–71.

— "So, Hume Did Read Berkeley," in *The Journal of Philosophy* 61 (1964): 773–778; reprinted in *Highroad to Pyrrhonism*: 289–296.

Rabbe, Felix. *Étude philosophiqe. L'abbé Simon Foucher chanoine de la sainte chapelle de Dijon.* Paris: Didier, 1867.

Radner, Daisie. "Descartes' Notion of the Union of Mind and Body," *Journal of the History of Philosophy* 9 (1971): 159–170.

— *Malebranche: A Study of a Cartesian System.* Assen: Ban Gorcum, 1978.

— "Is There a Problem of Cartesian Interaction?" *Journal of the History of Philosophy* 23 (1985): 35–49.

Rée, Johnathan. *Descartes.* London: Allen Lane, 1974.

Régis, Pierre-Sylvain. *Réponse aux réflexions critiques de M. Du Hamel sur le systême cartésien de la philosophie de M. Régis.* Paris: J. Cusson, 1692.

— *Systême de philosophie, contenant la logique, la metaphisique, la physique et la morale,* Lyon: Denys Thierry, 1690; facsimile reprint, New York: Johnson Reprint Corporation, 1970.

— *L'usage de la raison et de la foy, ou l'accord de la foy et de la raison.* Paris: Jean Cusson, 1704.

Revel, Jean-François. *Descartes: inutile et incertain.* Paris: Stock, 1976.

Rex, Walter. *Essays on Pierre Bayle and Religious Controversy.* International Archives of the History of Ideas 8. The Hague: Martinus Nijohoff, 1965.

Richardson, R. C. "The 'Scandal' of Cartesian Interactionism," in *Mind* 91 (1982): 20–37.

— "Union and Interaction of Body and Soul," *Journal of the History of Philosophy* 23 (1985): 221–226.

Robinet, André. *Le langage a l'age classique.* Paris: Klincksieck, 1978.

— *Malebranche et Leibniz, relations personneles, présentées avec les textes complets des auteurs' et de leurs correspondants revus, corrigés et inédits.* Paris: J. Vrin, 1955.

— *Malebranche vivant: documents biographiques et bibliographiques.* In Robinet, ed., *Oeuvres completes de Malebranche* 20. Paris: J. Vrin, 1967.

— ed. *See* Malebranche, *Oeuvres completes.*

Rochot, Bernard. *Les travaux de Gassendi sur Epicure et sur l'atomisme, 1619–1658.* Paris: J. Vrin, 1944.

Rodis-Lewis, Geneviève. *See* Lewis.

— ed. *See* Malebranche, *De la recherche de la vérité.*

— *L'Oeuvre de Descartes.* Paris: J. Vrin, 1971.

Roger, Jacques. "The Cartesian Model and Its Role in Eighteenth-Century 'Theory of the Earth,' " in Lennon, *Problems of Cartesianism* (1982): 95–112.

Rohault, Jacques. *Entretiens sur la philosophie.* Paris: Michel le Petit, 1671.

— *Rohault's System of Natural Philosophy, Illustrated with Dr. Samuel Clarke's Notes taken mostly out of Sir Isaac Newton's Philosophy, with Additions,* translated by John Clarke, London: James Knapton, 1723; facsimile reprint, New York: Johnson Reprint Corporation, 1969.

— *Traité de physique.* Paris: Vve de C. Savreux, 1671.

Rome, Beatrice K. "Created Truths and *causa sui* in Descartes," in *Philosophy and Phenomenological Research* 17 (1956–1957): 66–78.

Rosenfield, Leonora Cohen. *From Beast-Machine to Man-Machine: Animal Soul in French Letters from Descartes to La Mettrie.* New enlarged ed. New York: Octagon Books, 1968.

— "Peripatetic Adersaries of Cartesianism in 17th Century France," in *Review of Religion* 22 (1957): 14–40; reprinted in Rosenfield, *From Beast-Machine to Man-Machine*: 303–334.

Russell, Bertrand. *A Critical Exposition of the Philosophy of Leibniz.* London: George Allen & Unwin, 1900.

— *History of Western Philosophy, and Its Connection with Political and Social Circumstances from the Earliest Times to the Present Day*. New York: Simon, 1945.

— *The Problems of Philosophy*. London: Oxford University Press, 1912.

Santayana, George. *Scepticism and Animal Faith: Introduction to a System of Philosophy*. New York: Scribners, 1923.

— "*La liberté cartésienne*," in Sartre, *Descartes*: 9–52.

Sartre, Jean-Paul. *Descartes*. Paris: Trois Collines, 1946.

Sebba, Gregor. *Bibliographia Cartesiana: A Critical· Guide to the Descartes Literature 1800–1960*. International Archives of the History of Ideas 5. The Hague: Martinus Nijhoff, 1964.

— *Nicolas Malebranche 1638–1715: A Preliminary Bibliography*. Athens: University of Georgia, 1959.

— "What Is 'History of Philosophy'?" in *Journal of the History of Philosophy* 8 (1970): 251–262.

Segond, J. *La sagesse cartésienne et la doctrine de la science*. Paris: J. Vrin, 1932.

Sellars, Wilfrid. *Philosophical Perspectives*. Springfield, Ill.: Charles C. Thomas, 1959.

Serrus, Charles. *La méthode de Descartes et son application à la métaphysique*. Paris: Felix Alcan, 1933.

Sextus Empiricus. *Against the Logicians*. In R. G. Bury, *Sextus Empiricus with an English Translation 2*. London: Wm. Heinemann, 1935.

Shotwell, James Thompson. *A Study in the History of the Eucharist*. London: Eyre and Spottiswoode, 1905.

Sirven, J. *Les années d'apprentissage de Descartes (1590–1628)*. Paris: J. Vrin, 1928.

Sortais, Gaston. *La philosophie moderne depuis Bacon jusqu'a Leibniz*. Paris: Paul Lethielleux, 1920.

Spink, J. S. *French Free-Thought from Gassendi to Voltaire*. London: Athlone, 1960.

Temple, William. "The Cartesian Faux-Pas," in *Nature, Man and God: The Gifford Lectures 1932–1934*. London: Macmillan, 1934: 57–81.

Thomas, P.-Félix. *La philosophie de Gassendi*. Paris: Felix Alcan, 1889.

Trevor-Roper, Hugh. *Hermit of Peking: The Hidden Life of Sir Edmund Backhouse*. New York: Alfred A. Knopf, 1977.

Turnbull, Robert G. "Aseity and Dependence in Leibniz's Metaphysics," in *Theoria* 25 (1959): 95–114.

Vernon, Thomas S. *The Metaphysical Role of Ideas in the Philosophy of Descartes*. Ph.D. dissertation. University of Michigan, 1963.

Walsh, F. A. "The Decline of Cartesianism," in *Cartesio* (1937): 793–801.

Walton, Craig. "Malebranche's Ontology," in *Journal of the History of Philosphy* 7 (1969): 143–161; reprinted in Walton, *De la recherche du bien*: 22–42.

— *De la recherche du bien: A Study of Malebranche's Science of Ethics*. International Archives of the History of Ideas 48. The Hague: Martinus Nijhoff, 1972.

Watson, Richard A. "Berkeley in a Cartesian Context," in *Revue internationale de philosophie*, no. 65 (1963): 381–394.

— "The Breakdown of Cartesian Metaphysics," in *Journal of the History of Philosophy* 1 (1964): 177–197.

— "Cartesianism," in *Encyclopaedia Britannica* 3, 15th ed.: Chicago: Benton, 1964: 968–970.

— "Cartesianism Compounded: Louis de La Forge," in *Studia Cartesiana* 2 (1982): 165–171.

— "In Defiance of Demons, Dreamers, and Madmen," in *Journal of the History of Philosophy* 14 (1976): 342–353.

— "Introduction to *Critique de la recherche de la verité* by Simon Foucher," in Simon Foucher, *Critique de la recherche de la verité*, New York: Johnson Reprint Corporation, 1969: v–xlix.

— "Introduction to *An Entire Body of Philosophy* by Antoine Le Grand," in Antoine Le Grand, *An Entire Body of Philosophy*, New York: Johnson Reprint Corporation, 1972: v–xii.

— "Introduction to *Systême de philosophie* by Pierre-Sylvain Régis," in Pierre-Sylvain Régis, *Systême de philosophie*, New York: Johnson Reprint Corporation, 1970: v–xx.

— "Jacques Rohault," in Paul Edwards, *Encyclopedia of Philosophy* 7, New York: Macmillan, 1967: 204.

— "A Note on the Probabilistic Physics of Régis," in *Archives internationales d'histoire des sciences*, no. 66 (1964): 33–36.

— "Pierre-Sylvain Régis," in Paul Edwards, *Encyclopedia of Philosophy* 7, New York: Macmillan, 1967: 101–102.

— "A Short Discourse on Method in the History of Philosophy," in *Southwestern Journal of Philosophy* 11 (1980): 7–23.

— "Simon Foucher," in Paul Edwards, *Encyclopedia of Philosophy* 3, New York: Macmillan, 1967: 213–214.

— *Simon Foucher and the Cartesian Way of Ideas.* Ph.D. dissertation. University of Iowa, 1961.

— "Transubstantiation Among the Cartesians," in John M. Lennon, *Problems of Cartesianism*: 127–148.

— "What Moves the Mind? An Excursion in Cartesian Metaphysics," in *American Philosophical Quarterly* 19 (1982): 73–81.

— and James E. Force, eds. *The High Road to Pyrrhonism. See* Popkin.

Weinberg, Julius. *Abstraction, Relation, and Induction: Three Essays in the History of Thought.* Madison: University of Wisconsin Press, 1965.

Williams, Bernard. *Descartes: The Project of Pure Enquiry.* Harmondsworth: Penguin, 1978.

Wilson, Margaret Dauler. *Descartes.* London: Routledge and Kegan Paul, 1978.

Wolfson, H.A. "Causality and Freedom in Descartes, Leibniz, and Hume," in Sidney Hook and Milton R. Konvitz, eds., *Freedom and Experience: Essays presented to Milton R. Konvitz.* Ithaca: Cornell University Press, 1947: 97–114.

Yolton, John W. *Locke and the Way of Ideas.* Oxford: Oxford University Press, 1956.

— "Locke and the Seventeenth-Century Logic of Ideas," in *Journal of the History of Ideas* 16 (1955): 431–452.

— *Perceptual Acquaintance from Descartes to Reid.* Minneapolis: University of Minnesota Press, 1984.

— *Thinking Matter: Materialism in Eighteenth–Century Britain.* Minneapolis: University of Minnesota Press, 1983.

Name Index

237